Asad

The Sphinx of Damascus

Asad
The Sphinx of Damascus

A Political Biography

Moshe Ma'oz

GROVE WEIDENFELD
NEW YORK

Published by Grove Weidenfeld
A division of Wheatland Corporation
841 Broadway
New York, NY 10003-4793

Originally published in Great Britain in 1988 by George Weidenfeld and
Nicolson, Ltd. First American edition published in 1988 by Weidenfeld
& Nicolson, New York.

Library of Congress Cataloging-in-Publication Data

Ma'oz, Moshe.
    Asad: the Sphinx of Damascus: a political biography/Moshe Ma'oz.
    p.   cm.
    Bibliography: p.
    Includes index.
    ISBN 1-55584-433-2
    1. Assad, Hafez, 1928–   . 2. Syria—Politics and government.
3. Syria—Presidents—Biography.   I. Title.
DS98.3.A8M36 1988
956.91′042′0924—dc19
[B]   87-36539
                                                   CIP

Manufactured in the United States of America

Printed on acid-free paper

First Evergreen Edition 1989

10   9   8   7   6   5   4   3   2   1

To Albert Hourani
who introduced me to the study of modern Syria
and led me to a deeper appreciation of Arab history and society

Contents

Preface

The Sphinx of Damascus

This book is an attempt to compose a political biography of an outstanding ruler of modern Syria, one of the most powerful, intriguing and controversial leaders of the contemporary Middle East.

His is indeed an exceptional life story, a boy from a poor peasant family named Wahsh ('wild beast' in Arabic) who changed his family name to Asad ('lion'), and achieved an unprecedented rise to the supreme position of Syria's president. More significantly, although a member of the esoteric, heterodox and rural Alawite minority sect which represents only 12 per cent of the total population, Asad rules over this predominantly Sunni (Orthodox) Muslim country which was controlled for generations by its urban upper class. Members of this class traditionally regarded the Alawites as socially and culturally backward heretics and employed them as servants in their households. Yet Asad's regime has managed to stay in power since 1970 – longer than any previous regime in Syria's modern history. Asad has succeeded in eliminating the Sunni Muslim urban oligarchy, promoting in its place a new political elite composed mostly of lower-class young people from villages and small towns.

Asad accomplished this remarkable political and economic upheaval (which was periodically accompanied by brutality and bloodshed) at the same time as he transformed Syria from a notoriously weak and vulnerable state into one which was strong, stable and assertive. In a country which for decades had been a breeding ground for military coups and counter-coups, Asad established an unchallenged, highly centralized regime. Moreover, he transformed his country from an object of encroachment on the part of neighbouring countries into a regional power, challenging or affecting a number of countries and other forces in the region and beyond. For example, in response to Sadat's peace with Israel in 1979, Asad has defied Egypt's predominance in Arab politics and has endeavoured to become the new leader of an all-Arab confrontation with Israel. From co-leader of the 1973 war against Israel, he has become the first Arab ruler who now aims singlehandedly to challenge Israel's military superiority in the Middle East; and he has reached this point by working systematically for several years to achieve a 'strategic balance' with the Jewish state.

The 1982 Israeli offensive in Lebanon, despite its initial military success vis-à-vis the Syrian army, paradoxically served to enhance Asad's position, enabling him to turn his military predicament into a political victory. Not only did he impose the abrogation of the Israeli–Lebanese agreement of May 1983, but in 1985 for the first time in the annals of the Arab–Israeli conflict, he prompted a unilateral retreat by the Israeli army (which withdrew from most of Lebanon in the face of Asad's use of proxy guerrilla warfare). Subsequently, while turning Lebanon practically into a Syrian protectorate, Asad created a serious split in the ranks of the PLO, expelled Yasir Arafat from Lebanon, and organized the militant wing of the PLO into an instrument of Syrian regional policies. He has also played a significant role in foiling the emerging rapprochement between Arafat and King Hussein (embodied in the February 1985 confederation agreement), replacing it with the Syrian–Jordanian bilateral agreement of January 1986.

In addition to mending his fences with King Hussein, Asad continued to muster both political backing and financial assistance from Saudi Arabia, thereby demonstrating the weakness of Arab criticism of Syria's alliance with Iran, in the latter country's Gulf war with Arab-backed Iraq. Asad's support of Iran's Islamic fundamentalist regime is essentially designed to help him gain the upper hand in his intense rivalry with Iraq's Saddam Hussein over the leadership of the Ba'th and eventually for hegemony over the Fertile Crescent region.

Although Asad's domestic and regional achievements were realized with substantial Soviet military, political and economic support, he has by no means become a client of the USSR. Periodically he has even managed to manoeuvre the Kremlin into reluctantly accepting as *faits accomplis* several of his crucial actions with regard to Lebanon, the PLO and Iraq. Furthermore, while maintaining Syria's alliance with the Soviet Union as a counterbalance to the US–Israel alliance, Asad has sometimes dealt directly with the US (especially in the case of Lebanon and Israel) apparently without co-ordinating his moves with the USSR. Even though he has labelled the US Syria's arch-enemy, Asad has never closed the door to independent bilateral relations with Washington. Since 1984, he has forced the US to acknowledge Syria's permanent influence in Lebanon by demonstrating the critical role of Damascus in the regional and international politics of the Middle East.

True, Asad's external and domestic policies have faced grave problems and suffered serious setbacks. On balance, though, his achievements, especially in regional affairs, seem to be quite remarkable, all the more so when one considers that most, if not all, of those achievements have been accomplished singlehandedly by Asad himself. Naturally he is assisted by scores of advisers, ministers, army officers, but he makes all the important decisions and runs the country as a one-man show. He is as close to a one-person regime as one can envisage, the almighty of Syria.

Yet in many respects Asad is still the sphinx of Syria, an enigma to many of his fellow countrymen and to most outsiders. Asad presents two conflicting images. His followers and admirers in Syria and elsewhere describe him as an exceptionally gifted person who possesses a rare combination of talents: intelligence, shrewdness, bravery and strength, nobility and loyalty, patriotism and states-manship. According to this view, Asad is a genuine Syrian Arab patriot and a devoted Ba'thist, whose only motivation is to serve his nation in line with the Ba'th's nationalist progressive doctrines. His supporters argue that this 'uniquely talented, strong and noble person, the Lion of Syria, historical leader', has succeeded in establishing a durable regime, whose legitimacy rests on new political institutions as well as on broad popular support. Asad and his Ba'th regime not only have advanced the Syrians' national aspirations, but also have greatly improved the country's economic conditions within the framework of the Ba'th revolution. And the ultimate goals of Asad still remain to be achieved: all-Arab unity and the destruction of the 'neo-Crusader' state, Israel. Indeed, Asad is often portrayed by his admirers as the modern Saladin of the Arab world (the legendary Saladin succeeded some 800 years ago in unifying the Muslim world, defeating the Crusaders – in the historic battle at Hittin – and conquering the Crusaders' Kingdom of Jerusalem).

Diametrically opposed to this glorious and heroic characterization of Asad is the highly negative view held by his enemies, notably among the Syrians, Lebanese, Palestinians and Iraqis. By these Asad is seen as primitive and cunning, a coward and a liar, a traitor and a fascist, a tyrant and a butcher. He is described by them as 'the new pharaoh of Damascus, the fox or wolf of Syria, the mouse or rabbit of the Golan'. To his enemies, Asad is a heretic Alawite disguised as a Syrian Arab who has established by force a ruthless personal–sectarian–military regime in the name of the Ba'th and has brutally suppressed the basic human rights of the Syrian people, terrorizing and butchering thousands of innocent men, women and children. The uprising in Hama in February 1982, when Asad's troops, in the process of quelling the rebellion of the Muslim Brothers, killed indiscriminately up to 30,000 Syrian civilians, is cited as an example of this readiness to resort to violence. Asad's enemies further accuse him of destroying the Syrian economy and impoverishing large sections of the population, and of betraying the cause of the Arabs by his alleged accommodations with the enemies of Arabism, including Israel and Iran.

These two opposing images of Asad and his policies are both extreme, even biased, but they are widely reflected in press reports and other accounts by journalists, writers and politicians in the Middle East and in other parts of the world. The absence of balanced accounts on the subject presents a challenge to an Arabist to attempt as objective and scholarly a biography of Asad as available sources permit.

This is certainly not an easy task. Many biographers tend to identify with their hero intentionally or unintentionally. By contrast, an Israeli portraying his country's arch-enemy might be inclined to demonize Asad or misjudge him. Aware of these pitfalls, I have tried to remain as detached as I can, but without losing empathy for the study of Syria and Asad, with their interests and aspirations. Born and raised within the same geographical region and within the same generation, I experienced in my youth political upheavals and aspirations similar to those of many young Syrians. And being a student of Syrian (and Arab) history and society since 1956, I have studied Asad's rule since 1966 when he became the co-leader of the neo-Ba'thist Alawite regime in Syria. Then, after his ascent to power in 1970, I began more systematic work on the subject, some of which has already been published.

Yet when I started preparing this biography a few years ago I discovered that very little is known about Asad's childhood, his parents or his family. Asad himself does nothing to encourage an interest in his personal life. Foreign journalists who seek such details about him are handed a short curriculum vitae containing only the barest facts about his involvement in public life since he joined the Ba'th Party at the age of sixteen.

Even the two laudatory semi-official biographies virtually start at that point in his life.[1] Therefore, as it is, most of the material available on Asad concerns his political and military careers as well as his views and actions on various domestic, regional and international issues. In my study I have used many, if not most, accounts of him and his policies in Syrian, Lebanese, Israeli, Jordanian, Iraqi, Egyptian, European and American newspapers, journals and books. Among those of special interest are the remarks made about Asad in the books of several politicians who have conducted talks or negotiations with him – Henry Kissinger, Kamal Junblatt, Karim Paqraduni and Jimmy Carter. In addition to using official Syrian documents captured by the Israeli army in the 1967 and 1973 wars and made available for my research, I have read (or listened to on the radio) most, if not all, of the speeches and interviews given by Asad since 1966. I have also interviewed several American and British officials who met Asad and had various discussions with him. Among them are: Richard Murphy, US assistant secretary of state for Near Eastern and South Asian affairs and former US ambassador in Damascus; Joseph Sisco, former US under secretary of state for political affairs; and Talcot Seelye, former US ambassador in Damascus. I wish to thank them and other persons (who preferred not to be mentioned) for their useful remarks.

During the last stages of my research, I was considerably helped by my research assistants Yehudit Rahmani and Hana Yerusalemski as well as by the secretaries at the Harry S. Truman Research Institute, the Hebrew University, Jerusalem. Starting to write the book in the summer of 1985, I enjoyed the hospitality and help of the staff of the Middle East Centre, St Antony's College, Oxford. Yet my greatest debt is to William B. Quandt, acting director, Foreign Policy Studies, as well as to the director and staff of the Brookings Institution, Washington, for enabling me to complete my work in a highly scholarly and stimulating environment. I wish to thank Dr Quandt also for reading the entire manuscript and making useful remarks; and Mrs Virginia Riddel for her devotion and efficiency in typing the manuscript. Dr Yahya M. Sadowski and Dr Thomas L. McNaugher, research associates at the Brookings Institution, and Dr Jacques Roumani, a Middle East specialist, read parts of the manuscript and made important suggestions. While I remain grateful to them, I wish to point out that they do not bear any responsibility for what is said and argued in the book. Last but not least I wish to thank my wife Miriam for her patience and understanding.

This study will trace the evolution of Asad as a person, politician and leader since his days as a high-school student in Latakia, when he began identifying himself as a Syrian Arab nationalist. One of the main questions which will be dealt with is how did an Alawite peasant boy rise from a poor and backward social environment to a brilliant military career, and then become at the age of forty the supreme leader of this Sunni Muslim nation? Has he been motivated by a genuine sense of nationalist mission on behalf of Syrian patriotism and Arabism, as well as by an ideological commitment to Ba'thism? Or is he an Alawite whose enormous lust for power and great manipulative abilities have enabled him to establish a personal dictatorship in the name of Ba'th? Other intriguing issues will be examined. For example, how has Asad been able to rule this divisive and restless people for such a long time and, for the first time in its modern history, to give this notoriously feeble and fragmented state a remarkable measure of stability and strength? Is it a false stability, artificially created by a powerful military machine? Or is this regime founded on a new popular and progressive system with a democratic infrastructure? Similarly, how has Asad succeeded in making a small country of 12 million into an assertive regional power? Does this impressive change reflect the authentic political strength and potential of Syria? Or is it rather the product of the master manipulator Asad, who has skilfully magnified his country's position beyond its real capacity? What enabled him to achieve all these important changes which his predecessors had failed to effect? Can he be compared to Nasser of Egypt, or Saddam Hussein of Iraq? Is he a new Arab Bismarck or merely a Syrian Machiavelli? What are his ultimate goals in Syria and beyond, and how have his policies affected Syria and the other Middle East countries? Does he merely wish to use his strong military power to build a new cohesive nation-state and defend it against external threats? Or is Asad truly a modern Saladin, who with Soviet support aspires to unify the Arab east and lead it to an historic victory over Israel?

Unable to provide all the answers, I have tried to shed light on the above questions without rushing to premature conclusions or un-warranted speculations, because Asad's life story is still unfolding.

1 The Syrian Setting

Asad's unique rise to power in Syria, his long and impressive record as leader, the remarkable transformation that he has brought about in the political structure of his country, as well as in her regional and international position – none of these phenomena can be properly understood without knowing the historical background of Syria, particularly her political, social and ideological developments. Asad's own social and religious roots in the minority Alawite community and its interplay with other Syrian communities, notably the Sunni Muslim majority groups, deserve special attention.

From the end of the Muslim Arab Umayyad Kingdom in the eighth century, whose capital was Damascus, up to the beginning of the twentieth century, Syria was virtually never a separate political or administrative unit with a central government of her own. Rather, she was part of vast empires with remote centres, and was ruled for many generations in a loose way, subdivided into a number of provinces. This was especially true in the long Ottoman period (1516–1918) and is largely responsible for the political characteristics of modern Syria. Thus in the provincial capitals and in other regions of the country, mainly in the mountainous and desert fringes, there were foci of autonomous power which were separated from each other and held themselves aloof from the imperial centre.

Rural and tribal sheikhs, feudal overlords, chiefs of big clans, communal and religious notables and powerful patricians ruled in various parts of the country, sometimes providing a degree of security which the imperial government could not maintain.[1] These leaders based their status not merely on the old social structure which had prevailed in the areas from early times, but also on an ancient concept of rule recognized by the Ottomans. Accordingly, the central

1

government avoided any direct involvement in the social life of the local population and allowed them to exist in autonomous fashion, according to the traditional framework of the extended family, the tribe, the quarter, the religious community and the like, provided they recognized the sultan's authority and paid taxes.

Apart from social influence, some of the local leaders also commanded substantial military and economic power, by virtue of their rule over armed peasants or urban semi-military organizations and their privilege under Ottoman feudal rule of tax collection and jurisdiction in the rural regions.

Among the centres of political and social autonomy perhaps the most conspicuous were those of the Muslim heterodox sects and ethnic-minority groups in the outlying mountains of Syria: the Alawites (or Nusayris) of Jabal (Mount) Ansariyya in the Latakia region; the Druze of Jabal Druze in the Houran and in Mount Lebanon; the Shi'ites in the Anti-Lebanon region and mainly in Jabal Amil, southern Lebanon; the Ismailis in the Salamia mountains near Hama; and the Sunni Muslim Kurds and Turkomans in the passes of the Taurus range. Those groups exploited their geographical or topographical advantages and relied on their social or tribal structure to foster a semi-independent status, sometimes even challenging the regional Ottoman authority.

Furthermore, because of the communal and religious solidarity – developed as a traditional defence against zealous Muslim orthodoxy – political particularism was especially powerful among the heterodox Muslim communities.

These sects, together with ethnic minorities and the Christian and Jewish communities, contributed to the growth of two additional features of Syrian life: communal heterogeneity and sharp contrasts among the various groups. At the beginning of the 1870s, a British observer in Damascus described the intercommunal relations as follows: 'They hate one another. The Sunnites excommunicate the Shiahs and both hate the Druzes; all detest the Ansariyyehs [the Alawites]; the Maronites do not love anybody but themselves and are duly abhorred by all; the Greek Orthodox abominate the Greek Catholics and the Latins; all despise the Jews.'[2]

The axis of intercommunal conflict was naturally the Sunni majority (some 70 per cent of the population); its relations with the other communities and sects were determined not only by religious motives but also by political, economic, psychological and cultural factors.

Muslims versus Alawites and Druze

Relations between the Sunni majority and the heterodox communities were traditionally founded on the religious–sectarian contrast. The orthodox Sunnis regarded the Alawites, Druze, Shi'ites and Ismailis as heretics or deviators, avoided social contact with them, and strove to subdue or occasionally even annihilate them. However, the military power and topographical advantage of these mountain communities greatly hampered the Sunni aims.

Of all these heterodox sects, the Alawites were, as we shall elaborate later,[3] the major object of Sunni Muslim contempt and oppression, because of both their marked religious heresy and their relative political weakness.

True, the Ottoman Turks, the rulers of Syria for 400 years, did not, by and large, persecute the Alawites on religious grounds. But, periodically, notably during the nineteenth century, the Ottoman pashas dispatched military expeditions to the Ansariyya region in order to destroy the local centres of Alawite autonomy and impose central government authority. After a long series of armed clashes which continued intermittently for several decades, the Ottomans succeeded – by execution, arrests, deportation and disarming, as well as by conscription and taxation – in greatly weakening the military and political power of the Alawites, subduing them for the first time in centuries to direct government control.[4]

Unlike the Alawites, who formed only a narrow majority (some 60 per cent) in Jabal Ansariyya, the Druze enjoyed a heavy preponderance in their region, Jabal Druze of the Houran, south-east of Damascus. They were ruled by a few heads of clans (who were also the region's landowners) and displayed unity against exterior threats. So not only did they escape persecution by their Sunni neighbours, but they actually caused great damage to them, particularly in the Muslim villages of the Houran. The Druze successfully fought the Bedouin tribes in the Houran, as well as the Kurdish cavalry used by the Ottoman government to police the region. Furthermore, enjoying territorial concentration, topographical advantage, communal solidarity and social cohesion, the Druze evinced an obstreperous rebelliousness towards the central government itself and gravely damaged its authority and prestige. As Midhat Pasha, the governor of Damascus, reported in 1879, 'These people have completely lost all respect for the government, to which they no longer furnish any troops or taxes.'[5] The Druze were also able to fight back and defeat regular

Turkish troops who were periodically sent to subdue them.

Only during the last decades of the nineteenth century did the central government apply a systematic policy, with bigger forces and modern means, against the Druze and other centrifugal forces. A string of fortresses was built on the border of the Syrian desert, new roads were pushed into mountainous regions, railways were laid between the local centres, and telegraph lines were established between Istanbul and the Syrian cities. By these means, and by the continuous use of large military units, the government succeeded in penetrating the Druze mountain and establishing an Ottoman presence there.

Muslims and Christians

Relations between the Sunni Muslims and the Christian communities during the period under survey were of a different character from those between the Sunni and the heterodox Muslim sects.

Traditionally, the attitude of Muslims towards non-Muslims – Christians and Jews – was one of contempt. According to the Islamic rules these inferior subjects paid a poll tax (*jizya*), were not permitted to carry arms, and were subjected to other social and political limitations. Muslims occasionally humiliated their Jewish and Christian neighbours, maltreated and inflicted physical injuries on them, exposed them to blackmail, and forcibly converted their children. During the nineteenth century, Muslim feelings of scorn for the Christians turned into a deep and burning hatred, while relations between Muslims and Jews hardly changed. In various places in Syria, a number of violent outbreaks against Christians occurred; the outstanding incidents were in Aleppo (1850) and Damascus (1860). In Damascus, for example, Muslim masses, incited by the *ulama* (Muslim sages) and reinforced by Druze rioters, attacked the Christian quarter and killed and wounded thousands of men, women and children, while looting, burning and destroying churches and houses. They did not attack Jews.

This radical change in the Muslim attitude to the Christians in the mid-nineteenth century had a number of causes, mainly connected with the reforms forced upon the Syrian population first by the Egyptian ruler Muhammad Ali during the 1830s and subsequently by the Turkish government. These regimes, each in its own way, granted freedom of worship and equal rights in state institutions to non-

Muslim subjects, for the first time in the history of the Muslim world. Muslim notables feared that the equal status granted to Christians would damage the Islamic character of the country and endanger their own positions in government institutions and in the political community of the Muslim Ottoman state. Muslim merchants, artisans and officials objected to non-Muslim merchants controlling a large portion of the foreign trade, and to the influence of Christian (and Jewish) officials over certain government offices. Muslim masses looked enviously upon the new houses, churches and monasteries rising in the Christian quarters. In sum, many Muslims of different classes shared a common fear that the relatively large Christian element, being better educated and commanding substantial economic means, were likely to assume political control over the country with the external help of the European powers.

The tendency of Syria's Muslims to identify local Christians with the European powers and to consider them a 'fifth column' had been prompted by Napoleon's invasion of Egypt and Palestine in 1798–9. It was further enhanced during the Greek uprising in the 1820s and was turned into deep suspicion and increasing fear in the course of the nineteenth century by the Russian victories over the Ottoman Turks and the aid which Russia extended to Balkan nations in their revolts against the Ottoman empire. The Western Powers, Britain and France, though allies of the Ottoman empire for long periods, were not cleared of suspicion; the local Muslim population was convinced that they were hostile to the Turkish authority in Syria and 'in union with the Christians they wish to overset it'.[6] The Muslim fear of the European–Christian plot against their country was sustained by the cultural, religious, economic and diplomatic contacts of European states and organizations with local Christian communities. For example, European commercial firms appointed local Christians as their agents in Syria, and foreign consuls in the region gave protection to, and interfered on behalf of, the various Christian communities. The Western Powers even used military force, notably gun boat diplomacy, to protect the Syrian Christians: British and French warships patrolled Syria's coast at times of intercommunal tension, and a French expeditionary force landed in Lebanon during the civil riots of 1860. British and French forces conquered other Ottoman territories without provocation: the French occupied Algeria (1830), Tunisia (1881) and Morocco (1907); the British took Cyprus (1878) and Egypt (1882). These operations substantiated Muslim fears of European aggression assisted by local Christians.

Syrian Christians themselves, by openly relying on the foreign consuls and by their alienation from the Ottoman regime and their Muslim neighbours, greatly nourished these suspicions. Many local Christians undoubtedly preferred European to Turkish rule, even after being granted equal rights. Experience had taught them not to trust the intentions of the Ottoman government and they did not believe that they would be allowed to live on equal terms with their Muslim neighbours.

From all this it can be seen that not only did the Muslims refuse to accept the Christians as equal partners in a new social and political order, but the Christians themselves were reluctant to be integrated, though willing to enjoy equal rights. They preferred to be isolated in their communities and quarters and to rely on the protection of the Great Powers. On the other hand, they hastened to use their new rights – such as tolling of church bells, holding of processions – without taking into consideration the feelings of conservative Muslims, who had not heard or seen such phenomena since the beginning of Islam. Such conduct on the part of the Christians was hardly compatible with that of a minority aware of its limitations and sincerely wishing to reach an understanding with the majority; rather it was that of a group which overestimates its importance. For Muslims, this Christian behaviour constituted provocation, which actually sparked many of the outbreaks of Muslim–Christian violence in the nineteenth century.

Violence deepened the abyss between Christians and Muslims to an unprecedented degree in the history of Ottoman Syria. A considerable number of the Christians, concluding that it was no longer possible to live in Muslim Syria, emigrated to safer places in the Middle East – such as Egypt and the Sudan – or to places outside that region – England, America or Australia. This emigration, encouraged by economic prospects abroad, comprised some 330,000 people between 1860 and 1914.[7] Most of the Christians remaining in Syria continued to isolate themselves from their Muslim neighbours and relied on France and Britain until the end of the Ottoman rule.

The Ascendancy of the Urban Oligarchy
and the Decline of Other Classes[8]

Parallel to developments in the relations between the Sunni Muslim majority and the minorities, political processes within the Sunni community occurred in the larger Syrian cities and in their rural surroundings. The most important of these was the crystallization of the power of the traditional urban leadership, mainly in Damascus and Aleppo. This was accompanied by an economic strengthening of this leadership and by the impoverishment of the lower classes among the rural and urban populations.

It is true that the Egyptian regime of Muhammad Ali, which for the first time initiated modernization in Syria during the 1830s, launched an assault on the power of the traditional urban leadership – that is, the heads of the great families (ayan), the ulama and the feudal lords. This regime apparently tried to replace the old elite with a new urban leadership consisting of middle-class representatives, merchants and artisans, both Muslims and non-Muslims. In every town, such representatives were nominated as members of new provincial councils, assisting the governor with advice in matters of administration, commerce and law. But the authority of the council members was, nevertheless, meagre, and their social or religious (non-Muslim) origins could not have given them the requisite status or identification in the eyes of the Muslim populace during the short-lived Egyptian rule. Complete failure of this initial experiment was inevitable.

The new Ottoman regime also tried, upon its return to Syria in 1840, to fill the regional councils with representatives of the middle classes and the non-Muslim communities. But these were quickly removed or neutralized by the heads of the veteran elite, the ayan and ulama, who took over the advisory councils in the course of regaining their power. But the urban elite was not allowed to rebuild its military power, which had been an important source of political strength throughout the long period of pre-reform Ottoman rule. Under the Tanzimat reform regime, power relations indeed changed radically and the Ottoman army attained decisive domination over the urban militias. Armed power and violence, the previous pillars of the urban notables, were thus neutralized. They now had to gain their power from appointments in the administration, from public status and from wealth – and the new Ottoman regime offered such possibilities in abundance. The public administration, which expanded during the era of modernization, absorbed a number of educated notables and placed them in the provincial and municipal offices and in the judicature. The administration of religious institutions – the Muslim shari'a courts, the waqf (religious endowment), the mosques and religious education – were again left in the hands of the Muslim notables. Moreover, the Ottoman government in the Syrian provinces, which did not possess sufficient authority, needed the help of the indigenous elite for the introduction of unpopular reforms, especially military conscription and the new taxation. The representatives of this elite, the *ayan* and *ulama*, were thus allowed virtually to take over the councils established to assist the implementation of reforms; through the councils they received extensive powers in the administration, in the fiscal and economic structure, in the judicial system and in the supervision of law and order.

By controlling the councils and other public institutions, the urban notables managed to rebuild and strengthen their political status and to enrich themselves – largely at the expense of the common people, while widening the economic gap between themselves and the masses. These notables invested in farms, commerce, land and enterprises; their economic power was thus consolidated to an unprecedented degree and acted as a significant support to their political status. The middle class, on the other hand, was severely hit by a market overflowing with imported European merchandise of high quality and low prices (partly as a result of the low custom duties imposed due to the 'capitulations' agreements, whereby Ottoman Turkey granted legal and financial concessions to European powers). Muslim merchants and small traders did not benefit from this flowering commerce with Europe, for it was handled mainly by Christian and Jewish merchants (and by Muslims of the upper class). Groups of merchants and artisans could not defend their interests via their guilds, which were stagnant and disintegrating.

Furthermore, many of these occupational groups, as well as the masses of peasants and the urban proletariat, suffered from conscription and the new system of taxation. The drafting of young men for long periods reduced the number of earners in a family and caused impoverishment – only a few could pay the exemption fee from army service. The method of taxation was unjust and not progressive; the main burden thus fell on the middle and lower classes, aggravating existing poverty and contributing to the development of economic polarization between these classes and the wealthy urban elite throughout the late Ottoman period.

The Development of a Political Community

As we have seen, the political development which Syria underwent in the modern era enhanced communal conflict, widened the gaps between classes and fostered separatism and the isolation of various social groups in semi-independent autonomous centres. These grave developments presented an obvious obstacle to the crystallization of the Syrian population as a political community. In addition, modern Syria lacked other important conditions essential to a distinct political society, such as a central authority, ideological consensus and a territorial identity.

For hundreds of years Syria lacked an exclusive centre which could have served as a focus of identity and loyalty for the mass of the inhabitants and could have imposed its authority on the majority of the population. It is certainly true that, for generations, the Ottoman sultans constituted a centre of religious and political allegiance for the majority of Syria's population, the Sunni Muslims. This centre, however, was geographically distant and gradually became rather nebulous as a result of the lack of government authority and the inability of Istanbul to maintain internal security. Nearer and more concrete were the regional leaders, chiefs of tribe or village, who provided security to the people and thus held their basic loyalty, while weakening their political – if not religious – identification with the sultan. Needless to say, the non-Sunni communities and sects felt no loyalty whatever, whether political or religious, to the Ottoman regime. The only social group which fully identified itself with the sultan and the Ottoman empire were members of the religious and administrative establishment in Syria, who had been completely integrated in the Ottoman political community.

The aim of the Ottoman modernization movement in the nineteenth century was to expand the sphere of popular identification with the state to include the members of non-Muslim communities. The Tanzimat leaders and the Young Ottomans thought it best to establish a new political community; the basis of its identity was to be Ottoman supra-communal, and all the sultan's subjects, regardless of religion, were to participate. To achieve this end, the reform leaders strove to establish the sultan's authority in the provinces, improve the general standard of living and grant equal status to the non-Muslims. However, although the central role of the sultan gained strength in the Syrian provinces, by mid-century his spiritual authority had declined among the Muslim population because his policy injured their Islamic feelings. Turkish linguistic and cultural values could not have any attraction for the Syrian population, the majority of which was Arabic-speaking. Furthermore, the Ottoman empire was too extensive to ensure territorial identification of the Syrian population living in close traditional frameworks.

The values of Arabic language and culture and of Syrian territorial identity – which the policies of the Ottoman reform movement lacked – were in fact the very basis of a small cultural and ideological circle which originated in Syria in the middle of the nineteenth century. This circle was founded by a handful of Beirut Christian intellectuals, mainly Orthodox and Protestant, and expanded following the 1860 massacres in Lebanon and Damascus. In contrast with most local Christians, who preferred to continue their insular approach towards the Muslims and rely on foreign backing, or to emigrate, these few intellectuals looked for a joint life with their neighbours in other communities. They believed that the communal and religious loyalties which were splitting the population must be replaced by a secular patriotism based on the common Syrian homeland and on the Arabic language and culture. These Christian intellectuals devoted themselves to the revival of Arab language and culture. They established an Arabic literary society and theatre, wrote articles and conducted research in the Arabic language. By means of these tools these intellectuals – Butrus al-Bustani in particular – initially advanced the concepts of 'homeland' (*watan*) and of Syria. The concept 'Syria' was apparently borrowed from Christian or European sources, or possibly from the definitions used by the Byzantines and the Crusaders centuries before. Their notions of secularism and patriotism obviously originated in contemporary European national movements.[9]

The activity of this Syrian patriotic and cultural group increased in subsequent years and acquired a political undertone. In 1875 a few young intellectuals among Bustani's followers established a small secret society whose aims were to secure autonomy for Syria, including Lebanon, and recognition of Arabic as the official language.

These demands appeared in leaflets distributed by members of the society in various Syrian towns during the rule of Midhat Pasha (1878–81), consisting of such catchphrases as 'sons of Syria', 'Syrian devotion', 'Arab pride' and 'degenerate Turks'. According to some sources, the secret society included Druze and Muslims as well as Christians, had connections with Midhat Pasha, and had as its aim the independence of Syria based on Egypt's model.[10] At that stage, however, the Ottoman authorities intervened by arresting and deporting two members of the society. Shortly after this, Midhat Pasha was also deported, and the co-operation between him and the Syrian patriotic circle ceased.

Yet, apart from this episode, it should be emphasized that throughout the nineteenth century no sense of Syrian territorial patriotism developed among the majority of the local population. An experienced traveller and observer visiting Syria at the end of the 1850s described the situation as follows: 'Patriotism is unknown. . . . There is not a man in the country whether Turk or Arab, Mohammedan or Christian who would give a para [penny] to save the Empire from ruin. The patriotism of the Syrian is confined to the four walls of his own house; anything beyond them does not concern him.'[11] Even at the beginning of the twentieth century, no change in Syrian patriotism was evident. According to contemporary testimonies, of a Christian Syrian intellectual and a senior government official, 'the patriotic bond is weak and concerns only a few members of the upper class'; 'No symptom is noticeable which would tend to support the belief that any cohesion exists between the different classes of people. . . . religious differences are still as powerful as ever in effecting a cleavage among neighbours and fellow citizens'.[12]

Religious zeal and intercommunal enmity were indeed still strong among the majority of the population, due to the deep-rooted sectarian outlook and the general cultural and educational insularism. Traditional Muslim education in the *kuttab* and *madrasa* (religious schools) – which were attended by most of the Muslim students – provided Muslim values only. The Christian communal schools, on the other hand, furnished the community's youth with a narrowly sectarian Christian education. The new government's educational system, established after 1860, could not, or was not intended to, introduce values of Syrian patriotism and religious tolerance. This system remained limited, absorbed mainly Muslim pupils and had an Ottoman or (in the time of Abd al-Hamid) Ottoman Muslim orientation. Similarly, the missionary educational systems scarcely included non-Christian pupils, and fostered an attachment to European cultural values.

In addition the consolidation of the central Ottoman rule and the elevated administrative status of Damascus did not bring the inhabitants of the other Syrian districts any nearer to an identification with the concept of Syria. For example, Aleppo, the traditional rival city of Damascus, which included a substantial non-Arab and non-Muslim population, developed strong orientations towards Baghdad and Istanbul, rather than towards Damascus and Beirut.

The latter town developed after 1840 into an important commercial and administrative centre, the residence of European diplomats and a strong competitor with Damascus for regional seniority. In Mount

Lebanon a Maronite Lebanese political community was forming in isolation from the Syrian groups, notably the Sunni Muslims.

At this point it must be stressed that the entire political and religious Muslim elite rejected the idea of a secular Syrian patriotism and considered it dangerous to the Islamic character of the state and to their own positions in it. Simultaneously, however, the feeling of identification with the sultan and the Ottoman empire weakened among part of this elite during the mid-century precisely because of the idea of a secular Ottoman patriotism initiated by the Tanzimat leaders. Thus the reform policy of the Sultan Abd al-Majid (1839–61) provoked opposition among conservative Muslim circles in Syria, who began to question the right of the sultan to lead the Muslim world (they labelled this 'al- khain', the betrayal of Islam). In these circles, reform appears to have fanned the latent feelings of difference between Arab and Turk and emphasized the special role of the Arabs in Islam. In some places in Syria, during the sixth and seventh decades of the nineteenth century, hopes of 'separation from the Ottoman Empire and the formation of a new Arabian state under the sovereignty of the Shereef of Mecca' were expressed.[13] Later, under the tyrannical rule of Sultan Abd al-Hamid, Muslim intellectual leaders of Syrian origin, such as Abd al-Rahman al-Kawakibi and Rashid Rida, pleaded for the return of the caliphate to the Arabs. However, these expressions of Arab consciousness were too weak and sporadic during the entire second half of the nineteenth century, and became a major trend only at the beginning of the twentieth century, as a reaction to the secular Turkish nationalism of the Young Turks (1908–18).

Until that new era the majority of the religious and administrative establishment – the *ulama*, members of the government organs and senior officialdom – still regarded themselves as part of the Ottoman Muslim political community and remained loyal to the regime up to its last day. Although political and religious identification with the sultan weakened during the period of the reformer Abd al-Majid, it recovered under the conservative Sultan Abd al-Hamid II, who was a zealous Muslim.

Thus, by the eve of the First World War under the rule of the Young Turks, two political trends competed among the Muslim Syrian elite: a small undercurrent of Arabism, the manifestations of which were the secret Arab nationalist societies; and the mainstream of Ottomanism, which was especially strong in the circles close to the government and the public administration.[14] Among the majority Muslim population,

12

there persisted strong Islamic feelings on the one hand, and a rejection of Syrian patriotism on the other. These people considered themselves Ottomans and Muslims, and not Arabs or Syrians. For example, the nine representatives elected to the Ottoman parliament on behalf of the Syrian provinces did not act as one group, whether Syrian or Arab, and did not raise in the parliament any matters concerning Syria. By contrast, members of the Arab nationalist societies, many of whom were Syrians, considered themselves, above all, to be Arabs and demanded autonomy for all Arab countries and particularly for Syria. They regarded Syria as a centre of the Arab sphere, and Damascus – the past capital of the Umayyad Arab empire – as the future capital of the Arab state.[15]

It was only after the First World War that the notion of a Syrian Arab national entity became predominant among a growing number of Syrians, mainly due to the establishment of a separate Syrian political and territorial framework by the Great Powers, notably Britain.

The first step in the formation of this entity was reached during Amir (later King) Faysal's rule in Syria (1918–20) with the emergence of a semi-independent Syrian Arab government and local political parties. The names given to those organs indicate the notion of a Syrian identity. The governments of Faysal were, in chronological order: the Arab Military Government of Syria, the Arab Syrian Government and the Kingdom of Syria. The institution which was to serve as a kind of national assembly was called the National Congress and also the Syrian Congress, whereas the parties represented in that assembly called themselves the Independent Pan-Arab Party and the United Syrian Party. Faysal himself also endeavoured to integrate the various communities into a new non-sectarian Syrian Arab nation under the motto: 'Religion for God, the homeland for all'. He appointed leaders of the Muslim and heterodox communities to the regional administration and allocated seats in the Syrian congress and cabinet to Christians. Simultaneously, he promoted the Arabization of state institutions and the educational system and founded an academy for the Arabic language in Damascus.

Progress and Regression Under the French Mandate[16]

With the elimination of Faysal's kingdom in 1920 by the French occupation of Syria, an important ingredient in the creation of a national community in Syria was temporarily lost, while the prospects of establishing a new cohesive social system were suspended for another generation. Nevertheless, the sense of Syrian identity did not slacken among members of the national movement, thanks to the formation of Syrian government institutions – cabinet, parliament and so on – by the French authorities, and to the development of a national struggle for independence against the French.

The Syrian National Bloc (al-Kutla al-Wataniyya), which led the struggle against the French, included personalities and groups of various religious backgrounds and from different parts of the country. Among the Kutla leaders, mostly Sunni Muslims from Damascus and Aleppo, Orthodox and Protestant Christians were also prominent. They established close contacts with Druze leaders, notably Sultan al-Atrash, and co-operated with him during the 1925 uprising against the French.

The joint struggle of these personalities and groups against the mandatory rule undoubtedly contributed to the reinforcement of Syrian national consciousness among various circles of the population and in particular among the Muslim and Christian urban intelligentsia. Yet this consciousness was not as well developed nor as extensive as in other Arab countries, and thus could not have constituted a sufficient basis for a Syrian national community. Indeed, in contrast to what was happening in Egypt, Iraq and Lebanon, the mandatory regime greatly damaged the process of establishing a nation-state in Syria, not only by interrupting the initial Syrian steps towards independence and unity when it put an end to Faysal's regime, but also by reducing the areas of the historical Syrian provinces by annexing to Lebanon areas in the Tripoli, Biqa and Sidon districts in 1920, and by surrendering the district of Alexandretta to Turkey in 1939. The mandatory government also undermined the centrality of Damascus as well as the unity of the country by reviving and even deepening the communal conflicts and regional contrasts, and by strengthening non-Muslim sects. Thus at the beginning of the 1920s Syria was divided into four autonomous 'states': Damascus, Aleppo, and the Alawite and Druze districts. After several years, Damascus and Aleppo were united in the 'state of Syria', but the Alawite and Druze 'states' continued to exist separately until 1936. The Jazira region was also administered separately, whereas the Alexandretta district enjoyed broad autonomy until annexation by Turkey. Simultaneously, the French foiled the development of a cohesive Syrian society and intercommunal integration by encouraging and favouring the Christian communities. The autonomy of the Christian sects was revived and even expanded under the mandate, to include religious freedom, jurisdiction in matters of personal status and communal education.[17] These rights were officially recognized by the Syrian constitution of 1930, which also provided the heads of the Christian communities with an official status and granted these communities representation in official institutions. In fact, Christians enjoyed preferential status in public administration, both through French encouragement and thanks to their high educational level; they also benefited from a period of economic revival – not without help from the French. All of this contributed to the fostering of communal separatism, while further widening the economic, cultural and political rift between Christians and Muslims in modern Syria.

The economic gap between the wealthy Muslim elite and the middle and lower classes, both urban and rural, persisted during the French mandatory period without serious attempts on the part of the French to reduce it by initiating government reforms. In the cities, for instance, the process of decay in the traditional handicrafts and home industries continued, caused by competition from imported goods or from those manufactured in the modern local factories, which were established mainly by the Muslim upper class, as well as by local Christian and French investors. The rates of pay in industry likewise declined as a result of competition from Armenian immigrants who arrived by the thousands; working conditions were deplorable and social legislation rudimentary. There was unemployment among the middle class – who abandoned their traditional occupations and looked for jobs in the civil service – and among the unskilled proletariat, continuously reinforced by a host of peasants escaping the grim conditions in their villages.

Indeed, the French mandate did almost nothing to improve the conditions of the peasantry, which constituted some 70 per cent of the population. The French initially intended to improve conditions and aid the farmers: modern land registration was carried out, the *musha'* (joint ownership) lands were divided and registered, government land was put up for sale on convenient terms, and even an agricultural credit bank was founded. These reforms, however, hardly helped the small peasant, who could not afford to buy the offered state lands or was unable to fulfil the terms of a credit contract. Only the big landowners and wealthy farmers found a way to buy these lands and use the credits to increase the area under cultivation and its profitability.

The rich urban landowners did not confine themselves to agriculture and continued to invest their money in commerce and in the modern industries which developed in Syria towards the end of the mandate – mainly food and textiles. As during the Ottoman period, they invested part of their profits in secondary and university education, in Syria and abroad, for their sons and relatives. Those later occupied positions in the mandatory Syrian administration, while their families continued to possess great political and economic power, just as they had done in the Ottoman past.

At this point it should be mentioned that the economic contrasts which continued to develop in Syria after the First World War were not due merely to negligence on the part of the French mandatory regime, but resulted also from the attitudes of Syrian leaders who held the reins of self-rule and headed the national movement in Syria. The Kutla, like the 'moderate' Syrian parties, centred around personalities and families who had amassed great wealth since the Ottoman period. Representing narrow upper-class interests, these figures were keen to sustain the economic status quo and thus refrained from drawing up long-term plans to improve the conditions of the rural and urban masses. Similarly, unwilling to alienate the conservative sections of the Muslim population, the nationalist leaders did very little to provoke the Muslim *ulama* or to foster intercommunal accommodation. It is true that several Christian personalities were placed in the first ranks of the nationalist leadership, which periodically issued statements and slogans concerning freedom of conscience, religious tolerance and patriotic brotherhood, and that these notions were expressed in the 1930 Syrian constitution (clauses 6, 15 and 28, for example), which had been composed with the participation of the Kutla representatives. Yet most of these notions remained dead letters. An international subcommittee of the League of Nations thus stated in 1934: 'The commission regretted to note that the application of the Syrian legislation prescribing equality before the law is still sometimes impeded through the absence of a spirit of tolerance on the part of the autochthonous authorities.'[18] Four years later, in 1938, the law of personal status (1936), which expressed the constitutional principle of freedom of conscience and religion, was annulled under pressure from the *ulama*.[19] As in the Ottoman past, the Muslim masses continued to express, through acts of violence against Christians, their objections to intercommunal equality. During the uprising of 1925, for example, Christians suspected of collaboration with the French were attacked in Damascus, and in Homs the local Christian governor was assassinated by Muslims; in 1936 grave clashes occurred between Muslims and Christians in Aleppo and in Jazira. Some of these clashes resulted from French provocation, such as using Armenian troops against Muslim rebels and arming the Christian population of Damascus during the 1925 revolt. Nevertheless, the Syrian national leadership cannot be exempted from blame for these intercommunal conflicts. The leadership did not use its prestige to guide the masses towards values of mutual tolerance and patriotic brotherhood. Although the national leaders fought for Syria's independence, they did not invest enough thought and action in the formation of a national community by bridging the gaps between the various groups and by elevating the population from its narrow traditional loyalties towards a feeling of Syrian national identity.

As it was, most of the population in mandatory Syria did not identify itself as Syrian Arab. The minority communities – both Muslim heterodox and Christian, with the exception of Christian Orthodox and Protestant intelligentsia – still relied on the French mandatory regime. The rural and tribal groups and a considerable portion of the urban lower classes continued to abide by clannish and regional loyalties and considered themselves Sunni Muslim Arabs more than Syrian Arabs. Even among the more advanced urban members of the national movement, the feeling of a single Syrian entity was not as strong as were the parallel sentiments in some neighbouring Arab countries. Among these circles Islamic, regional or pan-Arab orientations were still powerful. And unlike in Egypt and even Iraq, Syria did not produce during that period a leader of national stature who could have served as a focus of national unity. Instead most of the Kutla leaders represented regional rather than national interests, particularly after the 1936 agreement (with France), when the struggle against the French met with partial success and Syria started to move towards independence. To some extent, certain leaders at that time acquired nation-wide prestige (men like Ibrahim Hananu, Hashim al-Atasi or Shukri al-Quwatli), but they were either too old or too weak to play the role of nation-builders successfully.

Thus, when Syria became an independent republic in 1946, she was formally a state but essentially was not yet a nation-state – a political entity which had neither a cohesive political community nor an integrated society.

Nevertheless, once the French had gone, a new generation of young Syrian leaders were in a better position to embark upon the appallingly difficult task of achieving national unity and of bringing about the necessary social and political change.

Among the young leaders who rose to power in independent Syria, the most prominent, powerful and effective, as well as the leader who has enjoyed the longest tenure of office, has been Hafiz al-Asad. Not only has he been able to engineer a fundamental social and political upheaval in the country, he has also succeeded in transforming Syria from a notoriously weak and vulnerable polity into a strong and assertive state, a regional power in the Middle East.

Asad's remarkable achievements are particularly striking in view of the fact that he is a member of the Alawite minority, which, as we have seen, has been considered an heretical religious sect and an outcast social group by large sections of the Sunni Muslim majority population.

This then raises intriguing and complex questions: what were the effects of these Alawite roots and environment, his social and geographical milieux, his cultural and political education, on the shaping of Asad's personality, views and aims?

2 Alawite Heritage and Arab Ideals

Alawite Roots

Asad's Alawite origins, background and loyalties have had a crucial impact on his personality and beliefs as well as on his career and policies.

Founded as a religious sect apparently during the late tenth century in Jabal Ansariyya near Latakia, a predominantly Sunni Muslim town and Mediterranean port in north-western Syria, the Nusayris – later known as Alawis or Alawites – have professed an esoteric secret faith. This was a blend of ancient Syrian or Phoenician paganism (mainly the worship of the triad: the sun, the moon and the stars or sky), possibly influenced by Christian Trinitarianism (Holy Trinity) as well as by various Christian ceremonies and feasts, and largely manifested in a Shi'i-Ismaili fashion, namely an adherence to Imam Ali, the first cousin and son-in-law of the prophet Muhammad and a divine incarnation (according to the Shia) of the Prophet, as well as an adherence to Salman al-Farisi, one of Muhammad's Persian followers. The name 'Nusayris' derives, according to one interpretation, from Abu Shuayb Muhammad Ibn Nusayr (a Shi'i religious scholar who lived in Basra, Iraq, in the ninth century), while the name 'Alawis' might indicate the worshippers of Ali.

Within their religion the Alawites are subdivided into three main sections: the Shamsis – a derivative of Shams, or sun; the Qamaris – after Qamar, or moon; the Ghaybiyyas – worshippers of air or the sky. The Alawite community is further divided into four tribes or clans (which do not necessarily correspond with the religious sections): the Haddadin, the Khayyatin, the Kalbiyya and the Matawira. This clannish and sectarian fragmentation during long periods not only exposed many Alawites to exploitation by their tribal heads and religious leaders, but made them particularly vulnerable to extortion and oppression by their Sunni Muslim neighbours. Indeed for generations the Alawites were landless serfs, agricultural workers or servants of urban Sunni (and Christian) landowners and proprietors. Furthermore, many among the Sunni Muslim majority population in Syria for centuries detested the Alawites for their religious heresy and cultural backwardness. As early as the fourteenth century Ibn Taymiyya, a distinguished Sunni Muslim scholar, issued a *fatwa* (a religious opinion or judgement) stating that the Nusayris were greater infidels than Jews, Christians and many other idolaters and that waging war against them should please Allah.[1]

Accordingly, certain (Sunni Muslim) Mamluk sultans of Egypt (who ruled Syria from the mid-thirteenth to the mid-sixteenth centuries) periodically attempted to Islamize the Alawites forcibly or exterminate them. Under the Ottoman Turks (who succeeded the Egyptian Mamluks as rulers of Syria) the Alawites by and large were not persecuted on religious grounds. But during that period they were still regarded as 'a wicked race' who deserved 'no mercy, no protection'.[2] Consequently 'they were abused, reviled and ground down by exaction, and on occasions their women and children led into captivity and disposed of by sale'. Indeed, their economic conditions gravely deteriorated towards the end of Ottoman rule to the extent that Alawite peasants developed after the First World War 'the practice of selling or hiring out their daughters to affluent [Sunni Muslim] townspeople. Some were sold in their childhood for life as servants but most were, for an agreed price, merely indentured, so to say, for a given period of time.'[3]

These deplorable conditions, coupled with the deep religious and cultural animosity directed towards them by their Sunni Muslim neighbours, seem to have contributed over a long period to develop or sharpen among Alawites certain traits or modes of behaviour which were basically of two kinds. One trend of Alawite reactions to their Sunni surroundings consisted of feelings of hatred and revenge, unruly and rebellious conduct coupled with a strong tendency to social and religious seclusion and political autonomy. The other current, or rather undercurrent, of Alawite conduct may be called *taqiyya*, that is 'dissimulation', 'caution' or 'disguise' (*taqiyya* is an Islamic term for dispensation from the requirements of religion under compulsion or threat of injury). This describes the cautious behaviour of the Alawites towards a powerful, fanatical or threatening ruler or neighbours, and a tactical, superficial adaptation to these outside forces. During the Ottoman era and under the French mandate the first current was predominant; the second appeared after the First World War and gained momentum thereafter. As for their more overt conduct, a knowledgeable contemporary observer wrote in the late 1850s: 'As the Ansaireah are oppressed by the government, so like most semi-barbarous mountain tribes they take their revenge by descending and plundering in the plains; and requite the hatred of the Mussulmans by robbing and murdering them without mercy, when pretty sure of escaping punishment.'[4]

In addition to such vindictive raids, Alawite chiefs would periodic-ally rebel against government attempts to impose conscription, disarmament and direct rule, while striving to solidify their own self-rule, and occasionally seeking European help or protection.

As we have seen, these Alawite endeavours to gain political autonomy were essentially unsuccessful until the end of Ottoman rule. Yet during the 1920s these tendencies towards independence were greatly encouraged by the French to the extent of creating an Alawite 'state' in the Alawite district, in accordance with the French colonial policy of 'divide and rule'. In fact, as Arnold Toynbee suggested in the 1920s, the Alawites were the only sect that benefited from the mandate[5] since they were also 'extremely useful, perhaps even indispensable' to the French as a military instrument.[6] Consequently not only were they able to foster their social and religious particular-ism, but the French helped them to develop a modern economic infrastructure in their region. In essence, young Alawite peasants, motivated by economic and personal ambitions, were encouraged by the mandate authorities to enrol in relatively large numbers in the French-controlled Troupes Spéciales, the local Syrian army. Being regarded by the French as 'warlike savages and bandits',[7] Alawites thus formed three out of the eight infantry battalions of this military force, and were employed by the French to help suppress the Syrian Arab nationalist struggle for independence, including the 1925 revolt.

Even after the French had left, the Alawite tendencies to seclusion, autonomy and rebellion continued while an independent Syrian national government was established in the country. Several insur-rections broke out in the Alawite district (with French encouragement) against the new Syrian government, in attempts to maintain a measure of regional and communal autonomy. Yet these uprisings, headed by Sulayman al-Murshid, an Alawite religious and political leader, and his son Mujib, were quelled with the capture and execution of

Sulayman in 1946 and with the killing of Mujib in 1952. Only then was the Alawite region for the first time subdued and subjected to central control. Since then more and more Alawites have sought to integrate into the Syrian Arab political community and to adjust to the fresh conditions. In fact the tendency among certain Alawites to adapt to the new political realities – the *taqiyya* conduct – was already apparent after the First World War when various Alawite chiefs pursued policies which were oriented to please not only the French (and the British) but also the Syrian Arab government of Faysal in Damascus.

These multifarious policies represented not merely Alawite attempts to regain their autonomous political position under the new circumstances, but simultaneously reflected the diversity and disunity among the Alawite community. For example, Sheikh Salih al-Ali, an Alawite chieftain involved in internal Alawite and regional rivalries, rebelled against the French, who supported his rivals. He formed alliances with the anti-French forces in Syria, namely Amir Faysal and Ibrahim Hannanu, the Syrian nationalist leader from Aleppo.[8] The rebellion was put down in 1921, and Sheikh Salih surrendered to the French. But his insurrection and his alliance with the Syrian Arab nationalists by no means demonstrated an Alawite tendency to integrate into a new Syrian Arab nationalist movement and to help it drive out the French. Such tendencies appeared only in the mid-1930s, particularly following the 1936 French–Syrian pact, which provided for the establishment of a unified and independent Syrian state.

While the majority of Alawites continued to adhere to the concept of Alawite autonomy under French protection, a growing number of young Alawites adopted a different position. Motivated by *Realpolitik* considerations or influenced by the ideas of Syrian or Syrian Arab nationalism, these young Alawites claimed that they were true Syrians, true Arabs and true Muslims. Apparently they regarded assimilation as a prerequisite for successful integration in the Syrian political community.[9] As in the case of other non-Sunni Arabic-speaking minorities, these young Alawites adopted the new nationalist ideas through both the expanding educational system and the recently established nationalist and secularist parties, the Syrian Nationalist Party and the Ba'th Party. Young Alawites were indeed attracted to these parties, notably the Ba'th, in greater numbers than the Druze for example. This was not only because the Alawites comprised a larger proportion of the population, but possibly also because of the greater diversity and disunity among the Alawite community, which perhaps contributed to the weakening of sectarian cohesion among educated Alawites. Nevertheless, as we shall see later, these young people by no means wished, or could afford, to dispose of their Alawite connections. They would draw a great deal of support from other members of their community in the remarkable process of their integration and political ascendancy in the new Syrian nationalist politics. One of these young Alawites was Hafiz al-Asad.

Asad was born in October 1930 and was brought up in that crucial era of cross-currents among the Alawite community. On the one hand, there was the old and deep-rooted tradition of sectarian seclusion, social alienation and political autonomy vis-à-vis the Syrian Sunni majority; on the other hand, there was a new political and cultural orientation towards integration into the developing Syrian national community.

These diverse tendencies were reflected in Asad's own clan and village. His village, Qardaha, had been a traditional centre of the Qamari sect and belonged to the Numailatiyya clan of the Matawira tribe. This tribe produced one of the greatest Alawite heroes, Ismail Bey, who for several years during the 1850s successfully fought the Ottoman Turkish government and was able to establish autonomous rule in large parts of the Alawite region. Another Alawite hero, Sulayman al-Murshid, initially belonged to the Qamari sect. By contrast Asad's village, Qardaha, served in 1946 as a meeting place for Alawite religious and political leaders who publicly advocated the integration of the Alawite region into the Syrian state.[10] Not too far from this village, there are the ruins of Crusaders' castles, which were conquered and destroyed in the twelfth century by Salah al-Din (Saladin), the legendary hero in Arab Muslim history. Presumably these diverse features of his historical background as well as his social, religious and political milieux contributed to the shaping of Asad's personality and *Weltanschauung* as a child. Unfortunately there is very little information about Asad's childhood, his parents, his friends, his teachers or his early education. (At both elementary school and secondary school he was reputedly a diligent, well-behaved student, very interested in history and geography, particularly of the Arab world, though weak in mathematics and sport.) But Asad himself is very reluctant to talk about these things.

Transformation

Hafiz was the oldest son in a family of eight children – six boys and two girls. At birth he was called Abu Sulayman, after his grandfather Sulayman, who had reportedly fought the Turks. Hafiz's father Ali, a hard-working farmer, was also known for his opposition to Syria's French rulers during the 1920s and 1930s. In one of his rare references to his childhood, Asad credited his father with instilling a strong Syrian Arab nationalistic fervour in him, at the same time reminding him to take pride in his Alawite heritage. Such testimony might substantiate the assumption that as a boy Hafiz received both at home and in his village elementary school an education which was both Alawite sectarian and Syrian Arab nationalist.

Yet, when he left his home and village at the age of fourteen and moved to Latakia for his secondary schooling, Hafiz further developed and consolidated his Syrian Arab consciousness, while possibly distancing himself from his Alawite past. The family name was changed around that time. His original family name had been Wahsh; in Arabic this literally means 'wild beast', but it can also be pejorative, connoting a bad, vulgar and uncivilized person. This was changed to Asad – 'lion' in Arabic – a symbol of both strength and dignity, indicating perhaps the measure of self-confidence and pride in the bearer. (Theoretically his full name is Hafiz al-Asad, 'the lion's guard', but in practice he is known simply as Asad, 'the lion'.)

The new environment, the largely Sunni Muslim town of Latakia, as well as the Arab nationalist secondary education he had received and his keenness for Arab history and geography – all these factors undoubtedly contributed to shaping Asad's nationalist and political tendencies. Plunging into student politics, he soon became the leader of the local student group. He was also involved in anti-French activities: he delivered fiery speeches against the mandatory rule and was reportedly jailed by the French.[11]

At the age of sixteen, this ambitious, proud and stubborn young man was ready, like many of his contemporaries, to join one of the parties which struggled for Syrian nationalist goals. Obviously, his choice could not have fallen on either of the veteran conservative nationalist parties. These parties came to be despised by many young Syrians for their failure to oust the French and gain independence, for their non-progressive economic policies, and for their ideological shallowness and organizational weakness. Furthermore, to a (former) member of a non-Sunni sect like Asad, these parties represented the traditional notions of religious predominance, contempt and oppression which the non-Sunni sects had for so long endured.

Precisely because of these shortcomings, young Alawites, Druze and

Christians tended to join one of the modern ideological parties, which also professed progressive policies for improving economic conditions and determining the role of religion in Syrian society. Four such parties fitted these criteria, since they preached national independence, social (or socialist) and economic reform and secularization of public life. They were the Syrian Nationalist Party (PPS – later known as the Syrian Social Nationalist Party, SSNP) and the Syrian Communist Party, both of which were established in the early 1930s; the League for National Action, formed in 1935, and the Arab Resurrection (Ba'th) Party, founded in 1940 and merged in 1953 with the Arab Socialist Party (founded 1950). The Communist Party had very little appeal among the Alawites (and Druze) because of its radical philosophy and its foreign (Soviet) links; this party was also hardly active in the Alawite region. By contrast, the PPS, founded by Antun Sa'adeh, a Lebanese Greek Orthodox Christian, drew to its ranks not a few Alawites, as well as other non-Sunni Syrians. Its appeal lay in its clearly defined and attractive principles: the adherence to a distinct Syrian national entity embracing geographical Syria; the separation of religion from the state and the removal of the barriers between the various sects; the abolition of feudalism and the protection of the rights of labour, and so on.[12]

Attractive to young Alawites in a different way was the League of National Action, or rather one of its leaders, Zaki Arsuzi, an Alawite intellectual and thinker originally from Alexandretta. Although initially he had shared the radical doctrines[13] and the pan-Arab and anti-French platform of this party, Arsuzi broke away from the League in the late 1930s. In 1940 he founded a small movement called al-Ba'th al-Arabi (the Arab Renaissance). The headquarters of this new group was in Damascus but it was active in Latakia during the mid-1940s. Most of its followers were Alawites. Among them, possibly, was young Hafiz al-Asad.[14] But Arsuzi's Ba'th group soon ceased its activities and most of his Alawi followers as well as other Alawites – Asad among them – joined the rival, or twin, Ba'th Party. Young Asad reportedly organized the Ba'th students' cell at his secondary school in 1947 at Latakia.

The Ba'th Party, like Arsuzi's Ba'th group, had been formed in 1940 in Damascus, and subsequently established branches in Aleppo, Homs and Latakia. Founded by Michel Aflaq, a Syrian Greek Orthodox Christian, and Salah al-Din al-Bitar, a Syrian Sunni Muslim, both French-educated intellectuals from Damascus, the Ba'th Party professed three main principles: unity, socialism and freedom.

Primarily and essentially, the Ba'th doctrine of Arab nationalism referred to the unity of the Arab nation, which is an eternal entity in history and should be united in one state in order to continue its contribution to world civilization. Arab unity is also a precondition for the solution of Arab problems. These problems must be then tackled through the application of Arab socialism, which is neither Soviet communism nor materialist Western socialism, but stands for social justice and economic reform. All this in turn will generate freedom, or liberation from sectarian and class conflicts and the application of individual rights and liberties, although these are ultimately subjected to the higher interests of the Arab nation.[15]

Although the Ba'th doctrines were not as clear-cut and well defined as those of the PPS–SSNP, the party nevertheless drew to its ranks a considerable number of young Alawites as well as Druze, Christians and even Sunni Muslims. Many of them, like Asad, were secondary-school students who had been exposed to the ideas of Arab nationalism. Emotionally and enthusiastically they embraced the romantic and heroic nationalist message of the new party. The non-Sunni students among them who were also attracted by the secularist notions of the Ba'th wished to integrate as equals into a new non-sectarian Syrian Arab community. Other members or followers of the Ba'th Party were university students and professionals from the big cities – Muslims and Christians alike – who were enthused not only by its pan-Arab ideas, but by the Ba'th notions of economic change, social justice and parliamentary democracy. Disillusioned by the poor political performance of the veteran nationalist leadership and resentful of its conservative policies, these young urban intellectuals regarded the Ba'th Party as an avenue for their own political ascendancy and social mobility.

The ranks of this party of predominantly young urban intelligentsia and members of the minorities were swelled in 1953 by scores of Sunni Muslim *fellahin* from the Syrian lowlands. They had originally been followers of Akram Hawrani's Arab Socialist Party, now amalgamated with the Ba'th. These peasants were particularly motivated by the urge to struggle against their feudal landlords for their own lands and for better economic conditions. In sum, as a result of its growing membership (2,500 in 1954) and its modern and efficient organizational machinery, the Ba'th Party succeeded in outnumbering its rival modern parties (the PPS–SSNP and the Communists), and in the 1954 elections it won 22 seats out of 142 in the Syrian parliament. Despite this important achievement, the majority of the parliamentary seats were still held by members of the traditional conservative nationalist parties, and the road to political ascendancy through parliament and electoral politics seemed to be too long and agonizing. A shorter and more promising avenue to power was the army officers' corps.

Indeed, in 1949, only a few years after Syria had become an independent republic with a parliamentary system, senior army officers – Hosni Za'im, Sami Hinawwi and Adib Shishakli – had successively seized control of the country by means of military coups or counter-coups. These military actions reflected the army's discontent with the civilian leadership's conduct during the 1948 war with Israel: it was blamed for failing to prepare the army for the war, and so inviting the defeat which followed. Yet beyond these complaints some officers shared the social and political grievances of the middle and lower classes from which they came. Some officers of course were motivated by a sheer lust for political power. Meanwhile upper-class officers supported the attempts of the veteran leadership to regain or maintain the status quo.

The democratic parliamentary system was reinstated in 1954, following Shishakli's overthrow by the army, backed by most political parties. Nevertheless the struggle for power in Syria continued among groups of army officers associated to the various political parties.[16] Of these military factions, the officers' group affiliated with the Ba'th Party appeared to have the upper hand. This affiliation had been initiated and cultivated by Akram Hawrani, the resourceful and rather opportunistic politician from Hama. Several years before he joined forces with the Ba'th Party, Hawrani had developed close ties with a group of young officers, graduates of the Military Academy at Homs. Through these contacts he played a significant role in the 1949 coups, particularly in those of Zaim and Shishakli, as well as in the anti-Shishakli rebellion in 1954. Thus when in 1953 he amalgamated his Socialist Party with the Ba'th, he provided a 'dowry': a group of military partisans, among them officers holding key army positions, such as those of deputy chief of staff, chief of military intelligence and leader of the 1954 coup against Shishakli.

Asad, a young Ba'th member, was serving at that time as a cadet in the Syrian Air Force Academy.

3 A Soldier Climbs to Power

The Soldier

The young and ambitious Asad, a Ba'thist activist and a student leader in Latakia from the age of sixteen to twenty-one, was still restless; his sense of personal achievement and national fulfilment was far from satisfied. As he said in a later interview:

> I thought of going to university and studying medicine, but I also considered the military academy. The use of force and violence against my people convinced me that military service would be the most effective way to serve my country. . . . When I was still a child I saw French soldiers in my country beating my people . . . when I heard French planes were bombing our towns I chose to become a pilot because I thought that if I were a pilot I could stop this.[1]

Yet, even after the French had left and Syria emerged as an independent state, it was suffering grave problems. The veteran conservative leaders who were governing the young republic were weak, divided and inefficient. They were thus unable to deal effectively with the domestic difficulties and the external challenges, notably the 1948 war with Israel. By contrast, the young and modern political forces in Syria, particularly Asad's own party, the Ba'th, were numerically too small and politically too marginal to have any significant impact on the country's destiny. The only group which was able to effect a substantial change in the country was the army, which seized power in 1949 and subsequently dominated Syrian politics.

Hence it was unavoidable that young Asad, following his secondary-school graduation, would be tempted to join the army. Indeed for a would-be politician of Alawite peasant extraction, a military career seemed to offer not only social and economic mobility but, more importantly, the chance of personal elevation and involvement in Syrian national affairs. By then, many young Alawites had developed a generation-old tradition of military service. Under the French mandate, Alawites were encouraged to enlist in the Troupes Spéciales, as part of France's colonial policy of favouring the religious and ethnic minorities over the Sunni Arab majority. Consequently Alawites accounted for about 25 per cent of all soldiers – mostly in non-officer ranks in the Syrian contingent of the Troupes (which later developed into the Syrian army). Druze, Ismailis, Circassians, Kurds, Armenians and Syrian Christians were also over-represented in these Troupes (Druze in the officer corps). By contrast Sunni Muslim Arabs were greatly under-represented, particularly in the officer corps. This omission was not only due to the French anti-Sunni policy or to the refusal of young Sunni Arabs to serve in French colonial interests. Many respectable Sunni Arab families often despised military service and viewed the Military Academy of Homs as 'a place for the lazy, the rebellious, the academically backward, or socially undistinguished'.[2] Such an attitude, however, did not prevent several of these influential Sunni families from recommending their Alawite home servants for cadetship in the Academy. Following Syrian independence more and more Sunni Arabs, mostly from the middle and lower classes, enlisted in the army, some as officer cadets, while the percentage of Christians, Druze and Alawites fell correspondingly. Despite this trend, and although a number of minority officers were purged or dismissed and the top military positions were held now by Sunni Muslims, Alawites and Druze continued to be over-represented in the army, notably in its combat units. As a Syrian military report from 1949 stated, with some exaggeration, 'All units of any importance stood under commands of persons originated from minorities.'[3] For example, several Druze officers were actively involved in the military coups of 1949 and 1954, while two Alawite officers commanded the Syrian air force in 1950 and 1952 respectively.

Influenced apparently by the latter officers and motivated by his own tendencies, Asad registered in 1952 in the Military Academy at Homs and subsequently in the Air Force Academy in Aleppo. His flying talent won him the best aviator trophy upon graduation as a combat pilot early in 1955. He flew British-made Meteor jets and was credited in 1956 with downing a British Canberra bomber that strayed over Syrian airspace during the Anglo-French–Israeli Suez operation. Holding the rank of lieutenant, Asad, an exemplary pilot, continued advanced training in Egypt where he won a prize as the best Syrian pilot trainee (one of his Egyptian fellow-trainees was Hosni Mubarak). In 1957 he was promoted to squadron commander and later went to the USSR for a course in night-flying with MiG-17s.

Asad, however, had no intention of pursuing a purely professional military career, essentially because he still regarded military service as a national mission and as a means for political participation. As he later said to a Lebanese journalist: 'I do not regard myself as a soldier in the common meaning. I am a citizen of this country and a member of the nation who felt its agonies and shared its aspirations even before I had joined the army. I joined the army as a way to serve the nation. . . .'[4] Yet given the army's intense involvement in Syrian politics through the various party-affiliated factions, Asad had to belong to one of them. Obviously the Ba'th military faction was his choice owing both to his early membership of the party and to the predominant position of the faction among the officer corps. This renewal of his Ba'thist activities carried significant risk to his military career and political future. For the rival factions associated with the PPS–SSNP and the Communist Party held important military positions, and either of them could seize control or overpower the Ba'thist military faction. In such a case Ba'thist officers like Asad were likely to be purged, arrested or even killed.

Thus by reviving his political activities in the army Asad took a calculated risk, but presumably he did this also out of ideological commitment to the Ba'th doctrine. In the long run this move – be it motivated by ideology or by personal ambition or both – served Asad's military political career well. The powerful Ba'thist faction in the army succeeded in 1955, with the help of the pro-Communist military faction, in destroying their common rivals, the group of PPS–SSNP officers, and in bringing to an end their activities in Syria. Subsequently, however, the Ba'th Party and its army partisans were faced with a more serious challenge. This time it was the pro-Communist faction in the army, which was allegedly preparing a Communist takeover in the country.

While Soviet influence was growing in Syria after 1955, pro-Communist and leftist politicians strengthened their positions in the government and were able to appoint as chief of staff of the army one of their sympathizers among the senior officers, General Afif al-Bizri. This pro-Communist threat, real or alleged, coupled with external pressures applied by the Western Powers and by Syria's pro-Western neighbours (Turkey and Iraq), possibly by Israel too, contributed to the Ba'th initiative in 1958 to seek a union between Syria and Egypt. This union – the United Arab Republic – dealt a heavy blow not only to the leftist and pro-Communist elements in Syria, but particularly to the traditional conservative elite and its military associates. Significantly, however, contrary to the Ba'th leaders' expectations, the party's position in Syria was likewise greatly weakened during that period. Indeed the Ba'th, alongside all other parties, was dissolved, and its leaders were not allowed to administer the UAR Syrian region, which in turn was subject to strict Egyptian control. Likewise, the pro-Ba'th army officers were partly dismissed and partly transferred (or 'exiled') to Egypt, while Egyptian and pro-Egyptian officers took command of the Syrian army.

Paradoxically these developments worked in Asad's own favour. On the one hand he was at that juncture too junior in military rank (captain) and in party politics to be purged by the Egyptian authorities. On the other hand, the purges carried out by the Egyptians during 1958–61 (affecting some 11,000 officers) mostly hit the class of senior army officers, Sunnis and non-Sunnis alike (this was true of all the purges since 1949). And as a result of the erosion in that officer class, junior officers like Asad could quickly fill the vacuum and rise in rank as circumstances developed. Asad exploited such circumstances and made his way up remarkably fast, not only because of his strenuous and consistent lust for power, but because his qualities – hard-working, pedantic, discreet and skilful – coupled with his Ba'thist and Alawite affiliations – were precisely those required for upward mobility at that time.

So it was that by the late 1950s Captain Asad became a leader of the Ba'thist Military Committee established in Egypt, alongside senior officers, the Alawite lieutenant-colonels Muhammad Umran and Salah Jadid, the Druze colonel Hamad Ubayd and Major Salim Hatum. This committee waited for an opportunity to rectify the situation in Syria. When Syria seceded from the UAR in September 1961 Asad was detained for some two months by the Egyptian authorities, and upon his release he returned to Syria. The new rightist regime in Damascus took no chances with the Ba'th officers, and Asad was eased out of military service and given a minor clerical position at the Ministry of Transportation.

However, Asad continued his clandestine activities in the Ba'th Military Committee. Having played a significant role in the March 1963 Ba'thist coup he was then recalled to the army, promoted to the rank of major and appointed commander of the major military airfield of the Syrian air force (the air force being a section within the Syrian army). Losing no time and using both his personal drive and his political standing, he was promoted again within several months to lieutenant-colonel, and by the end of 1963 was virtually in charge of the Syrian air force. At the end of of 1964 he was officially appointed air force commander with the rank of major-general. He began to turn the air force into his power-base by lavishing special privileges on its officers, appointing his confidants to senior and sensitive positions and establishing an efficient intelligence network, independent of Syria's other intelligence operations and given assignments which were not all of immediate air force concern. Asad was now ready to take an active and crucial part in the struggles for power which characterized Syrian politics until 1970. Demonstrating a winning combination of traits – leadership, consistency, patience, caution, coolness and shrewdness – Asad managed to become Syria's ruler within the next six years.

During the first stage of the power struggles[5] which lasted until February 1966, Asad remained the junior partner in the leading Alawite triumvirate with Muhammad Umran and Salah Jadid. This powerful and still cohesive committee was able to purge the two groups of pro-Nasser and nationalist unionist officers who had initially participated in the March 1963 coup, but who had later become a menace to the Ba'th bid for power. In order to overpower these groups and to withstand growing external Egyptian political pressures, the Alawite- led Military Committee had invited Brigadier-General Amin al-Hafiz, a Sunni Muslim veteran Ba'th officer serving as military attaché in Argentina, to become the figurehead of both the Committee and the government. This courageous and charismatic officer, who held the crucial posts of minister of the interior, deputy military governor and later also deputy premier, chief of staff and acting defence minister, succeeded in crushing an attempted military coup carried out by pro-Nasser officers on 18 July 1963. Subsequently assuming the positions of premier and head of the newly formed Presidency Council, Hafiz became the supreme leader of Syria, drawing his support from the Ba'th Military Committee as well as from a group of young radical Marxist politicians.

Amin al-Hafiz, together with these new military and civilian leaders who in the recent past had been junior Ba'th members or merely party sympathizers, established a new Ba'th regime in Syria, which deviated significantly from the original Ba'th ideas and policies. Largely drawn from lower Sunni Muslim classes, from small towns and villages as well as from the Alawite, Druze and Ismaili communities, the new

Syrian leadership gave priority to the concept of a Syrian nation-state rather than to pan-Arab unity. It also preferred socialist Marxist doctrines to the traditional Ba'th social reformist notions. These tendencies of the new Ba'th regime irritated the old-guard Ba'th leaders, notably Michel Aflaq and Salah al-Din al-Bitar, who were granted only token positions in the new regime; by the end of 1964 Bitar was ousted from the Syrian cabinet, and Aflaq went into voluntary exile in protest.

Yet the emergence of Amin al-Hafiz as Syria's strongman and supreme authority soon provoked the personal jealousy and resentment of General Muhammad Umran, initially the leader of the Military Committee and commander of the crack 70th Armoured Brigade, which had served as the backbone of the Ba'thist military force. Although he was appointed at the end of 1963 as deputy premier, Umran challenged Hafiz's leadership on the ground that his regime had been diverted from the true Ba'th course. Umran took steps to rally the Alawite and other non-Sunni officers in an attempt to topple his Sunni Muslim rival.

The outcome of this power struggle depended to a great degree on the attitudes of Umran's co-leaders in the Military Committee, his fellow Alawites Salah Jadid, now chief of staff, and Hafiz al-Asad. Although, like Umran, Jadid and Asad largely drew their support from the Alawite officers' cadre, they sided with Hafiz against Umran (who now associated with the former Ba'th leadership), both of them wishing to blur their Alawite sectarian identity. And while Jadid was also motivated by his leftist and ideological inclinations, Asad's position apparently derived from his pragmatic evaluation of the power balance between Hafiz and Umran. Yet, once Umran was removed from Syria and 'exiled' as ambassador to Madrid at the end of 1964, a new power struggle started between Hafiz and Jadid. This personal rivalry soon developed into a sectarian and inter-Ba'th conflict with Jadid backed by most Alawite and Druze officers as well as by the new Ba'th Syrian leadership (the Regional Command) while Hafiz mustered the support of most Sunni officers and of the old Ba'th pan-Arab leadership (the National Command). At the end of 1965 it appeared that Hafiz and his camp (which now included Umran) had obtained the upper hand in the power struggle, by means of political manoeuvres and the decisions of the National Command. In response Jadid and his predominantly Alawite and Druze followers staged on 23 February 1966 'Syria's thirteenth and bloodiest army coup in seventeen years. Its success was assured by the switch of General Hafiz al-Asad, the Alawite commander of the air force and former supporter of Hafiz, to the side of the insurrection.'[6]

Becoming second-in-command in the new neo-Ba'th regime with the portfolio of defence minister in addition to the air force command, Asad was now in a better position for the second stage of the power struggle in Ba'thist Syria which in 1970 culminated in his final victory.

Climb to Power

Asad, it can be assumed, had sought the supreme leadership of Syria ever since the February 1966 coup, and possibly even earlier. Beyond the lust for power that he was imbued with, Asad also felt that he had a vital mission to fulfil for his country and people – the unification of Syria under his leadership and her evolution into a regional power. To implement his prime goal, Asad used to the full his remarkable traits of patience, caution, flexibility and coolness. He did not at that stage share his plan even with his friends. He trusted only a few people and was loyal only to those who had proved their absolute allegiance to him and would not compete with him. Towards his close comrades who were his real or potential rivals, Asad had no loyalty whatsoever. He would wait for the opportunity to liquidate them and reach the top. In his eyes, this end justified the means.

Accordingly, Asad did not sustain his loyalty even to his fellow Alawites, Umran and Jadid (certainly not with his Military Committee co-leaders Hafiz the Sunni or Major Salim Hatum the Druze). He would shift alliances according to the changing circumstances, ignore his various affiliations with his sect, party and military factions, or make use of them, to achieve his goals. Likewise, Asad was by no means selective in the methods that he adopted to fight his rivals and gain predominance. These would range from ideological argument-ation and political manipulation to arbitrary arrests, brutal use of power and, in crucial moments, sheer bloodshed.

Following the February 1966 coup, Asad's first concern was to help his fellow Alawite, Jadid, to consolidate the new regime in the face of its first challenge, an attempt by senior Druze officers who had actively participated in that coup to form separate military power-bases and demand major positions in the government. The officers in question were General Fahd al-Sha'ir, a veteran Ba'th officer, and Major Hatum, the member of the Ba'th Military Committee and commander of the army's elite commando battalion. With the co-operation of leaders of the Ba'th old guard, these officers had initially tried to set Asad against Jadid, demanding senior positions such as that of defence minister; having failed in that attempt, they plotted with other Druze officers to overthrow Jadid's regime. Hatum and his followers even managed to detain Jadid as a hostage when he arrived with other leaders in Jabal Druze to negotiate with his Druze opponents. Asad, who had stayed behind in Damascus, was not tempted to seize this opportunity of deposing Jadid in co-operation with the rebellious Druze officers.

It is true that before the 1966 coup Asad had maintained close relations with Hatum in an attempt to create a balance of power between Jadid and the Druze officer, which in turn would have enabled him to manoeuvre between these two rivals and gain predominance at the opportune moment. But at this point he seems to have calculated that if he entered into an alliance with the powerful and cohesive Druze military factions, it would turn to Hatum's advantage and render Asad himself vulnerable vis-à-vis both the Druze and the Alawites. So he cast his lot with Jadid. He thus dispatched strong military forces to Jabal Druze and threatened to bombard its provincial capital, Suwayda, if Jadid were not released. Hatum fled to Jordan, and upon his return to Syria during the 1967 war with Israel he was promptly executed. Many other Druze officers were earlier arrested or dismissed from their military positions. As a result the Druze threat to the new Jadid–Asad dual regime was eliminated. Indeed, with the destruction of the Druze challenge, Asad not only strengthened his own power and prestige but emerged virtually as an equal partner to Jadid in the new neo-Ba'th regime.

Asad now moved to gain the upper hand in his contest for power with Jadid, who was regarded 'a master of manipulation . . . similar to . . . Stalin'.[7] Using his positions as defence minister and air force commander, Asad systematically directed his efforts towards extending his control over the army, notably its combat units, which he regarded as the focus of the regime's power. By contrast, Jadid, who had served since 1963 as chief of staff of the Syrian army, had resigned his military post after the coup of February 1966 and chose to control the regime through the party apparatus – from the position of assistant secretary-general of the Ba'th Party. He sought to continue his hold over the army through his followers in the Ba'th military organization, whose Military Committee, as we have seen, had dominated the armed forces since the 1963 Ba'th revolution. He also promoted the paramilitary organizations affiliated with the party, to serve as further instruments of control: the National Guard and the companies of armed workers' militia, as well as the semi-Palestinian Saiqa ('thunderbolt') organization.

Thus the struggle for power between the two Alawite leaders, which started as a personal competition, soon became, in certain respects, a rivalry between the party and the army. Paradoxically, the Syrian army's defeat in the June 1967 war with Israel served to strengthen Asad's military backing vis-à-vis Jadid's party apparatus. For although the regular army command under Asad were said by the Ba'th leadership to have been discredited on account of losing the war, they in turn accused the party leadership of 'having ruined the army by political purges' and by granting preference to the party interests over those of the army, which coincided with those of the nation.[8] Under such pretexts Asad demanded priority for military augmentation at the expense of economic development. He also asserted his command over the party's paramilitary organizations by incorporating them into the regular army. He then used his growing influence to dismiss rival party and military leaders and appoint in their stead his own partisans; one such appointment was that of Mustafa Tlas, who became chief of staff early in 1968 in place of Ahmad al-Suwaydani, a veteran supporter of Jadid. During that year Asad, promoting himself to the rank of field marshal, managed to extend his hold over the army: on the one hand he took over the Military Committee, and on the other hand he disposed of the officers who were still loyal to Jadid, such as the chief of military intelligence, Colonel Abd al-Karim al-Jundi (who committed suicide early in 1969) and Lieutenant-Colonel Izzat Jadid, a relative of Salah Jadid and the commander of the powerful 70th Armoured Brigade.

With most of the army under his direct command, Asad turned his attention to the party and its two power foci: the Ba'th leadership and the cabinet. In the course of the Ba'th fourth regional congress in September 1968, however, Asad was unable to assert his control over the party, although he managed to effect a reshuffle of the cabinet to his advantage. Two of his chief rivals, Prime Minister Yusuf Zu'ayyin and Foreign Minister Ibrahim Makhus, were arrested, and three of Asad's aides were appointed to the government, including Mustafa Tlas, who became first deputy minister of defence. A few months later Asad became strong enough to challenge Jadid directly: he suspended the Ba'th Party activities in the army and on 25 February 1969, while his tanks occupied key points in Damascus, his aides seized control of the party and government newspapers – *Al-Ba'th* and *Al-Thawra*

('The Revolution') – and of the Damascus Radio station. The Ba'th leadership reacted by denouncing the army's coup against the party and called for an emergency session of the regional congress of the Ba'th. The congress met at the end of March and elected a new Regional Command composed of both Asad's and Jadid's factions, but the new political bureau which was set up, as the regime's supreme authority, included Asad and Tlas and excluded Jadid. Nevertheless, Salah Jadid, still the powerful party leader and backed by the Soviet Union, continued his struggle against Asad's drive for supremacy and demanded that he should give up one of his two powerful positions: defence minister or air force commander. Disregarding this demand, Asad continued to carry out purges of Jadid's partisans in the army, in the government and in various Ba'th Party branches.

By that time it was evident that the initial personal rivalry between Asad and Jadid which was developing into an army–party struggle for authority, was likewise evolving as a dispute between two schools of thought, two political orientations within the neo-Ba'th regime.

On the one side there persisted the doctrinaire school of Jadid (including President Atasi, Premier Zu'ayyin and Foreign Minister Makhus), which stood for a Marxist–socialist economic policy in internal affairs and an uncompromising radical leftist orientation in the regional and international spheres. On the opposite side there crystallized the pragmatic school of Asad, which advocated a moderate socialist line in social and economic issues as well as a flexible and realistic foreign policy. Asad also advocated enhancement of the regime's co-operation with the non-Ba'th left by incorporating such elements in the government and in the army. Yet it appeared that the crux of the political conflict between Asad and Jadid was their disagreement over Syria's inter-Arab and anti-Israel policies. The Jadid school continued after June 1967 to visualize the struggle against Israel in terms of a 'popular war of liberation' to be carried out mainly by the Palestinian armed organizations with Syrian support. This school furthermore denied the role of most Arab countries in the struggle against Israel because of their alleged 'defeatist', 'rightist', 'reactionary' or 'agent' regimes, and called for their overthrow.[9] Jadid even opposed Asad's suggestion that Syria should come to terms with the new Ba'th regime in Iraq, which was established in July 1968 by orthodox Ba'th leaders.

It is not surprising, then, that these policies, which led Syria by 1969 to an almost total isolation in the Arab world (the friendly exceptions were South Yemen [PDRY] and Algeria), were seen by Asad as highly dangerous to Syria's national security. He was deeply concerned lest Syria should stand alone against an Israeli attack, which might be provoked by the activities of the Palestinian armed organizations at a time when the Syrian army was unprepared for war. Asad conceived the war against Israel as a classic military campaign to be launched at the appropriate moment by all Arab 'confrontation states' regardless of their regimes. As he stated in his address before the Ba'th congress of March 1969:

> I have repeatedly stressed the importance of Arab military co-ordination – notably among the Arab states which border with Israel – regardless of the differences and the contradictions in their political positions, as long as it would serve the armed struggle. . . . the defensive capability of the Syrian front is closely tied with the capability of other Arab fronts . . . and the same mistake prior to 5 June [1967] could be repeated and Israel would be able to strike in each of the Arab fronts separately one after the other. Therefore, the escalation and continu-ation of the *fidai* [Palestinian guerrilla] action is largely tied with the defensive capability of the Arab fronts.[10]

These interrelated issues of Syria's inter-Arab position, her confrontation with Israel and her relations with the Palestinian organizations became the critical factors which motivated Asad, or gave him the pretext, to overthrow Jadid's regime and seize control. In fact, Asad ordered his tanks to occupy strategic points in Damascus and take control of government and media centres on 25 February 1969, one day after Israeli air raids on Palestinian military bases at Al-Hamma and Maysalun near Damascus. Those raids once again brought to light Syria's military inferiority vis-à-vis Israel. Following this move, which resembled a military coup, Asad exerted pressure on the Ba'th emergency regional congress, which was then convened, to adopt resolutions that new efforts should be made to establish an Eastern Command, that criticism of rightist and agent Arab regimes should be muted, and that initiatives should be taken to co-ordinate between the Arab fronts and to implement union with the progressive Arab states.[11] The Ba'th government, still controlled by Jadid's faction, agreed to carry out these decisions, but on two major issues it adopted positions which contradicted Asad's pragmatic line. It thus rejected, in the summer of 1970, the new American proposals for a political settlement in the area, which Egypt and Jordan accepted. This Ba'th position, although compatible with the regime's rejection of Resolution 242 of the UN Security Council (of November 1967), was likely to isolate Syria and expose it to an Israeli threat. No less detrimental to Syria, according to Asad, was the military intervention of Syrian forces in the September 1970 war in Jordan, on the side of the Palestinian organizations and against the Jordanian army. Asad, who had reportedly opposed the decision to intervene, denied air cover to the Syrian units, which were later forced to withdraw in the face of American–Israeli military threats, suffering heavy losses at the hands of the Jordanian army.

If Jadid's setback in Jordan was not a sufficient cause for a final takeover by Asad, there occurred another crucial event in the region which apparently hastened Asad's decision to oust Jadid from power and assume the overall rule of Syria. This was the death on 28 September 1970 of President Gamal Abd al-Nasir (Nasser) of Egypt, which threatened to aggravate further Syria's vulnerability to Israel, since Nasser had been committed, in Asad's view, to defending Syria against an Israeli attack. Moreover, shortly after his succession, Anwar Sadat, the new Egyptian president, decided to conclude with Libya and Sudan an Arab federal union which Asad – but not Jadid – was anxious to join. Against this background Asad decided to act: he put Jadid's supporters under house arrest, discharged or transferred Jadid's military followers and seized control over the Saiqa, the only remaining military organization of the Ba'th leadership. In protest, Atasi, Jadid's chief supporter, resigned on 18 October as head of state and prime minister, forcing Asad to agree once more to the convocation of an emergency national congress of the Ba'th Party. The discussions and decisions of the congress, which was held between 30 October and 12 November 1970, demonstrated the upper hand that Jadid and Atasi still maintained in the party.

Asad was accused of creating a 'duality of power' in violation of the party decisions and of introducing a 'defeatist reactionary line'; he was also labelled 'a fascist' by Jadid. The congress finally decided on 12 November to remove Asad and Tlas from their posts in the government and the army. Asad reacted on the following day: he employed his troops to arrest the top Ba'th leaders, including Jadid, and their aides, and to occupy the party and government offices. He then established a provisional Regional Command of the Ba'th Party consisting of his own supporters. One of them, Ahmad al-Khatib, was appointed by the Command as Syria's new president, and he in his turn invited Asad to form a government. A few months later, in February 1971, the Command appointed the 173 members of the People's Council, which promptly nominated Asad as the sole candidate for the presidency. This nomination was endorsed on 12 March by a people's referendum, and opened a new era in Syrian history and politics.

4 The Man and the Leader

Most of those – politicians, diplomats, journalists and so on – who have met or have had any dealings with Asad are impressed. Even those who fear or hate him cannot but admire him, as a man and as a leader. There are few who can be neutral or indifferent.

In his dark suit, Asad at first sight looks like a country schoolmaster who lives an ordinary *petit-bourgeois* life. He is fairly tall, a strong-jawed man with a fair complexion, a moustache, a high forehead and a flat back to his head. He is married and has five children (four boys and a girl), and lives a fairly austere personal life. He neither smokes nor drinks and he likes to listen to Western classical music. He reads, swims and plays table tennis. Although he is a good family man, Asad essentially is a powerful political person, a natural leader. Indeed, his flashing dark eyes reflect firmness and shrewdness, while his bearing shows coolness, calmness, dignity and authority. He speaks in a quiet but resolute voice with a certain hoarseness and a rough shyness; he does not waste words and says only what he wishes to say. He is a tough and proud man with nerves of steel, self-controlled and self-confident. He is secretive, aloof and enigmatic to the extent that even his close aides have dubbed him 'the sphinx'. But he can also be brutal and merciless towards his opponents and enemies. He is persistent and stubborn, but he can also be pragmatic, flexible and cautious – depending on the circumstances.

Asad is a patient listener, a careful thinker with an excellent memory and the ability to concentrate. He is also highly intelligent and inquisitive, with an original mind as well as common sense. President Nixon once described him as having 'elements of genius', while President Carter referred to him as a 'brilliant' man. Henry Kissinger defined Asad in the mid-1970s as 'the most interesting man in the

Middle East'. Hassanein Haykal, the prominent Egyptian journalist and former adviser to President Nasser, once said that Asad had 'a comprehensive view of the world and knows exactly what he wants'. Apparently Asad has a strategic way of thinking, clear perceptions and an obvious sense of history. But he is also a seasoned politician, a master manipulator, a tough negotiator with an exquisite sense of timing. He prepares his ground without haste, 'with the meticulous care of a mine sweeper', according to a British observer in Damascus. A Western diplomat serving in Syria says, 'He thinks three or four moves ahead . . . gives his thoughts away bit by bit, like peeling an onion.' And, according to Kissinger, Asad negotiates 'daringly and tenaciously like a riverboat gambler to make sure that he had exacted the last sliver of available concessions'.[1] 'He would not back out when he is weak and would not indulge when he is strong,' says Karim Paqraduni, a Lebanese politician and an Asad watcher. He has a remarkable capacity for brinkmanship in his negotiations and can be decisive when necessary.

In his daily state business, as in his diplomatic deliberations, Asad works long hours – until three or four in the morning – and expects his ministers and staff to work similar hours. There is a saying among his ministers, 'The president is always standing behind your desk.' As a boss Asad is indeed very pedantic and harsh. He pays attention to detail and requires his aides and subordinates to be industrious and disciplined. Those who make mistakes are severely punished (but occasionally might be pardoned). Asad will never forgive those who insult him. Likewise, he does not tolerate anyone with independent views or ways, people who are so ambitious or clever that they could endanger his rule or overshadow his personality. Those possessing these traits are transferred to unimportant positions, sent to jail or 'to heaven' (executed). Asad's confidants and close associates are therefore by and large people with modest personalities, but intelligent enough to be trustworthy and loyal. Yet few – if any – are Asad's personal friends. He stands high above his comrades in the government, army and party. He is the supreme leader of the country and nation.

Asad's Personality Cult

A common joke in Damascus explains Asad's order to ban US films by Metro-Goldwyn-Mayer (which has as its emblem a roaring lion) on the grounds that there is already a 'lion' (Asad) in Syria. Despite his austere personal life Asad has indeed encouraged the formation of a personality cult around himself; according to *Middle East Insight*,

> In no other country in recent memory . . . not Mao's China, nor Tito's Yugoslavia, has the intensity of the personality cult reached such extremes. Asad's image, speaking, smiling, listening, benevolent or stern, solemn or reflective, is everywhere. Sometimes there are half a dozen pictures of him in a row. His face envelops telephone poles and trucks, churches and mosques. His is the visage a Syrian sees when he opens his newspaper.

He is reported to have instructed his aides to have photographers observe certain angles in taking his picture. Similarly he directs the daily references to himself in the press, radio and television. In the media as well as in various publications Asad is depicted as the 'boss' (*al-mualim*), the president (*ar-rais*), the 'general' (*al-fariq*), the 'comrade leader' (*ar-rafiq al-qaid*), the 'historic leader' (*qaid tarikhi*), the 'hero of the correction movement' (*batal al-haraka al-tashihiyya*), and 'Syria's Asad' (Suriyya'al-Asad).[2] In the Syrian army, slogans in rhyme are chanted about Asad, 'our leader for ever'.

Asad's own great heroes and models are apparently Saladin, the legendary Muslim (Ayyubi) leader of the twelfth-century victory over the Crusaders, and Nasser, the late president of Egypt. Both of those leaders have symbolized to generations of nationalist Arabs the quest for Muslim or Arab unity and the elimination of the 'Crusader' or Zionist state in Palestine. It is possible that in using these symbols and in endeavouring to imitate these two heroes, Asad seeks to gain legitimacy and support from Sunni Muslims in Syria and elsewhere for his role as a genuine nationalist leader whose prime aspiration is to fulfil the grand aims of Arabism and Islam. However, such tactics aside, it is likely that Asad is ideologically committed to the ideas of Arab unity and of the struggle against Israel.[3] His commitment as well as his identification with the figures of Saladin and Nasser are probably rooted in his upbringing, experience and *Weltanschauung*.

Asad grew up in a part of Syria which is spotted with the ruins of Crusader castles crushed by the armies of Saladin. In secondary school Asad was indoctrinated by Ba'th Party instructors in the ideologies of Arab nationalism and anti-Zionism. When he was seventeen and eighteen he witnessed the 1947–8 Arab–Israeli war, and participated in it according to his own testimony in a recent speech.[4] During his military service in the 1950s he closely watched and greatly admired the emergence of Nasser as a pan-Arab leader attempting to unify the Arabs and fight against Israel. Although these attempts failed, Asad, like many Arabs, continued to cherish the Nasser legacy. During the Egyptian–Syrian union in 1958–61 Asad himself was stationed in Egypt as a combat pilot and had the opportunity to observe and be inspired by Nasser's ideas and style of leadership. Only a few weeks after Nasser's death in September 1970 Asad seized power in Syria, almost as if to fill the vacuum left by his hero's death. As various nationalist and Nasserite groups in Syria and elsewhere in the Arab world were not impressed by Anwar Sadat, Nasser's successor, Asad presumably felt capable of seizing that challenge, and responded to the yearnings for a new Arab leader of Nasser's calibre. In December 1970, soon after his rise to power, Asad addressed a public rally in Damascus in which the crowd feverishly chanted, 'Nasser, Nasser, Nasser,' and then, 'Asad, Asad, Asad.'[5] In subsequent years, while trying to shape his presidential system in the Nasser mould, Asad would occasionally in public ceremonies hail Nasser's exemplary leadership and allow Nasser's photographs to be displayed alongside his own.

Yet Asad's ambition is to do better than Nasser, since the late Egyptian leader failed to achieve the fundamental goals of Arabism: the unification of the Arabs and the defeat of Israel. Nasser's failure makes the more remote but legendary figure of Saladin a more suitable model for Asad. This Muslim hero not only put an end to the Crusader kingdom in Jerusalem in 1187, but went on to establish a unified Middle East empire stretching from Cairo to Baghdad. Asad is indeed greatly inspired by Saladin. On the wall of his office there hangs a large painting depicting Saladin's Hittin victory in 1187, and Asad has held public ceremonies at Saladin's tomb in Damascus to commemorate the anniversaries of his death. Similarly, in recent years a new Syrian currency note was issued carrying the profile of Saladin; and, significantly, a ruined Crusaders' castle near Asad's birthplace, Qardaha, was given the name Qalat Salah al-Din (Saladin Castle) in place of its original name Qalat Sahyun (Zion Castle).

Does Asad actually regard himself as a new Saladin? President Carter, who visited him in the summer of 1984, writes,

> As Asad stood in front of the brilliant scene [of the painting of the Hittin Battle] and discussed the history of the Crusaders and the other ancient struggles for the Holy Land, he took particular pride in retelling the tales of Arab successes, past and present. He seemed to speak like a

modern Saladin, feeling that it was his dual obligation to rid the region of all foreign presence while preserving Damascus as the only focal point for Arab unity today.[6]

Henry Kissinger, who negotiated with Asad in 1974 following the 1973 war, also refers to the painting of the Hittin victory in Asad's office and says: 'The symbolism was plain enough: Asad frequently pointed out that Israel would sooner or later suffer the same fate.'[7] In his conversations with various foreign visitors – statesmen, diplomats and journalists – Asad equates Israel with the Crusaders and remarks that the Zionist state will not last longer than the Crusaders' state. Likewise in most of his speeches and interviews for Arab audiences, Asad emphasizes two intertwined goals that he considers vital: to fight Israel and to achieve Arab unity.

Asad's Philosophy and Strategy

The dual goals of Arab unity and the struggle against Israel are indeed the cardinal notions of Asad's philosophy; to those ends his strategy is to create a political and military network of Greater Syria. To begin with, in Asad's view national unity, namely Syrian unity and especially pan-Arab unity, is the only way to solve the problems that beset the Arab nation and to enable it to render its great contribution to humanity.[8]

Interwoven with Arab unity is the struggle against Israel, which is, for Asad, a zero-sum struggle, a matter of life or death, of being or not being a true Arab. It is not merely a territorial struggle to liberate the occupied Arab lands, notably Palestine, and it is not only a Syrian or Egyptian or Jordanian issue. It is an all-Arab war against an enemy which is portrayed as aggressive and as aiming to occupy the Arab east 'from the Nile to the Euphrates'. The Arab–Israeli conflict is seen as a fatal strategic confrontation against a country which is supported by international Zionism and imperialism, promoted notably by the United States, and which strives to destroy the Arab homeland and culture by pushing the Arab people into a state of backwardness. Israel is thus characterized as a racist country representing the forces of evil, a 'neo-Nazi' invasion of the civilized and progressive Arab nation.[9]

Asad's public adherence to the notions of Arab unity and of the struggle against Israel obviously reflects the major doctrines of the Ba'th Party as well as deep emotions among Arabs, especially Syrian Arabs. Asad's fiery speeches on both these issues are thus intended to rally his countrymen as well as other Arabs to support his legitimacy as an authentic nationalist and pan-Arab Ba'thist leader.

Yet, beyond this nationalist Ba'thist rhetoric, Western diplomats and statesmen have been impressed by Asad's strong ambition to lead the Arab world into a military victory over Israel. The question which arises now is whether Asad, who is a highly realistic leader, truly believes that he can fulfil these almost impossible missions. Can he bring about the unification of the Arab world which is now more polarized than ever before? And can he and his Arab allies defeat Israel, the strongest military power in the region? In regard to Israel, it is not inconceivable that even the cool-headed and pragmatic Asad has a blind spot when it comes to his attitude to the Jewish–Zionist state – he is apparently imbued with deep and intense feelings of animosity towards it and does not share the empathy of other Arab leaders towards Israel's legitimate interests. Added to this emotional attitude is presumably a strong conviction, not mere rhetoric, that Israel constitutes a substantial and critical danger to the Arab east, notably to Syria – its territorial integrity, political independence and cultural heritage. Asad believes that among the leaders of the Arab states he is the most aware of this fatal Israeli peril, the most capable of withstanding and even eliminating this danger. For Sadat achieved a rapprochement with Israel in 1974 and signed a peace treaty with her in 1979, Iraq has been engaged in the Gulf war and King Hussein has had *de facto* peaceful relations with Israel – only Asad has stood firmly by his beliefs that he could do even better in the future in leading the all-Arab confrontation against Israel. Indeed for the last decade he has been the only Arab leader who carried on a policy of confrontation with Israel and was able successfully to repulse Israeli military inroads into southern Syria in 1974 and into southern Lebanon in 1982–4.

With Soviet help, Syria is believed to be nearing a military balance with Israel. This would mean that Syria may shortly be able to confront Israel on the battlefield, without any help from her neighbouring Arab countries, and perhaps successfully withstand an Israeli Defence Forces (IDF) offensive. The military strength also means that, while capable of resisting political and diplomatic pressures from the neighbouring countries, including Israel, Asad would be able tactically to negotiate with Israel from a position of military strength. His short-term aim would be to reach a political settlement whereupon Israel would withdraw from the Golan Heights, the West Bank and Gaza in return for a non-belligerency agreement. The new territorial configuration would make Israel more vulnerable to an intra-Arab military offensive led by Syria. (Such an offensive would be even more likely to occur if Israel refuses to give up Arab territories, particularly the Golan Heights and the West Bank.) With these aims in mind Asad has been preparing his army for a long military struggle against Israel while simultaneously seeking to unite the Arab world behind this struggle. In Asad's mind, unity would ensure victory over Israel and also advance Arab development in various other ways.

Unity would be the cure for the malaise of the Arab people in the military, political, cultural and economic fields. Since Asad believes Arab problems to have been essentially created or exacerbated by the existence and expansion of Israel, it would follow that Arab unity equals the destruction of Israel, and this would enable the Arab world to move towards the solution of its major problems. Whether Asad really believes that he would be able to unify the Arab world, or even part of it, and lead a pan-Arab campaign against Israel is questionable. Nonetheless, it should be pointed out that Asad is convinced that he can achieve some sort of Arab unity: not of the entire Arab world, perhaps not even of its eastern part, the Mashriq, but more likely of its critical sub-regions, like the Arab Fertile Crescent (al-Hilal al-Hasib), certainly of Greater Syria (Surriyya al-Kubra). The plan for a united Fertile Crescent (Iraq, Syria, Lebanon, Jordan and Palestine) was an 'imperialist' idea conceived by the Hashemite rulers of Iraq, who were under British influence. Nevertheless, Asad is prepared to adopt such a plan. Following his great teacher and mentor, the Ba'th Alawite philosopher Zaki Arsuzi, he is ready to implement this 'old, imperialist' idea for the sake of Arab unity even if it means union between states with different regimes,[10] rather than the desired unified Arab nation with one political system.

Asad has apparently adopted a parallel approach to the idea of Greater Syria – that is, the union of Syria, Lebanon, Jordan and Palestine. It need be no more than a loose union with different regimes, as long as it is under Asad's leadership. In Asad's view, Greater Syria lies in a geographically strategic area which is at the core of any potential Arab unity and should thus serve as the focus of an Arab political–military network against Israel, for both defensive and offensive purposes. It is true that like the Fertile Crescent plan, the scheme for a Greater Syria was revived in the 1940s by another Hashemite ruler, the late King Abdallah of Jordan, also under British aegis. Yet the notion of Greater Syria or Geographical Syria or the Land of Syria (Barr Ash-Sham or Bilad Ash-Sham in Arabic – the 'Northern Land') is a centuries-old concept in the Islamic and Arab history of the region. Many Syrian Muslims are attached to the notion of Greater Syria as a geographical and cultural unit, while certain Syrian and Lebanese Christians – notably members of the PPS–SSNP – have expanded the concept of Syrian nationalism as a distinct entity embracing the whole population of Greater Syria. Asad is thus pursuing the idea of Greater Syria in order to appeal to the profound sentiments of his fellow countrymen – Muslims and non-Muslims alike.

In conclusion, it would appear that these three interrelated notions of Greater Syria, Arab unity and the struggle against Zionism and imperialism constitute the cornerstones of Asad's political philosophy and strategy.

Asad may well believe that it is his life's mission to achieve those grand historic goals of the Arab people. At the same time, however, he shrewdly propagates and manipulates those goals and concepts to broaden his power-base as the legitimate ruler of all Syrians by obtaining the consent of the Sunni Muslim majority as well as of his own Alawite group. By extolling Arab unity and the confrontation with Israel, Asad seeks to erase the image of a sectarian military regime, which seized power by the force of arms and has since critically damaged the political heritage, religious feelings, social prestige and economic interests of a great many of his fellow Syrians. While he needs to diffuse the strong opposition to his regime, Asad simultaneously seeks to build a new order resting on the under-privileged rural population and the urban workers as well as the intelligentsia and the younger generations. These sectors of the population are linked by a shared passion for Arab unity, for Greater Syria and for the struggle against Zionism and imperialism. Asad, therefore, makes use of these concepts even if he does not stand any chance of implementing them in his lifetime. His primary purpose is to continue ruling his country as a legitimate and popular leader. To this end, he endeavours to portray his regime as a nationalist, socialist, progressive government and a popular democracy.

The Quest for Legitimacy

From the moment he seized power, Asad sought to project an image of his regime as constitutional and democratic, and of himself as a national and popular leader deriving his authority from his people. He insistently and systematically avoided giving the impression of relying on military support or of endorsing a single-party system.

Asad thus presented his coup against Jadid in November 1970 as a 'corrective movement' which 'came to light in response to our people's demands and aspirations'; the 'people are the chief concern, the organ and the goal of the revolution'; they have been 'registering the bright pages in the history of this homeland'. Asad described himself as a 'citizen of Syria, a member of the people with whom he shares unprecedented identification'. He stressed in one of his press interviews that he was not an 'ordinary soldier', but had joined the army in order to serve the people, not by means of military coups but through a 'positive struggle' hand in hand with the 'pioneers of the enlightened citizens who have faith in the nation'.[11] Soon after his military coup, Asad relinquished his army position and called for a citizens' referendum to approve his nomination as president, defining this action as a manifestation of popular democracy. Some two years later it was officially stipulated in the permanent Syrian constitution (drafted under Asad's directives) that the 'candidacy for the post of the presidency of the Republic . . . is to be put to referendum of the citizens' (article 84), and that 'the president of the Republic has the right to refer important questions related to the interests of the country, to a citizens' referendum' (article 112).

In March 1971, Asad was approved as Syria's president in a referendum which granted him 99.2 per cent of the vote. Subsequently he was endorsed in two more referenda: in March 1978 with 99.6 per cent, and in February 1985 with 99.9 per cent of the vote.

Two similar referenda were held in September 1972 and in March 1973 to approve respectively Syria's membership in the Federation of Arab Republics and Syria's permanent constitution. These measures, designed to demonstrate the people's participation in the regime and in its vital decision-making processes, were enhanced by seemingly free elections for positions in municipal and local authorities. The March 1972 municipal elections were described by Asad as 'the first elections in this country that were marked by freedom and fairness'. Elections were held in May 1973 (and again in August 1977, and February 1986) for the Council of People's Assembly – the Syrian parliament – in order, as Asad stated, to take 'the first step in implementing popular democracy'.[12] At least half of the assembly's 195 members were to be representatives of the workers and peasants. Serving also as a legislative forum, this assembly is composed not only of delegates of the Ba'th ruling party, but also of representatives of several leftist and nationalist parties: the Communist Party, the Arab Socialist Union, the Socialist Unionists and the Arab Socialist Party. On Asad's initiative, these parties, under the guidance of the Ba'th, formed in 1972 a National Progressive Front both in parliament and in the cabinet.

In the same vein, and in order to underscore national consensus and support for his regime, Asad encouraged the establishment of many popular organizations and professional associations which, according to him, would participate in the decision-making process.[13]

Notwithstanding this elaborate system of popular organizations and parliamentary institutions, Asad controls, both officially and *de facto*, all the state organs and instruments of power – the Ba'th Party, the National Progressive Front – as well as the various popular organizations. For all practical purposes, the Syrian ruling apparatus is the personal dictatorship of Hafiz al-Asad, a one-man regime, run by him with the assistance of a team of aides. Asad exercises his power through a dual system: official state institutions and several unofficial power organizations.

The central organ of his personal rule is the presidency, which Asad established in 1971 according to the Egyptian Nasserite model. The presidency has become a highly centralized institution which grants President Asad (according to the 1973 constitution) absolute powers in political and military matters as well as in legislative and administrative affairs.[14] For example, elected for a seven-year term (article 85) the president 'establishes the general policy of the state and supervises its application' (article 94). 'He appoints one or more vice-presidents, the chairman of the council of ministers, the ministers, and assistant ministers. Moreover, he undertakes the responsibility of receiving their resignations or effecting dismissals' (article 95). 'The president of the Republic declares war or calls for general mobiliz-ation' (article 100); he 'is the supreme leader of the army and armed forces' (article 103); he 'appoints civil and military functionaries and terminates their services in conformity with the law' (article 109). 'He presides over the Supreme Council of Magistrates' (article 132), and 'promulgates the laws passed by the Council of People's Assembly. He has the right to oppose those laws by a reasoned resolution' (article 98); he 'is entitled to dissolve the council by the promulgation of a reasoned resolution' (article 107). He 'makes draft laws and turns them over to the Council of People for adoption' (article 110); he 'exercises legislative authority in the intervals between ... regular sessions and during extraordinary sessions in cases of necessity pertinent to the national interests of the country' (article 111) and 'he has the right to refer important questions related to the interests of the country to citizens. The results of the referendum are binding' (article 113). In addition to his personal authority over the army, the government and the parliament, Asad is also the secretary-general of the Ba'th Party, 'the leading party of the society and the state', and head of the National Progressive Front.

It should be pointed out that such an absolute presidential regime is unprecedented and highly significant in Syrian political history. Asad not only does not share power with his comrades (as his predecessors Hafiz and Jadid had done since the Ba'th came to power in 1963), but he is the first head of state from the heterodox Alawite minority to monopolize power in Syria. He took this bold and unusual step in a country whose successive constitutions since 1930 (with two brief exceptions) stipulated that the head of state should be a Sunni Muslim, and whose Sunni Muslim majority population distrusted the Alawites as heretics. Unlike his Alawite predecessor, Salah Jadid, Asad did not attempt to control the country behind the scenes with a Sunni Muslim president as figurehead. Remarkably and courageously, Asad imposed himself both officially and in practice as the supreme ruler of Syria, the country's president. But to maintain himself in power Asad was soon caught in an inevitable dilemma: he badly needed the support of the Alawites in the military against potential Muslim opposition as well as to spearhead his long-term vision of creating a new non-sectarian Arab Syrian national community. Yet, coupled with his secularist policies, this heavy reliance on an Alawite sectarian military base triggered fierce resistance among the Sunni Muslim population. In an attempt to cut the Gordian knot of his regime, Asad had thus designed a dual-system government machinery – the formal state institutions and the informal instruments of power.

The formal system has been given a legitimate nationalist appearance with a marked Sunni Muslim colouring, whereas the informal power-base has been predominantly Alawite. Accordingly, as president, Asad made certain gestures towards the Muslim population, *inter alia* by presenting himself as a devout Muslim. In June 1971, for example, he restored to the Syrian provisional constitution the previous formulation of the presidential oath, 'I swear by Allah Akbar' (the Greatest God), replacing the earlier secular format in the 1969 constitution (under Jadid) 'I swear on my honour and my faith.' Asad also reinstated in the constitution of March 1973 the provision that the president should be a Muslim. This requirement had previously been deleted from both the 1969 constitution and the draft permanent constitution. At the same time he publicly participated in prayers and religious ceremonies at various mosques. In a press interview in March 1971 he said, 'I believe in Allah and in the spiritual heritage of our nation. I perceive Islam as a faith of love and justice, and thus it is a socialist religion. I pray, observe the fast and hope one day to make the Hajj' (pilgrimage to Mecca).[15]

Similarly, in an attempt to project his regime as predominantly Sunni Muslim, Asad appointed to senior positions in the cabinet, the army and the party, Sunni Muslims who were personally loyal to him. For example all prime ministers, defence and foreign ministers and most cabinet ministers under Asad's rule have been Sunni Muslims. The longest-serving are Mustafa Tlas, the defence minister and deputy commander in charge of the army (who reportedly has an Alawite mother), and Abd al-Halim Khaddam, foreign minister and deputy prime minister. Khaddam, who is married to an Alawite woman, was appointed a vice-president in 1984. Other prominent Sunni Muslim figures in the regime are Hikmat Shihabi, the chief of staff of the army, Zuhayr Masharqa, vice-president since 1984 and deputy secretary-general of the Ba'th Regional Command, as well as Abdallah Ahmar, deputy secretary-general of the Ba'th National Command. Under Asad, Sunni Muslims, as well as members of other non-Sunni Muslim communities, hold senior positions in the government, parliament, the army, the judiciary, the bureaucracy, the Ba'th Party, the education system and so on.[16]

The Jama'a

Behind this formal façade, which appears to be representative of the Syrian Sunni population, there exists an informal ruling machinery which is also headed by Asad. It controls the power centres in the country and is heavily staffed by Alawites. At the core of this unofficial network there is Asad's coterie or Jama'a, composed of some ten persons (they are nicknamed the 'Ten Great Ones' in the Damascus Suq, where vegetable merchants promote the sale of lettuces of the 'Great Ten Leaves'). Among them are several ministers, army officers and other functionaries in charge of the vital nerve centres and crack military units, as well as holders of senior government positions. They implement all the important decisions under Asad's guidance. This group is highly cohesive and consists of Asad's close and veteran comrades, Mustafa Tlas, Abd al-Halim Khaddam and Hikmat Shihabi, plus the prime minister, the interior minister – all Sunni Muslims and all personally loyal to Asad – and it includes four senior Alawite generals: Ali Aslan, Ali Duba, Muhammad Khawli and, until recently, Rifat Asad, the president's brother.

While the five Sunni officials hold the top formal positions in the cabinet and the army, the Alawite officers are substantially in charge of the security and intelligence networks of the regime. Major-General Ali Aslan, deputy chief of staff for operations, holds the real executive power in the army and has been assigned to important military tasks (he was the first commander of the Syrian troops in Lebanon in 1976). General Ali Duba is chief of the military intelligence in charge of monitoring all the movements and political currents in the regular army, in order to prevent any anti-Asad formations among the troops. General Muhammad Khawli is chief of the air force intelligence and head of the Presidential Security Council. Possibly the closest confidant of Asad, he has been the regime's trouble-shooter, and is said to have engineered the 1982 assassination of Bashir Jumayyil, the pro-Israeli Lebanese president, as well as the 1986 attempt to blow up an El-Al airplane at London airport. Brigadier Rifat Asad, appointed deputy president in 1984, has been the commander of a large praetorian guard known as the Defence Detachments, which was assigned to protect the regime's nerve centres, particularly in Damascus, and to carry out special operations such as the suppression of the 1982 Hama rebellion (see chapter 12).

With the possible exception of Rifat, none of the coterie members, nor any other officials or generals, possess an autonomous power-base which is likely to threaten Asad's leadership. Almost all of them, though nourishing mutual rivalries (sometimes encouraged by Asad), have shown complete loyalty to the president, and with one exception have shown no ambition to replace him: the exception is General Naji Jamil, a Sunni Muslim, who had served since the early 1970s as deputy defence minister and air force commander. He was removed from these positions in 1978 because he had accumulated so much power that he was within reach of the number-two slot in the hierarchy. It appeared that Rifat was then the only member of the Jama'a with the potential to succeed or replace Asad, commanding as he did a virtually independent and very well-equipped military force which was at odds with the regular army. This elite force with its distinctive uniform (called the 'Pink Panthers' or the 'Animals') consisted, until recently, of some 50,000 men. They included three armoured companies, a mechanized infantry brigade equipped with 350 T-72 tanks and artillery, anti-aircraft missiles, helicopter and paratroop units, plus intelligence services and prisons of their own.[17]

Rifat has a burning ambition to succeed his brother, the president, in the event that he becomes unable to rule the country. Thus when Asad was recuperating from a heart attack in late February 1984, Rifat displayed his military strength at key points in and around Damascus, apparently ready to assume power. But most members of the Jama'a as well as other generals – Alawite and Sunni alike – opposed Rifat's bid for power, partly because they regarded Rifat as dangerous both to themselves and to the continuity of the regime, and partly because they remained loyal to the ailing President Asad. Asad himself was angered and embarrassed by his brother's behaviour but reacted in a rather peculiar way. He appointed Rifat, together with Abd al-Halim Khaddam and Zuhayr Masharqa (Ba'th Party secretary) as vice-presidents, creating these high offices for the first time since the establishment of his regime in 1971. Rifat was given responsibility for security affairs, but several months later, following a new showdown between his Defence Detachments and the regular army, Rifat was sent abroad and his military force was cut to about 18,000 soldiers. In late November 1984 he returned to Damascus from Europe and was confirmed by Asad as vice-president. The Defence Detachments were reorganized by Rifat, but their original size was not restored.[18] Lately it has been reported that Rifat no longer commands these Detachments and is living in Paris.

Asad's attitude towards his brother seems ambivalent. On the one hand, he well knows that Rifat's ambitions and corruption have led to his being hated by many Syrians – including most members of the Jama'a. Some of the actions Asad took were therefore aimed at taming Rifat and weakening his military power, while appeasing his rivals. On the other hand, Asad has allowed his brother a significant military force and, by appointing him vice-president, has conferred on him a certain political respectability and constitutional legitimacy. Whether or not Asad regards his brother as his potential successor, he seems to want Rifat to be on his side and badly needs his support. This is not because Asad wishes to please his old mother, who, according to some sources, travelled especially from Qardaha during the intra-family crisis to speak up for Rifat. Nor can his attitude to Rifat be explained only by his love for his younger brother (he was born in 1937): 'The president gets all dewy-eyed whenever Rifat enters a room,' noted an observer. Essentially Asad recognized Rifat as an important factor in his delicate security apparatus, the effectiveness of which is assured by kinship loyalties as well as by a complicated system of checks and balances. Rifat has not only done the dirty work for Asad by brutally suppressing the opposition, but his well-equipped troops are the guardians of some of the most sensitive centres of the regime, and are capable of counterbalancing or overpowering regular military units which one day might try to topple Asad. Indeed, unlike the latter units which are manned mostly by Sunni Muslim soldiers, Rifat's companies, as well as similar security forces and networks, are staffed and commanded mostly by Alawites – members of Asad's family, clan, tribe and community.

The Alawite Security Belt

The generals in Asad's coterie who are in charge of the security and intelligence networks are all Alawites from his tribe, the Matawira. General Ali Haydar, the commander of the 20,000-strong Special Forces, another praetorian guard for Asad, comes from the same village, Qardaha, although not from the same tribe as Asad.[19] Most of these troops – commandos and paratroopers – are Alawites. So are most of the soldiers of Rifat's Defence Detachments. Many of them belong to the same tribe or village as Asad. This is also true of other security units, which like the Defence Detachments are under the command of Asad's close relatives. Two of his cousins, Colonels Adnan Asad and Muhammad Asad, are in charge of the Struggle Companies, a force of some 5,000 men detailed to attend to the security of the Damascus area. Asad's brother-in-law, Adnan Makhluf, commands the 2,000-strong Republican Guard which protects the presidential residence.

Other members of Asad's family hold sensitive positions in various parts of Syria, notably the Alawite region. Jamil, Asad's youngest brother, is the commander of the Murtada militia – a well-trained Alawite force of 4,000 men which is assigned to protect the Alawite community in the Latakia region. Jamil's son Fawwaz Asad is in charge of intelligence affairs at Latakia. Other family relatives, Yusuf Asad and Muhammad Asad, are respectively in charge of the Ba'th Party in the Hama region and the Defence Detachments in Aleppo, the two main centres of Muslim opposition to Asad's regime. Another sensitive position, that of head of Syrian military intelligence in Lebanon, is held by Colonel Ghazi Kan'an, another relative of Asad.

55

In sum, Asad's security and intelligence networks – about a dozen organizations – are manned mostly by Alawites and commanded by members of his family, clan or tribe. They are subject to his direct personal supervision and their chiefs are responsible only to him. The half-dozen major intelligence operations are engaged in spying on Asad's enemies and opponents as well as supervising and monitoring actions and movements in the various sections of the army and the population. While keeping a thorough twenty-four-hour watch over possible sources of trouble, each of these organizations is empowered to arrest anyone. Simultaneously, some six or seven well-equipped elite military units form a ringlike protection for Asad in person at his residence as well as at the headquarters of his regime. With his new fortress-like presidential palace on a rocky hill just outside Damascus, Asad is possibly the best-guarded leader in the Middle East.

Yet without the support of the regular army this multi-layered security belt, however strong and effective it might be, cannot endow Asad with the kind of security and power-base that he needs. He therefore personally controls his huge regular army, particularly its combat units, by means of an elaborate mechanism of checks and balances. At the core of this control system Asad has again placed Alawite officers from his clan, tribe, village and community.

5 Relying on the Army

Although Asad retired from the army once he became president in 1971, he has continued to regard the army as the cornerstone of his regime and the chief instrument of his policies. In a country like Syria where the army was for many years the source of political power and was involved in coups and counter-coups, it is vital for any ruler to secure the army's allegiance. This is particularly true of Asad, as a minority leader who has held the reins of government against the opposition of large sections of the population. Total control of the army has thus been essential for the survival of his regime, for its stability and for guaranteeing the uninterrupted implementation of his policies. A strong army is at times particularly crucial in defending the state and the regime against its external foes as well as enabling Asad to carry out his regional policies from a position of strength. This is of special relevance to Syria's confrontation with Israel. As Asad has put it: 'Our prime efforts are . . . to strengthen our military force for the purpose of defending the homeland and withstand the cruel enemy [Israel] which has been supplied by imperialism with various weapons in order to commit acts of aggression against our Arab land.'[1]

The Arab defeats by Israel in the wars of 1948, 1956 and 1967 which Asad observed or participated in had a strong impact on him, hurting his pride both as a soldier and as an Arab. He was determined when he seized power to stop the series of humiliating Syrian military failures, and to recover at least the Golan Heights which his army lost in the 1967 war when he was defence minister. To this end and in order to consolidate his own leadership in Syria, Asad joined Egypt in the 1973 war against Israel (as will be discussed below). His failure to recapture the Golan and defeat Israel in that war did not, however, discourage him from further adding to his military power. On the contrary, Israel's growing military superiority on the one hand, and Egypt's gradual disengagement from the conflict on the other, made it imperative for Asad to strengthen his army. Thus, since the mid-1970s and particularly after the Camp David accords between Egypt and Israel, Asad has embarked on a highly ambitious plan to achieve a 'strategic balance' with Israel, mainly by means of military parity. A formidable military force could be used to defend Syria as well as to score political and diplomatic gains vis-à-vis Israel from a position of military strength.

However, Asad also needs a strong army to deploy on Syria's other frontiers. On the eastern border Iraq tried for years to undermine Asad's regime and to compete with Syria for regional hegemony. To the north and north-east the powerful pro-Western republic of Turkey, which in 1939 annexed the Syrian province of Alexandretta, poses a potential threat to Asad's pro-Soviet regime. To the West, Lebanon represented for decades the antithesis to Syria's authoritarian regime and its radical socialist and anti-West policies. For this reason and others, Lebanon has historically been an object of Damascus's designs for hegemony. Similarly, the Kingdom of Jordan in the south-east poses a serious obstacle to Asad's ambitions of creating a Greater Syria union under his leadership.

To implement this grand strategy and to defend his regime, Asad has systematically built the largest and strongest military force Syria has ever had – one of the most powerful and effective armies in the Middle East. Unlike his predecessor Jadid, who had allocated the bulk of state expenditures to economic reforms, Asad has given top priority to the military budget. Only a few weeks after his ascendancy in November 1970, he declared in a public meeting that an astonishing 71 per cent of Syria's new budget would be assigned to the army, a proportion that 'no country in the world has reached'. In the following years, military expenditure was well over one-half of the annual ordinary budgets, and was even greater after 1978 when the Baghdad Arab summit allocated to Syria US$1.8 billion yearly for five years.[2] According to the surveys of the London-based International Institute for Strategic Studies (IISS), Syrian military expenditure in real terms (constant 1978 prices) was as follows: US$71 million in 1955, $185 million in 1960, $268 million in 1965, $384 million in 1970, $427 million in 1971, $624 million in 1974, $1,110 million in 1976, $1,165 million in 1978, $2,018 million in 1979 and $3,186 million in 1980. A large part of the Syrian military expenditure came from Soviet aid, which amounted to US$19,000 million during the thirty-year period from the mid-1950s to 1985. Indeed, the IISS and other sources report that the Syrian army has absorbed huge quantities of modern Soviet arms and has steadily grown in numbers and equipment: from 60,500 soldiers in 1968 (with 430 tanks and 150 combat planes) to 135,000 in 1973 (with 2,000 tanks and 330 planes), 230,000 in 1976 (with 2,300 medium tanks and 440 combat planes) and some 350,000 soldiers (with 3,600 tanks and 500 planes) on the eve of the 1982 Lebanese war.[3]

The 1982 Israeli invasion into Lebanon, the IDF surprise attack on the Syrian troops in Lebanon and its subsequent deployment in the Biqa area some eighteen miles from Damascus — all these events (which will be discussed below) led Asad to strengthen his army further. By adding three new armoured divisions after the Lebanon war, he turned his army into one of the largest military forces in the region — in 1985 there were half a million soldiers in the regular standing army.

This huge army is equipped with some 4,200 tanks, among them the modern T-72, new squadrons of MiG-29 planes, as well as modern ground-to-ground (SS-23, range 500 kilometres), anti-aircraft (SA-5, range 300 kilometres), and shore-to-sea (range 300 kilometres) long-range missiles.[4] Yet these are by no means the limits of the Syrian military potential. In 1980 Asad declared in a public speech: 'We in Syria have already passed nine million [population] and are moving towards ten [million]. If we mobilize 10 per cent, which is a normal proportion in many countries, we could enlist 900,000 to one million soldiers.'[5] Nor has Asad confined himself to equipment and manpower. With the help of 4,000 to 6,000 Soviet experts, he has tried to improve the military training of his troops, for example by encouraging them to learn from their own mistakes and, significantly, from the experience of the IDF.[6] In addition, Asad has placed great importance on the psychological and moral aspects of his army's training. Since the late 1960s he has systematically worked to do away with the traditional factionalism and politicization among the troops, notably in the officers' cadre, and to unify the Syrian army under his sole command. In the March 1969 convention of the Ba'th Party Regional Command, Asad attacked the 'various tactics' of the Ba'th (civilian) leaders among the military forces which 'caused the creation of blocs and factions with shifting loyalties . . . and negative influences' in the army. He also fiercely criticized the establishment by the Ba'th Party leadership (i.e. Jadid) of military and paramilitary organizations such as the Saiqa, the National Guard and the Armed Workers which caused 'a duality of authority'.[7] By incorporating these paramilitary organizations into the regular army, and reducing the Ba'th Party's activities among the troops, Asad gave a new interpretation to the Ba'th concept of the 'ideological army'.

'The Ideological Army'

The concept of an 'ideological army' first appeared after the March 1963 coup, but it was shaped and nurtured under the regime of Jadid who, more than his predecessor Amin al-Hafiz, needed to provide his military-based government with an ideological cast. He also had to counter the demand of the veteran civilian leaders to remove the army from political life and place it under civilian control. After the coup of February 1966, Jadid called a special congress of the Ba'th Party which

> condemned efforts aimed at converting the army from an ideological body into a professional army, as is the case in some developing countries, where such a professional army is used by capitalism and foreign monopolies to suppress progressive movements and to stifle the aspirations of the masses. The Congress also condemned efforts aimed at changing the class structure of the army and made *inter alia* the following basic recommendations:
>
> 1 Implementation of recommendations of party congresses concerning the role of the army and the separation of military from civilian authorities.
> 2 Maintaining the class structure of the army and developing its present framework along popular revolutionary lines.
> 3 Concentrating on ideological and political education, especially among the ranks of soldiers and non-commissioned officers.
> 4 Taking a firm attitude against luxury and bureaucracy, putting an end to over-expenditure and enforcing strict financial audit and control.
> 5 Giving the ideological army a chance to participate in formulating the policies of the party by implementing resolutions of former party congresses, followed in the representation of the civilian sectors of the party.
> 6 Non-commissioned officers and the soldiers constitute the fundamental basis of the army which should be in line with the Revolution and the party. . . . [8]

Although Hafiz al-Asad subscribed in theory to the concept of an 'ideological army', in practice he did not accept that the army's intrinsic identity should be tied with the Ba'th Party. He preferred to stress instead a sense of identity between the army and the people. Following his November 1970 coup Asad stated that the ideological army 'will always be with the people as a nationalist vanguard that shares the masses' distress, hopes and aspirations'. Internal guidelines of the Ba'th Party organization in the Syrian army issued in late 1972, apparently under Asad's direction, indicated that 'the army should educate its soldiers in the spirit of love of the homeland and the people'.[9]

Nonetheless, upon establishing his authority in both the army and the party, Asad used his own version of Ba'th ideology in the indoctrination programme that he introduced in the army, and he has been personally involved in implementing it. Employing a large cadre of officers trained in the Military Academy to carry out the programme, Asad has frequently visited military units, addressing them on matters of national policies and the Ba'th doctrines.[10]

Asad's frequent visits to army barracks and posts have also formed part of his method of exercising a close personal supervision over the military forces, notably the combat units. 'Nothing goes on in the army without my knowledge, right down to the promotion or transfer of a private,' Asad reportedly said once (with some exaggeration).[11] He certainly inspects and controls the important and sensitive movements in the army and personally approves the promotions of officers from the rank of major and up. Asad's endeavours to win over the loyalty of the officer corps, particularly of the combat units, include granting them special privileges:

> They receive higher salaries than individuals of comparable civilian status . . . get free medical care and generous travel allowances. Army co-operatives provide them with every conceivable article at cost price as well as duty-free foreign imports not available to the rest of the population. Interest-free loans enable them to buy houses and villas. . . . Every city has its officers' club, invariably the best in town. Careers involving social prestige and good salaries are open to officers on a wide scale [after retirement]. Some move into the diplomatic service . . . government ministries and departments and to state enterprises.[12]

These privileges are granted to most, if not all, Syrian military officers irrespective of religious, communal or ethnic affiliation. Some officer groups, however, receive special attention as Asad attempts to secure their allegiance and make them the backbone of his army and his regime.

Alliance With Non-Alawite Officers

One such group is the Sunni Muslims. Since the mid-1960s Sunni Muslim Arabs have been greatly under-represented in the officer corps, particularly in the combat units of the army. While the Sunni Arabs numbered over 60 per cent of the total population, during the years 1965–71, Sunni Arab officers controlled only 25 to 30 per cent of all army units. Many of these officers were systematically purged, dismissed, retired and, periodically, executed while others were assigned to unimportant positions. Most of those dismissed or retired had been part of the veteran Ba'th leadership or had been associated with the old conservative parties or upper-class families. Many of those officers came from the big cities. By contrast, many of the Sunni officers who were retained in the army or are newly enlisted are from small towns and villages or are of lower-class origins. Most of them are (or pretend to be) loyal party members or followers, and identify with Asad's regime. They regard Asad's as primarily Syrian Arab nationalist rule and do not see the regime in terms of Alawite partisan interests. As beneficiaries of the system, these Sunni Arab officers are for the most part appreciative of and grateful for their gains, and a number of them have risen to senior positions in various parts of the army, including the combat units. Yet Sunni Arab officers are mainly represented in professional functions in the non-combat units. Thus, in addition to Defence Minister Tlas and Chief of Staff Shihabi, some 60 per cent of the officers of the General Staff Command are Sunni Arabs, including the air force commander, chiefs of operations and logistics, of instruction planning and so on. Similarly some 45 per cent of the senior officer corps throughout the army (including the staff command) are Sunnis, as are three out of four commanders of the Regional Commands. Although they are under-represented in the officer corps, notably in the combat units, Sunni Arab officers do hold senior or sensitive positions in such units. For example, more than half of the wing commanders and other senior officers in the air force are Sunni Arabs. Several Sunni Arabs serve as commanders of armoured or infantry corps, divisions and brigades, while further Sunni officers have more junior commanding positions in these units.

In sum, Asad, consistent with his policy of satisfying the Sunni Arab majority and of giving a nationalist image to his power-base, has appointed more Sunni Arab officers in junior as well as in senior military positions than his predecessor had done. At the same time, Asad makes use of military service to integrate the minority communities of the population into a new cohesive political community behind his regime.

For these reasons, Asad, more than Jadid, has opened senior military positions, including combat positions, to Christian, Druze, Circassian and Ismaili officers. Christian officers, for example, are estimated to form about 15 per cent of the officer corps in the army, and about 5 per cent of the senior corps, including two senior officers in the General Staff Command, two in the combat wings of the air force, one in a Regional Command, and another as commander of one of the military academies. Druze officers, several of whom were rehabilitated by Asad after the 1966–7 purge and encouraged to re-enlist in the army, hold senior combat positions in the air force, or are commanders of armoured and infantry brigades. Unlike the Christians, the Druze are still slightly under-represented in the officer corps (less than 3 per cent), especially compared to their position during the 1950s and 1960s, when Druze officers were relatively numerous and rather noticeable in important military positions. This phenomenon also characterizes the Kurdish community (Sunni Muslims, non-Arab, some 8 per cent of the population). Their officers are greatly under-represented in the army compared to their strength in the pre-Ba'th period. By contrast, the Circassians (another Sunni Muslim, non-Arab community numbering several thousands only) are now greatly over-represented in the officer corps. They count a member of the General Staff Command, a commander of an armoured corps, as well as a significant number of soldiers in Rifat Asad's Defence Detachments (which include Druze and Christians, but consist mostly of Alawites).

It may very well be that the differential representation of these religious and ethnic communities in the Syrian officer corps is unintentional, or irrelevant as Syrian officials would allege. Yet such a mix would be consistent with the claim of various sources that Asad's recruitment and appointment policies in the army have been carefully designed and systematically implemented to serve his prime goal of establishing a powerful professional army with an effective officer corps loyal to him or closely supervised by him. In line with this policy Asad would entrust senior and sensitive military positions to the kind of officers who are less likely personally or collectively to endanger his rule. They would be committed to him in one or more of the following ways: through personal loyalty, family, tribal or communal (Alawite) affiliation, Ba'th ideological commitment, or political association and professional service. Accordingly, apart from the Alawites, Christian and Circassian officers would be the least likely to threaten his regime and the most likely to stand by him in times of danger. Many of these officers are professional soldiers who have a vested interest in Asad's regime and in the opportunities for career promotion and social status. They belong to tiny (the Circassians) or fragmented (the Christians) communities with a long record of apolitical tendencies. Christians would also tend to identify with Asad's domestic policies, notably the weakening of Islam in public life, and with the encouragement of private economic enterprise. They can be regarded as a very reliable element in any intra-minorities alliance with the Alawites at its core.

The Druze and the Kurdish minorities, by contrast, are not in the same proximity to the Alawites. Asad has sought to gain their goodwill and allegiance particularly for his external policies. He has used Druze solidarity with their brethren in the Israeli-held Golan Heights in order to foster anti-Israeli subversive activities there, just as he has tried to take advantage of ties between the Syrian Druze and the Lebanese Druze to cultivate pro-Syrian tendencies among both these Druze groups. In a similar vein, Asad has employed Kurdish elements in the Jazira (north-eastern Syria) to help their brethren across the border in their rebellion against the rival Iraqi regime (just as the Iraqi regime has occasionally used its Kurdish collaborators to support Syrian Kurdish subversive activities against Asad's government).

These minorities can still pose a serious threat to Asad's rule, given their previous involvement in domestic Syrian politics and their strong sectarian loyalties. Each of these minorities is socially cohesive and territorially compact: the Druze in Jabal Druze are imbued with strong religious and tribal solidarity, while the Kurds (mostly in the Jazira region) adhere to Kurdish nationalistic ideas and to Sunni Muslim beliefs. Coupled with their past record of co-operation with Sunni Muslim Arabs, these two groups could become a solid base for any Sunni-inspired military uprising against Asad's rule.

That is the source of the greatest danger to Asad's regime – the Sunni Muslim officers and troops backed by a Sunni Muslim majority population (some 70 per cent of the total including the Kurdish minority). Notwithstanding the number of senior Sunni Muslim officers in the army, a large but unknown number of Sunni NCOs and officers deeply resent Asad and his military regime. In addition to sharing the bitter grievances of their community against minority rule by the Alawite regime, many of these officers feel immensely frustrated in that they do not control the army and have no say over promotions or appointments to higher positions. The reality of their under-representation in the officer corps (27 per cent) is exacerbated by the feeling that their combat soldiers were sent to fight and be killed in the battles against Israel, when Alawite soldiers were spared. (Some Sunni soldiers who were prisoners of war in Israel felt that Asad's regime did very little to free them.)[13] All in all, many Sunni soldiers resent the arrogant behaviour of their Alawite colleagues, who seem to them to receive rapid promotion without having gained adequate credentials.

These feelings of frustration and deprivation among Sunni Muslim officers and NCOs have over the years provoked defections of Sunni soldiers from the army, several attempts to assassinate Asad and other Alawite officers, as well as planned military coups, all of which were doomed to failure.

The Alawite Military Support

Relentless Sunni opposition, latent or active, gives Asad no other choice but to rely heavily on his fellow Alawites in controlling the army, especially its combat units. Those officers, mostly members of his family clan and tribe, who are in charge of the security and intelligence networks are at the top of a pyramid whose higher, middle and even lower levels are filled with Alawites. They also hold senior or sensitive positions in the armoured, mechanized and infantry divisions and brigades. As stated earlier, Alawites constitute some 60 per cent of the entire officer corps, about 50 per cent of the senior officer corps holding commanding positions of most tank, artillery, infantry, navy and air defence units, most sensitive posts (i.e. operations and intelligence) in the General Staff Command as well as in personnel and indoctrination departments. Likewise, Alawite officers and NCOs staff most of the commandos and crack troops wearing distinct uniforms and enjoying special privileges. Finally, the majority of the cadets in military academies are Alawites and so are most of their commanders.[14]

As we have seen, the ascendancy of the Alawite soldiers in the Syrian army had started under the French mandate, was maintained after Syrian independence and gained rapid momentum after the 1963 Ba'th coup. Salah Jadid played an important role together with his fellow Alawites Muhammad Umran and Asad in ensuring the proliferation of Alawite officers in the Syrian army. As chief of army personnel and subsequently chief of staff of the army, Jadid encouraged young Alawites to join the military forces and sent many of them to the officers' academies. He also urged Alawite reserve officers to re-enlist in the regular army and assigned them to senior combat positions, appointing his relatives to such positions in some of the crack units. The 70th Armoured Brigade, for example, famous for its military achievements, was commanded by his cousin Izzat Jadid.[15]

When Asad began to oust Jadid in the late 1960s, he took advantage of his position as defence minister to appoint his own relatives and followers to key military positions from which he systematically purged Jadid's appointees, just as Jadid had previously done to his fellow conspirator Muhammad Umran. After taking power in 1970, Asad confirmed the purges, notably by putting Jadid in jail and allegedly by ordering the assassination of Umran (who had escaped to exile in Lebanon) in 1972.[16] These actions provoked intense feelings of resentment among the Alawite families, clans and tribes related to Umran and Jadid, as well as among other disaffected Alawites. A few officers associated with Jadid and Umran formed secret organizations and made several attempts to overthrow Asad, often with the help of the rival Iraqi regime. The most important of these attempts, in which several of Asad's supporters were killed, occurred at the end of 1972 soon after the assassination of Umran and in 1976 during Asad's first involvement in the Lebanese quagmire.[17] Asad managed to overcome this limited but powerful opposition among Alawite regular and reservist officers by arresting, purging or killing dozens of them, including seven high-level officers. At the same time he began to heal the breach with other formerly pro-Jadid and pro-Umran officers, and to consolidate an all-Alawite backing for his authority, by creating a strong vested economic interest in his regime. After rallying the support of Alawite spiritual leaders, Asad became for almost the entire Alawite community the guarantor of its economic well-being, political supremacy and even physical survival. Indeed, most Alawites seem to recognize that Asad's regime serves their vital interests, and that, should it collapse, they are likely to face a serious threat to their very existence.[18]

Alawite solidarity and the sense of a shared destiny with Asad are well reflected by solid Alawite support in the armed forces, which Asad regards as indispensable to the survival of his regime, regardless of how well he succeeds in broadening that support with other group allegiances. A close observer of Syrian politics and the Syrian military describes this situation aptly though perhaps too symmetrically:

Asad recognized that Syria, as a country at war, could not risk the military's performance being adversely affected by its internal policing role or by ethnic conflict, nor could the regime confidently dispense with the protection afforded it by the careful appointment of Alawis to key command positions. The solution seemed logical: create what amounts to two armies, one to look outward, the other inward; one in which professional competence was the primary criterion for promotion to all but the most sensitive posts, which continued to go to Alawis, the other in which unquestioned political loyalty was a precondition of membership; one whose cohesion depended on discipline and a sense of national mission, the other whose members were closely bound by primordial ties of family, region, and ethnic group; one to be a source of national pride and to embody patriotic ideals, the other to compartmentalize and quarantine the regime's Machiavellian excesses.[19]

However one describes Asad's policies towards the army, it is clear that for the first time in the annals of the Syrian republic, the supreme leader has been able effectively to control the army, rather than be controlled by it. Not only has Asad succeeded in eliminating politicization and factionalism among its ranks, but he has turned it into a powerful and fairly credible military force in the Middle East. Despite the defeats it suffered, the Syrian army fought bravely in both the 1973 and 1982 wars against Israel in the Golan and Lebanon respectively. Its cohesiveness is all the more impressive considering that its many Sunni Muslim soldiers had to fight in 1976 and 1983 against Lebanese and Palestinians, the majority of whom were also Sunni Muslim. Nonetheless the Syrian army has been unable to overcome a number of crucial flaws, notably its poor technological performance. This applies mainly to the air force, which is still greatly inferior to the Israeli air force – this despite Asad's great efforts to improve it (it has been the cornerstone of his military support).

Though indoctrinated by Ba'th Party concepts and described as an 'ideological army', the Syrian army has been shaped by Asad primarily as a good professional army. Unlike Iraq's, Syria's army is not controlled by the Ba'th Party. It is fully controlled by President Asad, and together with the security network it constitutes the pillar of his regime. The Ba'th Party forms a second layer in Asad's support system, but like the army it is also closely supervised and manipulated by him, an instrument for legitimacy, control and mobilization.

6 The Ba'th Instrument

As far as is known, Asad joined the Ba'th Party in Latakia during the mid-1940s at the age of sixteen. At that time this incipient pan-Arab ideological party, persecuted by the French mandate, was beginning to attract members from among Syrian intellectuals and high-school students and teachers. Although he was an active member both before and during his military service, Asad did not hold any official position in the party's apparatus until the Ba'th coup of March 1963. But as one of the co-leaders of the self-appointed Ba'th Military Committee which initiated this coup, Asad subsequently became a member of the Ba'th Party Regional Command. Significantly he was elected or appointed to the Ba'th National Command as late as 1965, months before the February 1966 coup, which he masterminded together with Jadid. Asad continued to serve as a prominent member of both Ba'th Commands even after the 1966 coup, when he began turning to the army as his power-base. He took an active role in the deliberations of the various Ba'th congresses, sharply criticizing party policies and its leadership (of Jadid, Atasi, Zu'ayyin and Makhus) and presenting his own ideas as alternatives. He accused the party leaders of adopting personal and parochial, rather than national, positions, of mishandling the country's and party's affairs, and of undermining the Ba'th doctrines by 'a kind of ideological dimness and terror'. He alleged that 'this leadership could not competently assume the historical responsibility of leading the party and gathering the masses around the party'.[1] In particular, as will be discussed below, Asad attacked the party–state leadership for their policies regarding the conflict with Israel and Syria's relationship with other Arab countries, and for their economic measures. In short, Asad alleged that Jadid and his clique had in fact paralysed and polarized the party and army, had greatly hindered the country's economic development, and had seriously damaged Syria's position in the Arab world, in the international community and vis-à-vis Israel.[2]

These grave accusations, made in the Ba'th Party's conventions of March 1969, November 1970 and September 1971, reflected more than Asad's concern for the well-being of the state, the army and the people. They were aimed at discrediting the party's former leadership in the eyes of the delegates and convincing them, not without arm-twisting, that Asad was the suitable and legitimate leader of the party. Though he was able to overthrow Jadid's regime by his sheer military superiority, Asad nevertheless wanted to earn also the Ba'th Party's formal approval of his ascendancy. Thus even before he was 'elected' as Syria's president, Asad had been 'chosen' as the secretary-general of the Ba'th Party's National and Regional Commands. Since that time he has continued to play an active part in party conventions as well as in other party activities. He has used the party congresses to promote a personality cult and an image as the legitimate, heroic leader of the country. The standing ovations greeting his entrance at conventions are immediately broadcast on television to the most remote corners of Syria. The television cameras carefully frame the president against a backdrop of gigantic wall-banners which proclaim him 'leader of the struggle, champion of steadfastness and confrontation'. Party leaders hail his exemplary leadership, which has transformed Syria into the country of 'heroism, liberation, unity and socialism' and elevated its position in the region and on the international scene.[3]

Having seized power by force of arms, Asad was obviously eager to use the name and the institutional framework of the Ba'th to legitimize and perpetuate his rule. The need for Ba'thist legitimacy was even more important to Asad than to his predecessors, Jadid and Hafiz. First, he needed to support his new presidential system of personal, centralized rule, established in Syria for the first time in her history. Second, as the third in a series of military officers who ruled Syria in the name of the Ba'th, Asad was under attack by all previous Ba'th leaders including Aflaq and Bitar, who tried to discredit and invalidate his regime. For example, Salah al-Din al-Bitar, the co-founder of the Ba'th Party, said in his last interview in 1980 a few weeks before he was assassinated in Paris:

> Two years ago, when I returned to Syria after thirteen years of exile I met Hafiz al-Asad. I said to him 'Your regime lacks legitimacy. . . . Today, Syria is dead. . . . Only political democracy which must be re-established can allow Syria to regain its vitality and play a role in the

Arab World. . . . The two real bases of the regime are dictatorship and confessionalism [sectarianism]. The Ba'th Party, as a party, does not exist. Likewise, there is not a real government . . . policy remains in the hands of Hafiz al-Asad.'[4]

Similarly Amin al-Hafiz, the leader of the Syrian Ba'th in the years 1963–6 and a current supporter of the Iraqi Ba'th regime, described Asad in a 1985 interview as 'the fox dressed as a saint' and accused him not only of misrepresenting the Ba'th Party but of having 'fought against the true Ba'th Party' and of being 'in league with Israel'. Asad is also alleged to have plotted against Iraq, which represents the 'original Ba'th', to have killed many Palestinians in an attempt to destroy the PLO, and to have tyrannized the Syrian people. Hafiz finally revealed that the newly established National Alliance for the Liberation of Syria, consisting of a Ba'th (pro-Iraqi) faction along with Nasserite and Islamic elements, had as its aim the overthrow of Asad's regime.[5]

Asad's Ba'thist opponents, followers of Hafiz, Bitar, Jadid and Umran, were not content just with trying to discredit him in various ways. Largely backed by the Ba'th regime in Iraq, and by antagonistic Ba'th members inside Syria, they have periodically attempted to topple him. All these attempts, however, failed and were followed by the arrest of many Syrian Ba'th members. Coincidentally, several former prominent Syrian Ba'th leaders were assassinated abroad after criticizing Asad, including (as we have seen) Bitar in 1980 in Paris and Umran in 1972 in Lebanon.[6] In addition, most, if not all, veteran Ba'th leaders have been jailed or exiled since Asad came to power. In order to ensure his effective control over the party, he appointed his followers, mostly junior members, to key positions in the Ba'th institutions. Beyond that, he reformed the party's apparatus and its activities in order to expand its membership and influence, and to turn it, along with the army, into one of the foundations of his regime and a major instrument of his rule.

Accordingly, one of Asad's first steps has been to mobilize and incorporate into the party the broadest possible array of social groups from the various communities, regions and classes. Special attention was given to members of the Sunni Muslim majority population, and particularly to the less privileged among them. The participation of these groups would project an image of the Ba'th as being, in Asad's words, the party of the 'toiling masses'. Put in another way, such participation would demonstrate that the regime's single party represents the Syrian people as a whole and not merely 'a select group/system'. It would thus emphasize and reinforce the populist, civilian character of Asad's regime and present it to the Syrian people and to the world at large as a 'popular democracy' rather than an Alawite military dictatorship.[7] In order to underline its popular and democratic nature, Asad boasted that in 1980 the Ba'th Party had 550,000 members,[8] although other reliable sources put party membership in 1982 at 300,000.[9] This membership, organized in fourteen regional branches with some 200 sections, has been recruited by some 100,000 cadres on the basis of friendship, kinship or ideology. But many party members are motivated largely by personal economic considerations.[10]

Thus, apart from a great many Alawites and a considerable number of Druze and Ismailis, mostly peasants, about one-third of the Sunni Muslim peasantry is reported to have been recruited into the Ba'th Party since Asad's rise to power. This significant enrolment can be attributed to the effective organization and persistent activity of the Ba'th Party in the Syrian countryside, which led to the training of young peasants in the party's schools and the creation of a system of peasants' associations. In addition to enabling peasant leaders to join the political arena at both the local and national levels, Asad's regime has gained the allegiance of many ordinary *fellahin* through a series of economic measures such as land reform, rural electrification projects, credit and modern machinery for their farms. Urban workers have similarly benefited from the Ba'th's new policies, which led to a marked improvement in their conditions, such as shorter working hours, better medical and welfare services, and so on. Other social groups or sections which became affiliated with the Ba'th Party in considerable numbers were the salaried middle class, school teachers and intellectuals. Many of them belong to the state bureaucracy and are thus critically dependent on the regime. And although many are discontented with the favouritism rampant in the public service, especially towards Alawites, with the pervasive corruption among the political elite and with the suppression of civil liberties, they see no viable alternative to the Ba'th regime. On the contrary, many of them, certainly the ardent Ba'th followers, take pride in Asad's strong leadership as well as in his well-balanced domestic measures and courageous foreign policies.

Finally, among the younger generation of Ba'th members – high-school pupils and university students – many enthusiastically support Asad and his policies, as they have been systematically indoctrinated to do for the last two decades by the party's apparatus. The party has motivated these students, as well as peasants, workers, women, artisans, professionals, and other groups in 'popular organizations', in order to achieve a visible demonstration of their backing for Asad's regime and to attract others to join the party's ranks.

Some of these organizations have also fulfilled the function of combating Asad's domestic enemies, for example when armed militias of peasants and workers have been called upon to assist the security forces in various operations. The peasant militia, comprising some half-a-million armed members, was reorganized in 1980 and given the role of 'liquidating gangs of reactionaries, killers and saboteurs'.[11] In 1982 these same peasant members participated in the brutal suppression of the Hama rebellion.

Asad allows his Ba'th members opportunity to voice their opinions, complaints and expectations on national issues, particularly regarding economic and social policies. As a way of testing the popularity and feasibility of the government's policies, the voicing of such opinions is encouraged in party gatherings, particularly during party congresses when some 800 party delegates debate for several days important but limited sets of issues. These congresses, which convene every four years, nominally fulfil another important function, the election of the party's highest organs, the Central Committee and the Regional Command. Yet like the resolutions passed in these congresses, the elections are in fact controlled and their results are predetermined by Asad. Nonetheless the composition of the twenty-one-member Regional Command is highly significant: it is made to reflect various 'representative' sections of the Syrian population, in the way that Asad wishes that representation to appear. Thus between 1970 and 1980 the Regional Commands consisted of some 70 per cent Sunni Muslim members, some 21 per cent Alawites, 4 per cent Druze and 5 per cent Christians as opposed to 52 per cent Sunnis, 23 per cent Alawites, 9 per cent Druze, 9 per cent Ismailis and 6 per cent Christians during the Jadid period. Furthermore, Asad has greatly increased the percentage not only of Sunni Muslims in the party leadership, but also of Sunni members from the Damascus area, which rose from zero (under Jadid) to an average of 25 per cent under Asad.[12] These telling changes are undoubtedly consistent with Asad's policy of bringing into the party the maximum number of Sunni Muslims from the countryside as well as from Damascus. His aim has obviously been to gain the loyalty of the majority Sunni population while transforming the image of the regime. In particular the increased number of Sunni members from Damascus in the Regional Commands has been encouraged by Asad in order to win the support of the Sunni urban population which, under

Jadid, had been alienated by a series of rigid and doctrinaire Marxist policies. While accusing the Jadid regime of deviation from the true Ba'th course, Asad could thus claim that he came to power only in order to return the party to its 'pure' course and to reorient its policies 'to serve the people's interests'. Labelling them a Ba'thist 'corrective movement', Asad initiated new domestic policies, aimed at consolidating his rule on the basis of widespread support for his grand project of nation-building.

7 The Six Good Years (1970–1976)

Nation-Building

There is little question that Asad dedicated enormous resources and energy to building a powerful army as the pillar of his rule. But this was not his only concern. Asad has been equally resourceful in shaping a dynamic foreign policy which has contributed significantly to mobilizing popular support and acquiring legitimacy for his regime. At the same time, Asad did not neglect the internal challenge of rebuilding the Syrian state and society. His systematic and direct attempts at nation-building were based on his new 'corrective movement' policies, inaugurated in November 1970 and embracing the Ba'th's tenets of unity, freedom and socialism. Asad's policies would thus, in theory, aim to achieve national unity through the creation of a popular democracy, granting civil liberties and building on the original socialist reforms of the Ba'th revolution. The organs used to implement these goals would be the National Progressive Front led by the Ba'th Party, and the People's Assembly, as well as various other popular organizations. They would foster civil liberties and socialist measures while mobilizing the people to unify and to dedicate their energies to the Syrian homeland. A unified Syrian people would in turn constitute a solid basis for pan-Arab unity and for the struggle against Zionism, imperialism and reactionary Arab regimes.[1] However, beyond these theoretical and rhetorical statements aimed at demonstrating his commitment to Ba'th doctrines, Asad's first priority has been to establish a basis of popular legitimacy for his regime.

To achieve these goals Asad sought to maintain political stability and to expand economic opportunities, thereby neutralizing most of the opposition or even cultivating the allegiance of some. However, aware of a perennial conservative Muslim opposition, Asad decided from the beginning of his rule to rely more on the relatively modern, secular sections of society. Through them Asad has endeavoured to establish a new political community encompassing many of the underprivileged elements of the past: peasants, workers and small-town dwellers, as well as military officers, Ba'th members, intelligentsia, students and the younger generations. Indeed, except for latent Muslim resistance which surfaced on only one occasion, many Syrians supported or tolerated Asad's leadership during the first six years of his rule (1970–6). This support was in part due to Asad's dynamic and courageous foreign policy (which will be discussed below) – notably his decision to enter the 1973 war against Israel. But it was also due to Asad's relative success at maintaining stability and liberal economic policies. Or in the words of a leading Arabist, writing in 1973, 'Asad has represented liberalization, modernization, normalization [and] a search for consensus.'[2]

To begin with Asad made small gestures to appease the traditional urban, Sunni Muslim middle class, composed of merchants, artisans, shopkeepers and religious functionaries, which had been deeply alienated by the harsh measures of the previous Ba'th regimes (1963–70). One set of measures had brought about the nationalization of medium-sized industries and commercial enterprises and strict governmental control of small businesses. These economically painful steps were aggravated by the more psychologically traumatic secularist policies of the pre-Asad Ba'th regimes, such as separating Islam from state institutions, restricting Muslim (and Christian) religious education at state schools, and downgrading the status of Islam and of its guardians, the *ulama*. These unprecedented measures had triggered (as will be elaborated upon in chapter 12) several cycles of fierce demonstrations during the mid-1960s by *ulama*-led Muslim middle-class people, which were bloodily suppressed by the regime's security forces.

Upon his ascendancy Asad made substantial efforts to mitigate the multiple sources of antagonism from the urban Muslim middle classes. First, he made a series of gestures to demonstrate his alleged devotion to Islam, and then he embarked on a new policy of economic liberalization. Asad's economic measures were aimed at revitalizing the small and medium-sized private sector enterprises. Restrictions on foreign trade were thus relaxed and Syrian merchants were now allowed to import raw materials and industrial and agricultural equipment as well as luxury goods. New and modern hotels were built in the cities, and free-trade zones were set up in different parts of Syria to enhance private sector trade and increase the national income. Wealthy Syrian entrepreneurs who had fled the country after the 1963 Ba'th revolution were now wooed back and offered inducements to invest their money in various projects. Asad personally invited a number of public figures to come back and contribute to the reconstruction effort, and he promised posts in the public service to technically qualified young men who had left Syria. In 1974 he issued a decree granting extensive bonuses to young engineers and other technicians in order to discourage their emigration abroad.[3] To satisfy the salaried lower-middle class and the intelligentsia, Asad created new jobs in the expanding bureaucracy, decreed price reductions on essential foodstuffs, lowered taxes and increased family allowances. He also eased travel restrictions abroad, lifted martial law, permitted foreign newspapers to enter the country and prohibited arbitrary arrests.

Asad's major efforts were, nevertheless, still directed towards the large rural population. He strove to carry on the economic revolution, which was started during the 1958–61 union with Egypt and subsequently enhanced by the Ba'th regimes after 1963. The main beneficiaries of these reforms were to be the masses of peasants and workers – 'the productive toiling people', in Asad's words, whose well-being 'has been the goal of the revolution'.[4] Thus, after land expropriation from the traditional big landowners was completed, limited land redistribution to landless and smallholding peasantry was continued under Asad's directions, encompassing about one-third or more of the landless *fellahin* by the late 1970s. The system of state-run agricultural co-operatives which had started in 1958 has also been greatly expanded under Asad's regime (there were some 3,400 with about 250,000 members in 1980). The co-operatives provide the peasants with seeds and fertilizers, technical assistance and training programmes as well as marketing facilities; the State Agricultural Bank allocates loans and credits to the farmers. More and more peasants came to enjoy greater security in land tenure and received other support in developing their farms. Those farmers, as well as many other landless peasants, have also benefited from opportunities opened to them in state education and employment in public projects both in their rural neighbourhoods and in the towns.[5]

Despite these reforms the majority of Syrian peasants (who are Sunni Muslims) still remain landless, and many continue to be poor. This is partly because Asad's government has overlooked the renewal of the practice whereby wealthy farmers buy small non-viable plots of land from poor peasants and cultivate them in an economically profitable way. But it is also because Asad's regime has deliberately chosen not to distribute the bulk of the land that the former Ba'th regimes had confiscated from the big landowners after 1963. One reason for this policy was economic: Syrian agriculture was modernized by means of mechanization and the cultivation of large plots of land, while unemployed peasants were transferred to industry.[6] Another goal was political, as it would appear that Asad preferred to keep a large part of the land as government property and lease it to landless peasants in order to establish, with the help of local village leaders, a patronage system covering hundreds of thousands of Syrian *fellahin* who could be mobilized on behalf of his regime. As it is, the Asad regime controls the Ba'th-led General Federation of Peasants, which includes some 40 per cent of the rural workforce. Many of these peasants are organized in the agricultural co-operatives and have received loans from the State Agricultural Bank, which helps to foster allegiance to the regime.[7] On various occasions the peasants' federations have indeed proved their loyalty to Asad's regime, particularly in times of crisis. They, as well as the labour organizations, were given arms and were organized as militias to support the security forces' struggle against the foes of the regime.

Urban workers have also enjoyed, to some extent, improved conditions in matters of family allowances, social security, higher pensions, health insurance and technical training. And many other sections of the population have benefited directly and indirectly from the big national development projects, most of which were started in the mid-1960s with foreign (notably Soviet) aid. The outstanding project – the Euphrates Dam – has been at the core of the development of a modern agro-industrial infrastructure. One of the biggest earth dams in the world, this huge project in Tabaqa, north-east Syria, which was completed with Soviet assistance in 1974, brought about the 'complete electrification of the country' (i.e. it supplied lighting) and provided 80 per cent of the electric power needed for the erection of modern industries. Simultaneously this dam, with its 250,000-square-mile reservoir, Lake Asad, greatly increased the irrigation of arable lands and eventually will more than double the land area under irrigation. This in turn has improved agricultural production in this fertile area, has attracted poor peasants to settle in the region and has contributed to the rise in living standards of its inhabitants as well as to enlarging the national consumer market.

Yet the share of agriculture in the Syrian economy decreased over the years as other sectors grew faster, particularly industry, which was given high priority in the 1971–5 five-year plan. With the help of foreign aid, the state invested heavily in various industries during these years, which increased the provision of domestic goods and commodities while accelerating the growth rate of national income and decreasing Syria's dependence on foreign imports. Energy has been one of the major sectors contributing to economic growth, as oil and phosphate industries in the Jazira region and elsewhere supplied large parts of Syria's domestic needs while contributing substantially to her GNP.[8] An important component of these big development projects has been the modernization of the national transport system which contributed to state-building by improving communications and linking remote parts of the country to the big cities and the port towns. Various projects which started in the mid-1960s have been continued or completed under Asad's rule, serving the expanding domestic transit and foreign trade in agricultural and industrial products, and facilitating internal and regional connections for both civilian economic and military strategic purposes. Another significant by-product of this industrial expansion was the training and employment of many skilled workers and engineers in mechanics, electricity, oil, chemicals and construction.

At the same time as he expanded and modernized the economic infrastructure, Asad, like his predecessors, made considerable efforts to improve the poor health and education systems in the country. Health services were expanded and medical insurance introduced, new hospitals were built or completed and old ones were renovated and newly equipped. Asad's ambition in 1972 was to erect during the following five years a network of health centres which would provide one medical clinic for every 25,000 people, both in the towns and in the villages.[9]

Equally ambitious (but unrealistic) was Asad's plan to eradicate illiteracy and improve the spread of education particularly among children and women.[10] Great attention and many resources were initially devoted to this project. In 1972 Asad enacted a law calling for the eradication of illiteracy within a mere six years. Simultaneously he urged the expansion of the educational system at all levels, with special reference to vocational and technical training. As a result of these efforts the proportion of children of primary-school age attending school gradually grew to 63 per cent in the early 1970s, including 92 per cent at the first-form level, according to Asad's figures. Secondary-school education was also increased during the 1970s, with high priority given to technical education, basic sciences and agriculture. Similarly, higher technical and scientific studies were greatly expanded while two new universities, in Aleppo and Latakia, were established, along with five new higher technical institutes in other towns. They include faculties or schools of science, engineering, medicine, petro-chemistry, agriculture and veterinary medicine. Asad's educational policies also gave high priority to developing the seminaries in order to train more teachers.[11]

To conclude this brief survey of Asad's economic policies it must be said that beyond any doubt he dedicated a great deal of thought, effort and resources to development goals. After he came to power in 1970, for at least the first six or seven years of his rule he was personally involved in the various development plans of the country. In many of his public speeches he would elaborate in great detail, citing figures relating, for example, to the number of chickens and livestock, and to production of pencils and electric bulbs, as well as data regarding agricultural and industrial production, medical services and educational facilities. Notwithstanding his obvious desire to impress his audiences, Asad has been genuinely interested in improving the well-being of the Syrian people, notably the under-privileged elements, irrespective of their religious affiliations. He has been equally keen to strengthen the Syrian economy, particularly its public sector – 'the leading sector'.

It is also clear, however, that Asad regarded these goals not only as an end in themselves but also as a vehicle for achieving his political ambitions – namely the consolidation of his regime on the basis of popular consensus and social stability, and the strengthening of Syria's regional position through economic independence and military power. Asad would occasionally state that his economic reforms were directed towards achieving 'national unity' and securing the country's defence. But Asad's approach to these economic reforms was not only politically oriented. It was also largely pragmatic, in comparison to his predecessors' doctrinaire socialist line. For example, criticizing his predecessors for refusing to obtain UN aid because it had been financed by the US, Asad mentioned that Bulgaria received UN aid despite US financial involvement. Similarly, Asad rejected criticism that Western oil companies were permitted to operate in Syria, stressing that even the USSR had invited such companies, including American ones, to search and produce oil in Siberia. 'Why then,' exclaimed Asad, 'if the USSR, the biggest socialist country, can do this, cannot we? Undoubtedly, the USSR is not going to give up socialism just because it is drawing on Japanese or American funding. . . . when the dollar reaches us it ceases to be American but becomes our property. . . . each plan and project is carried out according to purely economic criteria.'[12]

Similarly, Asad was candid and realistic enough to admit to certain obstacles and mistakes inherent in the planning and execution of various development projects. On several occasions he indicated that some projects had not yet produced any useful results, although they constituted an important basis for the long-term developments in the economic, educational, cultural and social arenas.

Indeed, despite the significant achievements of Asad's state-building policies, notably the remarkable growth during the first six years of his rule, the chronic economic problems of Syria have remained largely unsolved, while new ones have developed. For example, the failure to reduce illiteracy substantially, which was at about 60 per cent in the early 1970s, has hampered social and economic development efforts. The government in fact allocated very small sums of money for that purpose and, according to a neutral observer, at the rate that the anti-illiteracy programme was advanced in the early 1970s 'it would take not 10 years but nearer 150 to eradicate illiteracy'.[13] Similarly in the field of primary education, supposedly compulsory, a significant portion of the relevant age group either has not attended or has dropped out of school. In addition to the shortage of qualified teachers, classes are overcrowded, school buildings old and many more new schools are needed, particularly in the rural areas.[14] The serious and continuing problem of a brain-drain has also impaired Syria's development programme in the fields of education, science and health. Thus several thousand Syrian doctors (as well as thousands of teachers and engineers) are practising abroad, while many medical students fail to return home from overseas. These factors certainly contribute to the shortage of adequate medical services in the country. In rural areas in particular, doctors are few and hospitals scarce: the average in 1974 was one doctor per 10,000 people and one bed per 1,000.[15] This average has not changed much since then.

The population of the rural areas is also deprived in other ways. The majority of peasants are still unaffected by the agrarian reform despite the revolutionary change in land ownership, and the Ba'th slogan 'The land to him who works it' is far from being implemented. Many peasants rent land from urban landlords or rich farmers – the new *effendis* (bosses) – and are subject to their patronage and extortion; so are many agricultural workers. While a noticeable number of poor peasants suffer underemployment, a growing number of unemployed peasants emigrate to the cities and contribute to the widening of the economic gap among the urban population. Even those who had settled in the new villages were not satisfied with the living conditions, even referring to their homes as 'tombs'.[16] The state's co-operative system, despite the efforts devoted to its expansion, lacks dynamism and efficiency, is plagued with corruption and thus does not always stimulate agricultural production.[17] As it is, despite its steady growth, agriculture has not kept pace with the increasing demands of both the consumers and the food-processing and textile industries. So for several years there have been severe shortages in fruits and vegetables in this predominantly agricultural country.[18] Industry, although given great attention by Asad's regime, is still very short of qualified workers and engineers; it suffers from mismanagement and consequently does not show high productivity. One aspect of mismanagement is overstaffing in factories, which not only aggravates budget problems but also provokes dissensions among workers, lowers their morale and undermines discipline. Rapid inflation has eroded the salaries of industrial workers as well as of middle- and lower-level public employees and it has become increasingly hard for them to cope with the soaring prices of food and rent.

The only sector, apart from the officer corps, which has benefited significantly from Asad's regime has been a parasitic new class of *nouveaux riches*. It is engaged in luxury consumption, importing, housing speculation, black-marketeering and exploitation of the public sector through lavish contracts doled out by an increasingly corrupt officialdom.[19] Indeed, senior government and party officials have profited from various shady transactions. Thus sightings of senior officials cruising about Damascus in $25,000 cars or drinking whisky at $100 per bottle in bistros with names like The Crazy Horse are not uncommon and tend to encourage general corruption.[20] Of course, corruption among senior officials and speculation and black-marketeering had certainly existed before Asad came to power, but their incidence has substantially grown since the early 1970s, following Asad's economic liberalization policy and the influx of Arab oil capital and Western investments. As will be discussed later, Syria's involvement in Lebanon since 1976 enormously increased the black market, as many contraband goods were smuggled from Lebanon – frequently in army trucks – to enrich the middlemen as well as senior army officers and government officials. Corruption and bribery among these officials has been so widespread and infectious that since his accession to power Asad has personally led a continuous campaign against these practices, but apparently without success.[21]

Thus during the first six years of his rule Asad encountered serious obstacles in his ambitious attempts at nation-building. Corruption among the officialdom, the emergence of the parasitic class of *nouveaux riches*, as well as the severe economic problems which infected Syria up to 1976, went from bad to worse in subsequent years. Indeed, Syria's involvement in Lebanon from 1976 greatly aggravated her social and economic difficulties while rendering sharp blows to Asad's policies of nation-building. The most conspicuous of these problems was the emergence of a strong and popular Islamic opposition which threatened the legitimacy, indeed the very existence, of Asad's regime during the years 1977–82.

Among the important causes of this critical opposition and of the weakening of Asad's regime after 1976 was the grave deterioration in Syria's regional posture – with regard both to Israel and to Syria's Arab neighbours. For, like the remarkable economic growth and political stability that he was able to achieve within his country, Asad's dynamic and courageous regional policies enormously strengthened his position during the first six years of his rule as a legitimate and strong leader of Syria and the Arab world.

8 Preparing an Arab Crusade Against Israel

On the eve of Asad's re-election as president for his second seven-year term in January 1978 the Syrian parliament and the media (both closely controlled by the regime) discussed his record in his first term of rule. While mild criticism was voiced (as in previous years) with regard to domestic policies,[1] there was a full consensus concerning Asad's remarkable achievements in foreign policies, notably in the Arab world and towards Israel. Parliament and the media depicted Asad as the heir of Nasser and as a strong and unique leader of both regional (Arab) and international stature. Through his pragmatic and realistic policies he had delivered Syria from its regional isolation. Thanks to his ideological stance in the struggle against Israel, he had transformed Syria into a leading Arab country. Making his country the spearhead of the Arab confrontation with Israel, Asad had promoted Syria's intra-Arab status much above her relative weight in the Arab world.[2] Although inflated, these admiring evaluations of Asad's achievements were basically shared by a great many Syrians (and many other Arabs). The foreign-policy gains indeed contributed to the overshadowing of Asad's failures and difficulties in his domestic affairs, deflating the Islamic opposition to his rule and enhancing his image in Syria as a legitimate and popular leader.

The special attention which Asad gave to foreign and regional affairs was not calculated merely to score lightning gains at a time when the crucial economic problems of Syria required long-term and painstaking efforts (without immediate, positive results). Beyond his ambition to elevate his personal stature in Syrian and Arab politics, Asad initiated his new regional policies in order to strengthen Syria's defensive and economic position as well as her political power. These goals were interwoven with the historical and ideological aspirations of many Syrian Arabs, namely Syria's lead in the quest for Arab unity and the struggle against Israel. Not only did Asad's fresh foreign policy reflect the deep-seated sentiments of his people; his strong personal conviction, imagination and courage were evident when in the early 1970s he decided radically to improve Syria's relations with her Arab neighbours, and again in 1973 when he embarked on a highly risky war against Israel. Asad's decision to fight Israel, with the initial aim of regaining the Golan, was also motivated by his desire to restore his and his fellow Syrians' pride, deeply wounded by the loss of that territory in 1967.

The interrelated goals of Arab unity and war against Israel were indeed the major motivation and pretext of Asad's coups in 1969 and 1970 as well as the principal themes of his public speeches and political actions after his assumption of control. As already shown, during the late 1960s Asad had strongly opposed the policies of the then Syrian leaders, Jadid and Atasi, who had rejected the concept of an all-Arab war against Israel because most Arab countries were governed by 'rightist' or 'reactionary' regimes. Asad was concerned about Syria's political isolation in the Arab east and her military vulnerability vis-à-vis Israel. He launched his first military coup, on 25 February 1969, only one day after Israeli air raids on Palestinian military camps near Damascus had clearly revealed Syria's military helplessness. Several weeks later, as we have seen, in the Ba'th congress session of March 1969 Asad stated, 'The defensive capability of the Syrian front is closely tied with the capability of other Arab fronts. . . .'[3]

Subsequently Asad exerted pressure on the Ba'th congress to adopt a resolution that 'new efforts should be made to establish an Eastern Command', which apparently would include Iraq and Jordan. Yet in September 1970 Jadid, still in control, ordered Syrian troops to invade Jordan and help the PLO fighting against the Jordanian army. Rejecting this decision, which was likely further to alienate Jordan from Syria and weaken both Jordan and the PLO, Asad, then minister of defence and air force commander, denied air cover to the Syrian armoured troops in Jordan, who were later forced to withdraw in the face of Jordanian assaults and Israeli military threats. Significantly, Asad effected the complete overthrow of Jadid's regime in November 1970, several weeks after the death of Nasser (28 September) and shortly after Nasser's successor, President Sadat, had decided to conclude an Arab federal union. Possibly Asad aspired to fill the vacuum in pan-

Arab leadership caused by Nasser's death, and in the meantime to have Syria join the new federation, which Jadid had shunned. Indeed, the first foreign-policy decision Asad took after assuming power in Damascus was to join the Federation of Arab Republics (with Egypt and Libya). This step, later approved by a people's referendum (1 September 1971), initially aimed at political, military and economic co-ordination between these Arab countries. In Asad's words, the federation was established as a stage towards a comprehensive Arab union from 'the Atlantic Ocean to the Arab Gulf',[4] and, accordingly, Asad did not rest content with this union merely among three 'progressive' Arab regimes. While calling upon Sudan to join the federation, and mending Syria's fences with the rival Ba'th regime in Iraq, he endeavoured also to renew and improve Syria's relations with the conservative Arab regimes – Saudi Arabia, Kuwait, Morocco, Lebanon and Jordan.

Asad emphasized time and again that the major challenges to the Arab Federation and to all-Arab unity were: to face the 'aggressive and racist' Zionist entity that was a threat to the entire Arab nation; to liberate the Arab territories occupied in 1967; and to return to the Palestinian people the land they claimed as their own. Asad described Israel as supported by world Zionism and imperialism and as a danger not only to the territorial integrity of the Arab states from 'the Nile to the Euphrates' but also to Arab civilization and culture.[5] Thus, according to him (and to Syrian writers inspired by his attitude) the struggle against Israel was inevitable, a zero-sum struggle. 'It is a fatal confrontation, of life or death, of existence or non-existence. . . . It is not a struggle between Arabs and Jews . . . we do not hate Judaism as a religion but we hate Zionism as a colonialist invading movement.' The campaign against this movement should be pursued by various means but essentially through an all-Arab war against Israel.[6] He also advocated political and diplomatic actions in support of the military campaign.

In February 1971 Asad signalled, and in March 1972 declared for the first time, that he would no longer oppose the implementation of UN Security Council Resolution 242 (of November 1967) provided it would entail total Israeli withdrawal from the Arab lands conquered in 1967 and the realization of the (national) rights of the Palestinian people.[7]

This significant change in the position of Syria (Jadid had refused to accept Resolution 242 under any circumstances) reflected Asad's pragmatic thinking regarding the war with Israel. In an interview with

Aliyya al-Sulh, the Lebanese writer, in March 1971, Asad remarked, 'political activities could perhaps facilitate the military campaign. . . . sometimes political manoeuvres are important for the war efforts in order, for example, to gain time or to acquire the sympathy of international public opinion.' However, Asad stressed in the interview that ultimately only Syria's military capability would determine the struggle against Israel, since Israel openly rejected a political settlement by refusing to withdraw from the occupied Arab territories. Asad added that even if Israel withdrew from the Golan and Sinai, Syria would still continue to fight alongside the Palestinian people, as the 'Palestinian problem is the major issue' between the Arabs and Israel.[8]

Consequently, after he came to power, Asad's major priority was quickly and systematically to build a strong army and prepare it for a war against Israel – for both defensive and offensive purposes as well as to enable him to negotiate with Israel from a position of military strength. Allocating over 70 per cent of the 1971 budget to the army, Asad geared Syria's economic and human resources towards the military confrontation with Israel. Through his numerous speeches and his indoctrination campaign he also took steps to prepare his fellow countrymen psychologically for the fatal battle with the formidable enemy, Israel. (For example, in a meeting with his air force pilots he mentioned that the Vietnamese people had sacrificed 2 million people in order to achieve their goals.)[9]

While preparing the Syrian public for the imminent war with Israel, Asad made a trip to Moscow in July 1972 to sign a US$700 million arms deal which included MiG-21s, SAM anti-aircraft missiles, and FROG surface-to-surface missiles. The shipment of these arms later in 1972 was accompanied by Soviet advisers, whose numbers in Syria increased from about 700 to 3,000 in a few months.[10] More Soviet arms, including tanks, followed the visit in February 1973 of a Soviet military delegation to Damascus. In early May 1973 Asad secretly visited Moscow, returning to Damascus in the company of a Soviet air force commander, Marshal Kutakhuv, who led a military delegation to Syria. The Soviets subsequently delivered to Syria new batteries of SAM-6 anti-aircraft missiles, but refused to deliver the modern MiG-23 jet fighters. This may have been related to the Soviet attitude towards a possible Syrian–Israeli war. Although their policy was to help Syria to defend herself against an Israeli attack – hence the supply of anti-aircraft missiles – at that time the Soviets were not keen to see Asad initiating a war against Israel. (They were obviously aware of his military preparations.) They preferred a political settlement to the Arab–Israeli conflict and were possibly also concerned lest Syria be defeated by Israel as in the 1967 war, once more rendering a blow to Soviet interests and prestige in the region.

Yet, even if the Soviet leaders made attempts to dissuade Asad from waging a war against Israel – which is not very likely – they certainly could not have succeeded in this mission.[11] As we have seen, Asad had started preparations for a military confrontation with Israel immediately following his ascent to power on 13 November 1970 (although according to General Mustafa Tlas, Syria's defence minister, Asad started to prepare the army to fight Israel soon after the 1967 war while he served as defence minister under Jadid. Tlas has also alleged that Asad initiated the October 1973 war and suggested a joint venture to Sadat.)[12] In any case, barely two weeks after his ascendancy, on 26 November, Asad signed a military agreement with Egypt, apparently as part of his strategy to consolidate an all-Arab front against Israel. The 1973 assault on Israel was Sadat's initiative, rather than Asad's. Asad would have perhaps waited longer to prepare his army more thoroughly before attacking Israel. And, since the Syrian army was far inferior to the IDF, Asad would not have been likely to start a war against Israel without the participation of other Arab countries, particularly Egypt, or a front-line state such as Jordan (or Iraq). As it was, Sadat's invitation to Asad to join him in a co-ordinated military offensive against Israel came at a time when Asad was preparing his army and his people to fight Israel. Moreover, from Asad's viewpoint, Israel's attitude towards Syria and other Arab nations at that juncture left him no option but to resort to military action. In mid-December 1972 Asad told an Indian journalist that, if a political settlement was not achieved within six months, a war with Israel would be imminent. He added that since Israel's leaders bluntly refused to withdraw from the Golan Heights and from other occupied Arab territories, he had lost hope in a political settlement.[13] There was additional Israeli provocation in that, following the PLO's attacks on Israel, the IDF had inflicted heavy casualties on the Syrian army in a series of military engagements which lasted from November 1972 to January 1973.[14]

Therefore, when in February 1973 General Ahmad Ismail, the new Egyptian war minister, came to Damascus to suggest an Egyptian–Syrian offensive against Israel, Asad quickly agreed. The only reservation he expressed was regarding the date of the attack – May 1973. Asad argued that he would need several more months to have his army ready. Sadat agreed to postpone the operation until October 1973. After the initial agreement and further military co-ordination, Asad secretly visited Cairo in May 1973, and thereafter Moscow, in order to improve the tense Soviet–Egyptian relations (Sadat had expelled the Russian advisers from Egypt in 1972) and to renew Soviet military supplies to Egypt on the eve of the war. In the summer of 1973, in preparation for the war, Asad and Sadat tried to improve their relations with King Hussein of Jordan; diplomatic relations between Syria and Jordan, and between Egypt and Jordan, were subsequently resumed. Asad was particularly interested in linking Jordan to the military confrontation with Israel. Jordan has the longest border with Israel and is fairly close to the Israeli government headquarters, military bases and population centres. Using Jordanian soil to attack or threaten Israel could thus be advantageous to the Syrian-led Arab offensive on the eastern front. More important for Asad was the need to protect the southern flank of his army and prevent the IDF from advancing to Damascus through northern Jordan. It may be assumed that Hussein agreed to prevent such an Israeli counter-attack, but refused to commit himself to attack Israel from his territory. The only commitment he undertook was to dispatch two Jordanian armoured brigades to fight Israel in the Golan Heights.[15]

Regarding Lebanon, another front-line state, Asad did not expect this militarily weak country to attack Israel. But he certainly intended to use Lebanon's soil for two main purposes. First, to prevent an Israeli counter-attack through Lebanon's Biqa valley and along the Beirut–Damascus highway. Second, to engage Israeli troops along the Lebanon–Israel border in order to split the IDF war efforts further. While the second assignment was given to the PLO armed organizations, Asad presumably received the approval of Lebanon's president Taqi al-Din al-Sulh to allow Syrian troops to move into Lebanon in order to counter an Israeli attack via the Biqa valley. Such understanding might have been secretly reached in August 1973 when the Lebanese president visited Asad in Damascus. At the end of that meeting Asad declared, 'we [Syria and Lebanon] are one land and one nation with two governments.'[16]

From March 1973 on there were significant signs of war preparation in Syria. The Lebanese weekly *Al-Sayyad* reported from Damascus in mid-March that in addition to intense Syrian military training and exercises, which Asad also hailed publicly, urgent preparations (such as the building of new water reservoirs, the digging of new wells, and so on) were being made in the civilian sector.[17] In May 1973 the Lebanese press reported that King Hussein of Jordan had distributed a secret letter to his army officers telling them that several Arab countries were about to attack Israel.[18] In July 1973 a second contingent of several thousand Moroccan troops arrived in Syria by Soviet ships (the first shipment had taken place in March 1973). Along with these military preparations (which included new shipments of Soviet T-62 tanks and SCUD missiles) Asad, as well as other Syrian Ba'th leaders, Muslim religious functionaries and the media, fiercely attacked Israel, vowing shortly to wage a crucial war against the 'Zionist enemy'. Thus, for example, in his speech on 2 August 1973 Asad depicted the Zionists as 'the invaders who are threatening the entire human race not only the Arab nations'. The imam (preacher) of the Great Mosque in Damascus, called on 6 September 1973 for a *jihad* (Muslim holy war) against the Zionist enemy.[19]

In Israel, senior officers in the Syrian section of the military intelligence, as well as the officer commanding the Northern Command, General Hofi, were well aware of the Syrian military preparations and were worried about a possible Syrian attack in the Golan. They particularly expressed their concern after the Israeli air force shot down thirteen Syrian MIG fighter planes over the Syrian coastline 125 miles north of Israel on 13 September. This was a severe blow to Syrian morale, and particularly to Asad, the former commander of the Syrian air force, who had continued to pay special attention to this force. Israeli army intelligence officers, expecting an act of revenge from Asad, by late September and early October observed a growing Syrian military build-up along the Syrian border. While Syrian army units had been transferred from the Jordan border and from other areas to the Golan frontier, Russian-built bridging tanks, T-62 tanks and many anti-aircraft missiles were heading towards the front.[20]

Yet, notwithstanding this information and the warnings of an imminent Syrian attack given by the Syrian desk in the Israeli intelligence, by the CIA and by other sources, the head of the Israeli Intelligence Branch, General Zeira, had a different evaluation. His deputy, Brigadier Arye Shalev, explained to the Israeli kitchen-cabinet meeting on 3 October 1973 that 'Asad is a realistic, cool and balanced leader. . . . Syria won't go to war by herself. Asad is scared the IDF will reach Damascus. War just wouldn't make sense, and the Syrian deployment is apparently only because of fear of Israeli attack.' Shalev, backed by General Elazar, the chief of staff, concluded that since the Egyptian army deployment along the Suez Canal was merely a military manoeuvre, and since it was unrelated to the Syrian build-up, 'it is unlikely that a co-ordinated Egyptian–Syrian war will begin in the near future'.[21]

Israel's defence minister, Moshe Dayan, produced a different evaluation. While he believed that the Egyptians would not risk a Suez Canal crossing, the Syrians might try to launch a military offensive since 'they have both provocation and temptation'. Accordingly on Friday, 5 October, he ordered the highest state of alert in the IDF standing army and the reinforcement of the armoured brigades in the Golan. Accepting Dayan's evaluation, Premier Golda Meir decided to take no further action until the regular meeting of the full Israeli cabinet on Sunday, 7 October, a day after Yom Kippur (the Day of Atonement). Golda Meir closed her kitchen-cabinet meeting saying, 'On Sunday we'll lay these problems before the cabinet, and please God we won't have to. Meanwhile it would be good if were we able to send Asad to Synagogue on Yom Kippur. . . .'[22]

Asad was obviously not aware of Golda's condescending advice. He and Sadat were secretly preparing a Yom Kippur for the Israeli Jews which they would probably never forget.

Significantly for Asad, 6 October was his forty-third birthday, but it marked for the first time his ascendancy as a pan-Arab leader, a new leader of the Arab struggle against Israel.

The 1973 War

Indeed, Asad owed his prestigious new position as pan-Arab leader and hero to his full partnership with Egypt (the biggest, most powerful Arab country at that time) during the crucial 1973 war against Israel. His leadership was due just as much to his far-reaching war objectives, his courageous decisions – which involved serious risks to his regime and his country – and his bold and tenacious conduct of the war. Unlike Sadat – whose war aims were limited to crossing the Suez Canal, occupying the eastern bank up to the Sinai passes, and thereafter generating American pressure on Israel to give up the entire Sinai – Asad's goal was to reconquer the entire Golan Heights to the Jordan river and possibly occupy its bridges. In case of strong Israeli counter-attack Asad had planned to consolidate his hold over the Golan and have the Soviet Union negotiate with the US a ceasefire between Syria and Israel.[23] Indeed, by occupying the Golan Asad had undertaken the grave risk of a fierce and powerful Israeli counter-attack (including the use of nuclear weapons). In comparison with the expanse of the Sinai desert separating Israel and Egypt, Israeli and Syrian population centres are in relatively close proximity. It could be expected that the IDF would direct its major military thrust towards the Syrian battlefield, including an offensive towards the capital, Damascus. The IDF retaliation against Syria would be particularly sharp because, unlike the position vis-à-vis Egypt, the US was not likely to restrain Israel from punishing Asad, the Soviet ally.

Apparently taking such a scenario into consideration, Asad was nevertheless ready to risk this, and pay a high price if necessary. In addition to prearranging food and water supplies for the civilian sector, Asad ordered large graveyards prepared and had hotels converted to hospitals. Nonetheless, in order to minimize the toll of an Israeli counter-attack, Asad had shrewdly planned to take his enemy by total surprise. One way of achieving this was by way of a carefully prepared scheme of deception – partly in co-ordination with Egypt and possibly also with the USSR. Thus, for example, in late August 1973 Asad received UN Secretary-General Kurt Waldheim in Damascus, apparently to discuss a political implementation of Security Council Resolution 242. In parallel, Syrian sources leaked disinformation to the effect that their air force pilots were dissatisfied with the MIG planes, that there had developed disputes between the Syrian officers and Soviet advisers and that Damascus was interested in purchasing new weapons from the West.[24] Asad was possibly prepared to go further with his grand deception plan and to risk a limited air battle with the superior Israeli air force. Thus according to an American Middle East analyst, the air battle of 13 September 1973 which cost Syria thirteen planes was provoked by Syrian pilots (undoubtedly under Asad's orders) in order to demonstrate Israel's allegedly aggressive intentions against Syria.[25] This dogfight provided Asad with an excuse to step up the concentration of his military forces in the Golan under the guise of preparation to face an Israeli offensive there. In the same vein Syrian sources, followed by the Soviet media, systematically planted disinformation regarding Israeli army concentrations and Syrian counter-measures along the borders.

In Israel these alleged Syrian fears and military steps were 'understood', and late in September Asad ordered another diversionary move against Israel to draw her attention further from the war plans already made. The Syrian-controlled Saiqa organization hijacked a train carrying Soviet Jews from Moscow to Vienna. Prime Minister Golda

Meir flew to Austria and was preoccupied until 3 October with the hostage drama while Asad finalized his war plans.[26] Asad, as president and commander-in-chief of the army, apparently initiated this successful deception plan, and was likewise in charge of the entire military operation. He had told, and was helped by, only his defence minister and chief of staff. Even the Syrian military commanders in the field received no information up to one hour before the attack.

Without going into the details of the 1973 war, which is beyond the present study, it is clear that Asad (and Sadat) not only managed to take Israel by surprise on 6 October 1973 (although Israel was partly prepared for a Syrian attack in the Golan), but were also able to throw into the battle a larger, better-disciplined, -trained and -equipped combat force of armoured, infantry and anti-aircraft units. These forces, which were also highly motivated, succeeded in overcoming the small IDF forces, downing IDF planes and capturing most of the Golan and the Hermon Mount before Israel could mobilize and dispatch her reservist troops – the bulk of the IDF combat brigades – into the battlefield. The Syrian forces continued to fight boldly and were ready to make substantial sacrifices, even after the tide turned and the IDF inflicted heavy blows on them, pushing them all the way back and in addition capturing new Syrian territory close to Damascus. Syrian troops continued to fight obstinately, exacting more Israeli casualties during the Syrian 'war of attrition' in the spring of 1974, following the ceasefire agreement of 22 October 1973. Similarly, during the 1973 war a large part of the Syrian civilian population made an impressive show of stamina, solidarity and morale, despite the war losses and heavy Israeli bombardment of military and other strategic targets within Syria, all of which caused the population no little suffering. These new phenomena of Syrian military and civilian courage and pride may be largely attributed to the Syrians' urge – following the 1967 defeats – to recover both their captured territory and their wounded patriotic feelings.

Yet these emotions could not have crystallized nor have been translated into military performances and popular attitudes without the exemplary leadership of Asad and his intensive indoctrination campaign of the Syrian public and army. Indeed, in addition to his systematic efforts prior to October 1973 to prepare his people for the war – in psychological, ideological and military terms – Asad took the leading role during the war and thereafter in conducting the military and diplomatic struggle against Israel, as well as in preaching and persuading his troops and fellow countrymen of the vital national urgency of this war. Thus, along with his supreme command and active participation in military matters (he was present in the central operations room), during the war Asad made several speeches aimed at boosting the morale of the troops and the population at large and steering them from their deep-seated fear of Israel. Using historical Islamic symbols, Asad referred to his people as the 'descendants of Abu Bakr, Umar, Uthman and Ali [the first Muslim caliphs who defeated the enemies of Islam and established the first Muslim empire in the seventh century], of Abu Ubayda [the Muslim leader who defeated the Persians in the seventh century at Qadisiyya, Iraq], and of Salah al-Din'. Asad equated Israel not merely with the historical enemies of Islam, notably the Crusaders, but also with the alleged endangerers of human civilization, the Mongols. He hailed the heroic Muslim victories over both these enemies in Palestine – at Hittin (1187, near Tiberias) and at Ayn Jalut (1260, at Jezreel valley in north Israel). He said, 'Our ancestors were victorious through their faith, sacrifice and adherence to the *shahada* [martyrdom] defending Allah's religion. . . . Your efforts are blessed in this holy month, the month of Ramadan, the month of *jihad* . . . the month of victory. . . .' Styling the Syrian troops 'soldiers of Allah', Asad called upon them to fight for the sanctification of Allah using the slogan '*Shahada wa nasr*' (martyrdom for Allah and victory), depicting the war as *jihad* and referring to the battle of Badr (the war Muhammad fought against the infidels).[27] Interwoven with these evocative Islamic slogans, Asad appealed also to the feeling of national pride and honour of his troops, urging them to demonstrate their ability and to stand face to face as equals with the IDF, erase the Arab shame and recover Arab honour.

The emphasis on these Islamic and nationalist sentiments of the troops and the civilian population was skilfully employed by Asad to promote their morale and fighting spirit during the first days of the war – the days of victory – and, crucially, when the IDF subsequently defeated the Syrian army and advanced to positions only twenty miles from Damascus. During these critical days not only was Damascus under grave threat but Asad's rule was also in serious danger both from the external enemy Israel and from potential domestic opposition, notably the Sunni Muslim population. Consequently, in addition to his Islamic and nationalist indoctrination which was aimed at neutralizing such opposition, Asad agreed to a ceasefire with Israel on 23 October (earlier, on 8 and 9 October he had wanted a ceasefire in order to avoid any Israeli military gains). His military action against Israel on 6 October was now transformed into a tough political and diplomatic struggle, involving also certain acts of defiance towards Egypt and the USSR, and by contrast establishing working relations with the United States. First, as a highly realistic politician Asad accepted the ceasefire with Israel in order to save his army and capital from further destruction and to prevent his own downfall. Yet in his public speeches Asad stressed that he had strongly opposed the ceasefire but had had to accept it, as he hinted, because of Sadat's unilateral decision and Soviet pressure to accept it.[28] (The ceasefire was embodied in UN Resolution 338 of 22 October 1973, sponsored jointly by the US and the USSR.)

Asad further emphasized that the war against Israel had not come to an end and that it would continue as long as Israel occupied the Arab territories captured in 1967 and denied the national rights of the Palestinian people. Accordingly, despite Soviet, American and Egyptian pressures, Asad refused to participate in the Geneva peace conference of December 1973, which was attended by Egypt, Jordan, Israel, the United States and the USSR. Instead, for several months Syrian forces were frequently engaged in skirmishes with the IDF along the new ceasefire line. As new Soviet weapons continued to reach Syria during the first months of 1974, Syrian military clashes with Israel intensified, turning in March, April and May into a Syrian 'war of attrition' against the IDF. Asad designed and supervised this war of attrition in order to achieve two goals. First, to demonstrate to his people and to the Arabs at large that Syria remained the only Arab country which continued to struggle against the enemy. This fact could in turn increase Asad's prestige in his own country as well as in other Arab states, and for the first time possibly elevate him to the position of leader of the all-Arab confrontation with Israel. Second, to accompany the new phase of political negotiations with tough military action in accordance with Asad's belief in the 'importance of political action combined with military action' in the fight against Israeli military pressures.[29]

Indeed, parallel to the continued military actions against the IDF, which were mostly initiated by the Syrians, Asad embarked on a well-designed and shrewdly executed diplomatic campaign (or a war of nerves) against Israel, using various means, notably brinkmanship, in his negotiations. Asad's main partner for these negotiations was Kissinger, then the US secretary of state and the chief negotiator for the post-war agreements. It would appear that Asad intended to use Kissinger to achieve a settlement with Israel which would be better for Syria than the Egyptian–Israeli one, and could be demonstrated by

Asad as his political victory. At their first meeting (on 15 December 1973) to discuss the jointly sponsored US–USSR Geneva conference, Asad had already hinted to Kissinger that he 'would brook no superpower condominium', that 'he was not a Soviet puppet' and 'that a Syrian–Israeli disengagement should be negotiated through [Kissinger]'. Yet 'Asad left little doubt that he would not die unfulfilled if the Geneva conference never assembled' and that he was not 'dreaming about going to the conference'. 'What he really wanted', remarked Kissinger, 'was its fruits without contaminating himself by its process. . . . what Asad really wanted to know was not the procedures for the conference but its outcome. . . . he wanted the outcome settled beforehand. . . . That would determine Syria's ultimate participation, and in the meantime, in his prickly manner, he would keep his options open.' Asad was not content with a Syrian–Israeli disengagement that would be similar to the Egyptian–Israeli one. He wanted Israel 'to give up all the territory it captured in the 1973 war and virtually all the territory it captured in 1967'.[30]

Sadat, for his part, had not been prepared to keep his Third Army cut off in the desert by the IDF while Asad acted out his own tactics in a protracted negotiation. Sadat agreed to participate in the Geneva conference and subsequently reached a disengagement agreement with Israel without co-ordinating it with Asad, his partner in the 1973 war.

Dismayed with Sadat's 'duplicity', and afraid of being forced to accept Israel's encroachment towards Damascus, Asad was forced in late January 1974 to scale down his demands regarding the disengagement with Israel. Yet he still insisted on a full Israeli withdrawal from all the territory captured in 1973, plus a substantial withdrawal from the part of the Golan captured in 1967. Asad used two major arguments to press his point: one was Saudi pressure on the US, in the form of a threat that the oil-producing Arab countries would not lift the oil embargo that they had imposed when the war started until Israel started its withdrawal from the Golan. The other weapon he used was the sensitive issue of the IDF prisoners-of-war, whom Israel was so keen to repatriate. Asad took full advantage of this soft spot to put pressure on Israeli leaders headed by Prime Minister Golda Meir.[31] During the negotiations Asad himself behaved in a cool manner. He would play with his *misbaha* (a string of beads) and sip his Turkish coffee as if he had all the time in the world. According to Kissinger, he was a 'proud, tough, shrewd' negotiator and 'played out the string to absolutely the last possible millimetre. . . . His tactic was to open with a statement of the most extreme position to test what the traffic would bear. He might then allow himself to be driven back to the attainable, fighting a dogged rearguard action that made clear that concessions would be exacted only at a heavy price.' Eventually, after five months of hard negotiations accompanying a war of attrition, Asad settled for a fraction of his original demands, namely an Israeli withdrawal from the 1973 salient, plus the town of Quneitra and two small hills in the vicinity which had been captured by Israel in 1967. In Kissinger's evaluation this 'outcome represented a Syrian gain over what a strict calculation of the existing balance of forces would have warranted'.[32]

Asad's achievements from the 1973 war in political and psychological terms were far greater than his small territorial gain of Quneitra. Although from a purely military point of view Asad had lost the war, he managed to turn his defeat into a victory in the eyes of many Syrians and other Arabs (for example he personally hoisted the Syrian flag in Quneitra after its return to Syrian rule – to demonstrate his 'victory'). This was due not only to his efficient propaganda system but also to his proud and daring conduct of the war in both its military and diplomatic ramifications. His bold leadership, coupled with an elaborate ideological indoctrination, apparently made many soldiers overcome their 'barrier of fear' vis-à-vis Israel and bravely fight against the IDF. (Mustafa Tlas went so far as to declare during the war of attrition, 'Many of our people, our brothers and sons were killed in the October war of liberation while uttering these words, "For your sake, Asad." ')[33]

But beyond this and similar manifestations of his personality cult, Asad's prestige and popularity soared in Syria during the war and thereafter. Although not a few Syrians who opposed his regime apparently blamed him for losing the war, many of his followers now regarded Asad as the new pan-Arab leader, the worthy successor to Nasser.[34] In fact, Asad's position in the Arab world was elevated during that period, as will be shown later on, and several Arab countries dispatched military units to Syria or gave her financial and diplomatic support. In the international community Asad became a celebrity as major television stations and newspapers from various countries competed for his interviews. In addition to the Soviet bloc and Third World countries, West European countries (notably France) and the United States moved towards acknowledging Asad as an influential Arab leader. Thus following Kissinger's protracted negotiations with Asad, which received wide publicity, President

Nixon paid an official visit to Syria in mid-June 1974, and sub-sequently diplomatic relations were resumed between the US and Syria. Apparently this not only reflected US recognition of Asad's important role in the future Middle East peace process but also signified Asad's realization of the US's major influence on Israeli positions and policies. He wished to use his newly improved relations with the US in order to achieve a full Israeli withdrawal from the Golan as well as from other occupied Arab territories, and to bring about a solution to the Palestinian problem. In return he was perhaps prepared to sign a non-belligerency agreement with Israel under US auspices.

Asad's New Strategies Towards Israel

It may indeed seem that following the disengagement agreement with Israel (31 May 1974) Asad for a while entertained the idea of signing a peace agreement with Israel within a comprehensive political settle-ment of the Arab–Israeli dispute based on UN Resolutions 242 and 338. In early March 1974, before the disengagement agreement, Asad told *Time* magazine that he was not 'pessimistic' regarding the peace prospects in the Middle East and that the US was fulfilling an important function in this region. Asked whether Syria would accept a possible solution in which an autonomous and demilitarized Palestin-ian state would be established in the West Bank and Gaza, Asad answered that that was one option among several.[35] Then on 1 June 1974, one day after the signing of the Syrian–Israeli disengagement agreement and two weeks before Nixon's visit to Damascus, Asad gave an interview to *Newsweek* in which he stated his position, declaring that the disengagement agreement was an integral part of a 'comprehensive and just settlement' and that it constituted a step towards a 'just and durable peace', based on UN Resolution 338, which would entail 'a full [Israeli] withdrawal . . . safeguarding the rights of the Palestinian people'. He added that Syria would be ready to participate in the new Geneva conference if this conference could bring about the implementation of this UN resolution. Asad refused to commit himself to the idea of a Palestinian state in the West Bank and Gaza, leaving the decision up to the PLO, a decision which he would support. But when asked what would happen if the PLO decision were to be to 'dismantle the state of Israel', Asad's response was: 'I would imagine that what the PLO decides will not exceed the spirit of the UN

97

resolutions. And these do not call for the dismantling of Israel.' Finally, while implying that there were still differences with the US about what these UN resolutions meant, Asad seemed to give the US a central role in achieving peace in the area.[36]

Some eight months later, on 25 February 1975, Asad gave yet another exclusive interview to *Newsweek*'s Arnaud de Borchgrave, which reads as follows:

Q: Some Israelis would be prepared to return the Golan Heights to Syria in exchange for a longterm peace treaty. Does that kind of quid pro quo seem reasonable to you?

A: Yes, that would be acceptable. Provided of course that the final peace settlement includes the creation of a Palestinian state.

Q: Israeli leaders say that the next step with Syria should be an over-all peace settlement. Could this idea be profitably explored at a reconvened Geneva conference?

A: Of course. If the Israelis return to the 1967 frontier – *and* the West Bank and Gaza become a Palestinian state – the last obstacle to a final settlement will have been removed.

Q: Could this be a peace treaty with Israel?

A: Yes, it could. When everything is settled it will have to be formalized with a formal peace treaty. This is not propaganda. We mean it – seriously and explicitly. You look so surprised from the expression on your face. This is not a new logic in Syria's policy; it is our fundamental position, decided by party leaders.

Q: If Israel were to say at Geneva that it is prepared to help set up a Palestinian state and return to its 1967 borders in exchange for normal, longterm peace treaties with the Arab states, what do you think should be the Arab response?

A: To reach the stage you describe is our only objective. We are not looking for a limited agreement – but a lasting peace. But the actual duration of a treaty is a matter of procedure and it would be premature to discuss it at this stage. First, we must end the state of belligerency. That means the implementation of United Nations Resolution 242 [the withdrawal of Israeli troops from Arab territories occupied in the 1967 war in exchange for an end to the state of belligerency and acknowledgment of Israel's right to secure, recognized boundaries]. And the end of belligerency will mean the beginning of a stage of real peace.

Q: Do you see any merit to the idea of U.S. defense guarantees for Israel in return for the evacuation of Arab land?

A: Under a final settlement, this is acceptable to us. But not to guarantee a second step. If these American guarantees should be made before complete withdrawal and the recognition of Palestinian rights, the only result would be deep and lasting hostility between the Arabs and America. And in my assessment, these sort of guarantees, short of a final settlement, would make the U.S., in effect, a co-occupier of Arab land. Under these conditions, you would never be able to have friends in the Arab world.

Q: Would a further 5- to 6-kilometer slice in the south of Golan – now reportedly being discussed by Henry Kissinger and the Israeli government – be acceptable for a second-stage agreement with your country?

A: We have no interest in this at all.

Q: You would prefer to move straight to an over-all settlement with Israel then?

A: No, not necessarily. But a few more kilometers in the south of the Golan are not worth talking about. It would have to be a substantive move on the Golan, all along the line, as well as movement on the other two fronts.

Thus, for the first time since he came to power, Asad stated that he was ready to sign a formal peace treaty with Israel, provided Israel would withdraw from all occupied Arab territories, including the West Bank and Gaza, and would agree to the creation of a Palestinian state in the latter territories. Asad did not specify the exact nature of the lasting peace and its duration, nor whether the Palestinian state should be demilitarized or not, but indicated that two stages should precede the final treaty. He agreed to, first, an interim agreement which would be a substantive Israeli withdrawal on all fronts, and he suggested, second, a non-belligerency agreement with Israel following total withdrawal from the occupied territories.[37] These significant, even dramatic, conciliatory statements, which signified a major departure from Asad's previous hostile attitudes towards Israel, call for explanation. The main interpretation would be that through these moderate statements Asad, the pragmatic and shrewd politician, wished to impress the US government and have it bring about a substantial Israeli withdrawal from the Golan, preferably from the entire Golan region. Having realized soon after the war that only the US had been able to exert pressure on Israel and bring about the IDF withdrawal from the outskirts of Damascus, Asad was prepared to renew diplomatic relations with the US and even to integrate into the American diplomatic process in order to push Israel further back. This could explain his first interview to Newsweek on 1 June 1974, two weeks before the official visit of President Nixon to Damascus, and the subsequent renewal of Syrian diplomatic relations with the US. In that interview Asad did not mention the Soviet Union at all as a partner for the negotiations, but indicated the important role of the US in the peace process and that US views regarding certain components of this process were similar to Syria's.

Perhaps the most important component was total Israeli withdrawal from the Golan. According to Kissinger, 'During the May [1974] shuttle Asad had repeatedly asked me for a written assurance that we would support Syrian demands to regain all the Golan Heights. I had evaded it. Asad now returned to the charge with Nixon.'[38] Nixon was very impressed with Asad:

> he exceeded my expectations on the conversations I had had with Henry [Kissinger]. He was, as Henry had said, a tough negotiator, but he has a great deal of mystique, tremendous stamina and a lot of charm. He laughs easily, and I can see he will be a dynamic leader if he can just maintain his judgement. In our last conversation he came down very very hard against any separate peace. But on the other hand, he seemed to be quite reasonable with regard to the various regional approaches we were making. All in all he is a man of real substance and at his age – forty-four – if he can avoid somebody shooting him or overthrowing him, he will be a leader to be reckoned with in this part of the world.
>
> Pat [Nixon] noted that he had a flat head in the back which she said was probably because he hadn't been turned when he was a baby.[39]

In his account, however, Nixon does not give any details of their negotiations. But according to an experienced US observer, in a private meeting between the two 'Nixon informed President Asad . . . that the United States favored the substantial restitution of the 1967 frontiers on the Golan Heights . . . within a framework of a general peace.' And when Asad said that Syria would never relinquish the Golan Heights 'Nixon replied that the purpose of interim diplomacy . . . was to nudge the Israelis backwards upon the Heights, step by step until they reach the edge, then tumble over.'[40] No wonder then that Asad interpreted Nixon's words as a US commitment to Syria.[41] Encouraged by this change in the American position Asad sought to 'open a new page and begin a new phase [with the US] . . . improve relations with the US', further 'cultivate the American position', and deepen 'this American commitment' in an attempt to push a wedge between the US and Israel, or, in Asad's words: 'This development [in the US position] is compatible with the interests of the American people and contradicts the interests of world Zionism.'[42]

Subsequently further talks were held between US and Syrian officials and at the end of January 1975 the US State Department decided to give Syria a financial grant as an incentive for Asad to adopt a moderate approach to the Arab–Israeli conflict.[43] Possibly this US gesture, coupled with Kissinger's renewed efforts to explore, in mid-February 1975, a second-stage agreement between Egypt and Israel, led Asad to give his second and more moderate interview, on 25 February 1975, to *Newsweek* regarding peace with Israel. He apparently aimed at linking the new Egyptian–Israeli agreement with a similar Syrian–Israeli one which would entail a substantial Israeli withdrawal in the Golan. However, by mid-1975 Asad had become bitterly disappointed with the US position regarding the political process in the Middle East, and this for two interrelated reasons. First, because American efforts to bring about an agreement between Egypt and Israel culminated successfully in September 1975 in the Sinai II agreement, which involved a substantial Israeli withdrawal in Sinai but not a further Israeli pull-back in the Golan. Second, because Israel continued to receive massive US military and economic support, and yet the US refused to negotiate with the PLO, 'the legitimate representative' of the Palestinian people.[44] Asad expressed his dismay in yet another interview with *Newsweek*'s Arnaud de Borchgrave: 'The billions you are giving Israel for a few miles of Arab land [in Sinai] will only encourage Israeli arrogance and intransigence. . . . The U.S. has become a direct party in the Arab–Israeli conflict. This is not in the Arab interest and certainly not in the U.S. interest.'[45]

It can then almost certainly be assumed that Asad's unique statement regarding a formal peace treaty with Israel (in his interview with *Newsweek* on 25 February 1975) was in fact directed not towards Israel but rather towards the US. Its aim had been to dissuade the US from effecting a separate Egyptian–Israeli agreement on Sinai, or to link such an agreement with a substantial Israeli pull-back from the Golan (as well as from the Jordan river). The evidence for such an assumption is mostly circumstantial. First, the timing: the interview took place during Kissinger's renewed efforts (in February 1975) to bring about another Egyptian–Israeli agreement. Second, this unique interview of 25 February 1975, unlike all other interviews by Asad, was not broadcast on Damascus Radio, nor was it translated in any of the Syrian journals or newspapers. Third, Asad's spokesman denied after the interview (which was quoted by foreign news agencies) that Asad had mentioned 'a peace treaty' with Israel in his interview.[46] Fourth, Asad did not refer to a peace treaty with Israel in any other foreign media interviews that he gave around that time. In an interview with the BBC in September 1975, he mentioned a non-belligerency agreement but then said that this would not mean the recognition of Israel as a state. Furthermore, in most of these interviews he did not dissociate himself from the PLO's position, which denied the right of Israel to exist. Asad also strongly attacked Israel in many of his speeches and interviews, depicting her as an enemy of the Arabs and stating that no Arab was talking to Israel, but only to the US (about the peace process).[47]

Nevertheless, there is in theory a slim possibility that Asad's new conciliatory expressions regarding peace with Israel, which appeared in the few interviews Asad gave (in March and June of 1974, and particularly in February 1975), were directed towards Israel as well as the US. Asad's aim (in co-ordination with the US) might have been to try and persuade Israel to withdraw further from the Golan, as she was prepared to do in Sinai. Asad preferred to get back the Golan through diplomatic means, rather than by military action which he was anyway too weak to take at that time. Asad was possibly ready for a political agreement, as he himself said, 'If political action will give us back our lands – we would welcome it'; but this was provided he did not have to give Israel peace in return, only a non-belligerency agreement.

At any rate, whether or not Asad signalled to Israel that he was ready to give her a non-belligerency agreement in lieu of the Golan, Israel was not prepared then to withdraw further from the Golan. Golda Meir declared early in March 1974 that the Golan was an inseparable part of Israel. Subsequently, following the disengagement agreement with Syria, Israel refused to consider any more withdrawals from the Golan, but was prepared to pull back in Sinai, within the framework of another Egyptian–Israeli agreement. One major objective of these Israeli moves (according to Asad) was to widen the split between Egypt and Syria and deal with each separately. Asad was indeed deeply concerned about such a development, as the corner-stone of his strategy towards Israel – in both its defensive and its offensive aspects – rested on Arab unity or solidarity: the support or co-operation of other Arab countries, notably Egypt, the most powerful Arab state. Being militarily weak, especially before the 1973 war and in its aftermath, Asad's Syria was unable by herself to withstand Israeli might. She badly needed the military and political co-operation or assistance of Egypt, Iraq and Jordan as well as the diplomatic backing of the Arab oil-producing countries.

As we have seen, Asad succeeded in obtaining the military and diplomatic support of most Arab countries when he joined Egypt in the 1973 war against Israel. But as soon as the tide of war turned in favour of Israel, Sadat hurriedly signed a ceasefire agreement with Israel, without any co-ordination with Asad. Subsequently, being left alone to fight the war of attrition against Israel, Asad became seriously worried lest Sadat should go ahead in concluding more separate agreements with Israel, under US auspices, thus leaving Syria in the cold. In an unyielding attempt to prevent Sadat from taking such a course, Asad hailed Arab solidarity and its courageous manifestation in the 1973 war which had been led jointly by Egypt and Syria. And in interviews he gave to Egyptian newspapers during the post-war diplomatic process, Asad stressed the 'harmony' and 'consensus' between himself and Sadat, while denying stories about a rift between their two countries.[48]

However, Asad made intense efforts to muster the political and diplomatic backing of other Arab leaders and to persuade them to put pressure on Sadat in order to prevent him from making separate deals with Israel. Asad also directed the Syrian press and some of his comrades to voice indirect criticism of Sadat's deviationist policy, which had started with his decision to accept the UN ceasefire resolution of 22 October 1973.[49]

During the spring of 1975, while negotiations between Kissinger and Sadat were heading towards a new Egyptian–Israeli agreement, Asad and Sadat met in Damascus in an apparently unsuccessful attempt to co-ordinate their policies. Around that time Asad himself began to criticize Sadat, first indirectly by denouncing the 'split' and 'regionalism' in the Arab world which 'helps the enemy'.[50] On 2 August 1975 Asad complained in an interview with two Lebanese journalists that neither Egypt nor the US was keeping Syria informed about the progress in the Egyptian–Israeli negotiations.[51] Finally, after the Egyptian–Israeli Sinai agreement was signed (in September 1975) Asad personally criticized it as 'a submission to the Israeli occupation, a total submission to Israeli demands, a step backwards from peace. . . . It ignores the nature of the conflict by attempting to divide the problem into separate compartments. . . . It constitutes a breach in Arab solidarity . . . and a serious and dangerous attempt at foiling Arab struggles since 1948.'[52] Yet, although in public demonstrations in Syria (and Libya) Sadat was denounced as 'a traitor to the Arab cause', Asad was careful not to burn the bridges completely with the Egyptian leader. At the same time, however, he implied that the conflict with Israel was not a matter concerning leaders alone (Sadat) but an issue which concerned the 'Egyptian people and the Egyptian army'; and that it was not only an Egyptian or Syrian issue, but an all-Arab one.[53]

Consequently, having failed to rally the military and political power of Egypt in a continued struggle against Israel, and unable to retrieve the Golan through diplomatic means with US help, Asad had to formulate a new strategy towards Israel. The October war and its destructive results for Syria did not deter him from continuing the military struggle, nor did it abate his deep ideological antagonism towards, and possibly his personal hatred of, the Jewish state. On the contrary, the vulnerability, in his eyes, of the IDF, particularly during the 1974 war of attrition, led him to believe that in future wars the Arabs would be able to defeat Israel. The many casualties and great destruction caused by the Israeli counter-offensive had perhaps fostered Asad's desire to take revenge. Indeed, in his post-war speeches and interviews Asad fiercely attacked Israel and her Zionist ideology, alleging, for example, that:

> Zionism distorts the heavenly principles and misuses Judaism. . . . it is an instrument to destroy existing societies in many countries of the world . . . it is an ally of Nazism. . . . it is not an historical current . . . but a phenomenon which contradicts the historical logic. . . . it is an artificial, chauvinist phenomenon which manifests itself in the colonialist ideology, based on usurpation and expansionism in the region. . . . it incites Jews who belong to a certain national community to reject it and to emigrate from their homeland to a country that they have no link to, and there it mobilizes them to acts of aggression, killing and destruction.[54]

'Israel has been seen by the world as a racist fascist state. . . . Israel threatens the values and principles that the human being believes in . . . [and] the interests of the nations of the world.'[55] In these addresses and interviews, Asad again equated Israel with the Crusaders' state, indicating that 'Israel's age . . . is only one-sixth of the period of the Crusaders' dominion in our country.'[56] Asad concluded that if Israel continued to occupy the Arab lands, there would be 'a fifth war against Israel', 'another October war', wherein 'Syria would be the spearhead'. 'We know how to wait and to prepare ourselves to liberate them [the Arab lands].'[57]

In any attempt to interpret Asad's post-1973 intentions and goals regarding the struggle against Israel, among the intriguing questions is: could Asad have afforded to sign a peace treaty with Israel against the background of the systematic and extensive anti-Israeli indoctrination of the Syrian people? As he himself implied in one of his conversations with Kissinger: 'The Syrian difficulty is that people here who have been nurtured over twenty-six years on hatred can't be swayed overnight by our changing our courses. We would never take one step except in the interests of our own people. We are all human – we all have our impulsive reaction to things. But in leadership we have to restrain ourselves and analyse and take steps in our own interest. A just peace is in the interest of all people in this area.'[58] Would this peace include Israel? Would Asad have been content with Israeli withdrawal from all territories occupied in 1967 and with the establishment of a Palestinian state in the West Bank and Gaza and then let Israel exist in peace; or would his final goal be to destroy Israel once and for all? When asked such a question in 1974 by an American writer, Asad replied:

This is a very complex question. . . . I will admit that there is a mood in the Arab world to make some sort of settlement with Israel to allow Israel to exist within certain frontiers. There is a great struggle taking place between the heart and the mind. In our hearts we say 'No Israel – not on any terms.' In our minds we say 'We must turn to other things so let us give Israel a chance to withdraw to its original frontiers, let us give it a chance to prove that it will no longer try to expand.'. . . If Israel withdraws to its original borders, we will not wage a war against it. We will accept the United Nations resolutions of 1947 [the partition resolution] in the interest of getting on with other important business, and simply let nature take its course. . . . we will work [then] behind the scenes to overthrow the Zionist system in Israel and bring about a just return of Arab presence there so as to make this land an integral part of the Arab world. . . . The ultimate goal of all Arabs is an all-Arab world here [in Israel]. We do not know exactly how it will come about. But we know it *will* come about . . . once this problem is solved, then I can say that the Jews will be able to live here with no fears for themselves. ['As Jews but not as Israelis?' Asad was asked.] That is correct. . . . I do not have any personal animosity against the Jewish religion or the Jew as a religious person. But the Jews in Israel, this is different. The Jews are our enemy. . . . I feel about the Jew, the Israeli Jew . . . in the same way I feel about any people who comes and takes away my land.[59]

From this revealing interview – in which Asad referred several times to the need to eliminate Israel – as well as from various other deliberations by Asad and by his Ba'th organs after the 1973 war, it may be concluded that Asad's ideological and ultimate goals were (or remained) as follows: the elimination of the 'Zionist entity'; the liberation of the entire Arab land and the return of the full rights of the Palestinian Arab people over the whole of Palestine. There could not be a compromise or a durable settlement with the Zionist side, since the Arab–Zionist struggle is a 'fatal historic struggle', a struggle for life or death, to be or not to be.[60] This struggle, which is the core of the Arab war of liberation, deserves the highest priority. It should be conducted in a way which would integrate a 'realistic flexibility' with the 'doctrinal adherence to a national goal' – the combination of political and diplomatic measures and military action in the struggle against Israel. The military action could constitute the chief way to deal with Israel, and the next war must be more successful than the October 1973 war.[61] Yet since Israel cannot be destroyed in one stroke, it is imperative to achieve this strategic aim in stages, first to effect a full Israeli withdrawal from all the Arab territories occupied in 1967; then to establish a Palestinian national rule on any part of the liberated land (the West Bank and Gaza) while demanding the full implementation of UN resolutions (notably the 1947 partition resolution and the 1948 resolution to allow the Palestinian refugees to return to their homes). This Palestinian entity, helped by the Arab states, would subsequently be the spearhead of the continued Arab struggle against the Zionist entity.[62]

In sum, it is evident that the ideological goals of Asad (as well as of Sadat before 1977 and of most Arabs) were, and still are, twofold: the liberation of all Arab territories occupied by Israel and the elimination of Israel as a Zionist entity. Yet, whereas the former goal is also his strategic aim, it is not clear whether this would be true of the latter goal. It is very likely that in 1974–5 this ultimate goal might have been either a dream, sheer wishful thinking or an incremental, open-ended process to which Asad himself did not specify an end. To quote Kissinger:

> Asad would have liked to destroy the Jewish state but he recognized that neither Egypt, nor in the final analysis Saudi Arabia, would join him in that enterprise and that the cost of attempting it would hazard Syria's domestic structure, perhaps even its existence. . . . he was as prudent as he was passionate, as realistic as he was ideological. . . . he concluded that Syria was not sufficiently strong to unite the Arab nation, and needed to regain its own territory before it could pursue larger ambitions.[63]

One thing is crystal clear: in his strategic thinking Asad was very much concerned, perhaps obsessed, with the issue of the balance of power with Israel. Realizing that Syria by herself was far too weak to withstand an Israeli offensive, let alone to attack Israel, Asad put his trust in 'Arab solidarity' – the combination of the military power of the Arab countries, notably Egypt, and the political influence of the oil-producing Arab states, particularly Saudi Arabia. This military and political combination was effective during the 1973 war, when Syria fought together with Egypt while military forces from Iraq, Morocco, Saudi Arabia and Jordan were deployed or fought against the IDF on Syrian soil and while the Arab oil-producing countries imposed an oil embargo on the US and West European countries. But to Asad's deep frustration this impressive manifestation of Arab unity soon collapsed when Egypt unilaterally agreed to a ceasefire with Israel, and the Arab oil embargo was lifted.

In a tireless effort to bring back Egypt to the 'Arab fold' and reshape Arab solidarity, Asad, apparently for the first time, referred to the concept of 'strategic balance' with Israel, at the Arab summit meeting in Rabat, Morocco (October 1974).[64] At that juncture this notion referred to wide Arab military and political co-operation built around the Cairo–Damascus axis and facing Israel during the diplomatic process and thereafter.[65] But when Egypt unilaterally signed the Sinai II agreement with Israel in 1975, Asad was driven to seek an alternative to Egypt within this intra-Arab axis. It is highly likely that around that period Asad contemplated for the first time achieving, in the long run, a strategic balance or a balance of power with Israel with himself as the leader of a new intra-Arab alliance, and Syria its cornerstone. Yet Asad's initial intention was to establish or revive the Arab Eastern Front Command against Israel, which would ideally consist of Syria, Lebanon, Jordan, the PLO and Iraq. Ba'thist Iraq, however, was immediately counted out because of its fierce and increasing rivalry with Asad's Syria (as will be discussed below). Therefore the new strategic concept of the Eastern Front was to extend from Tyre in southern Lebanon to Aqaba in southern Jordan.[66] This was to be a military and political structure, led by Asad and essentially geared to serve Syrian strategic interests: to defend the flanks of Damascus from Israeli invasion, and to encircle Israel from the Mediterranean to the Gulf of Aqaba and apply military, political and economic pressures against her, including waging war at the appropriate time. Within this framework, Jordan's function would be primarily military, i.e. to block an Israeli assault via north Jordan towards Damacus, and to use Jordan's front line – the longest border with Israel – to launch an offensive against Israel.[67] Lebanon's southern border would serve similar defensive and offensive functions, except that in the absence of an effective Lebanese army these tasks would be carried out by Syrian and Palestinian forces. Last but not least, the PLO commandos would be employed to wage guerrilla warfare against Israel from Lebanese territory, while the Palestinian problem would be used in the international arena to conduct a political and diplomatic campaign against Israel. Asad's new plan was part of his grand strategy of creating a 'Greater Syria' union comprising Syria, Lebanon, Jordan and the Palestinians – and led by him.

9 The Lion of Greater Syria

Attempts at Arab Solidarity

For many years, Asad has been imbued with the notion of Arab unity. This notion, although strongly interrelated with the struggle against Israel, went beyond that strategic goal. It constitutes his and his generation's foremost ideology and highest credo. This belief has been greatly relevant to the leader of Syria – the 'beating heart of Arabism', the hotbed and cradle of Arab nationalism – and particularly to Asad, the Alawite ruler who has sought legitimacy by presenting himself as the 'most Arab of Arabs'. In Asad's words, Arab unity is 'not merely an emotional feeling, but is an eternal historical truth. . . . It is the source of strength for the Arabs. . . . It is also a struggle of the entire Arab people to achieve equality with other peoples of the world.' It is intended to enable the Arab nation to reach a position in which it can 'contribute to the enrichment of human civilization. . . . There is a strong feeling among Arabs, a spiritual feeling, that we are all a single nation of people. . . . But it will take a long time to convert that spiritual feeling into a material reality . . . perhaps not in my lifetime, for there are still too many differences between one Arab state and the next.'[1] In the meantime, Asad, the realistic Syrian leader, attempts to achieve a maximum degree of Arab solidarity (*tadamun* in Arabic), i.e. an intra-Arab co-operation to help Syria strengthen her military might, political position and economic conditions in her struggle against Israel, the arch-enemy of the Arabs. Within this process Asad endeavours to implement his combined personal ambition and national mission, to become a pan-Arab leader, a Nasser of the 1970s and 1980s, perhaps a Saladin of the late twentieth century. As already described, Asad's first political actions after his ascendancy in

November 1970 were to join the newly established Federation of Arab Republics (with Egypt and Libya, Sudan pending) and to sign a military pact with Egypt. While considering Egypt as the major and senior partner in the new intra-Arab co-operation, Asad also made great efforts to improve Syria's relations with all other Arab countries regardless of their domestic regimes and external orientations.

These new Arab solidarity-oriented policies of Asad bore fruit during the 1973 war against Israel. While elevated to the position of a pan-Arab leader, Asad succeeded in attracting a wide range of Arab co-operation and assistance. Military forces from Iraq, Jordan, Morocco, Kuwait and Saudi Arabia were dispatched to the Golan Heights. Generous financial aid was promised to Syria by wealthy Arab states, and the oil embargo was employed by oil-producing Arab countries to exert diplomatic pressure on the US and West Europe. Yet this highly impressive demonstration of Arab solidarity with Syria started to collapse within weeks of Sadat's unilateral decision (according to Asad) to accept the ceasefire with Israel on 22 October 1973. Asad and Tlas claimed after the war that Sadat designed and carried out from the outset a strategy different from that which had been agreed between the two countries. That is, Sadat's intention was merely to cross the Suez Canal, occupy its eastern bank and generate a political settlement with Israel.[2] Syria was subsequently left alone to fight Israel in the war of attrition, the Arab oil embargo was lifted, and Sadat took further steps to complete his 'defection' from his alliance with Syria: in September 1975 he signed the Sinai II agreement with Israel without linking it to the Syrian Golan.

Asad made intensive attempts to prevent the collapse of that Arab solidarity soon after Syria accepted the ceasefire with Israel. Communicating and visiting with Arab leaders, Asad initiated (according to Syrian sources) an Arab summit conference in Algeria in late November (24 to 26) 1973. (According to neutral sources it was Morocco which called for that conference.)[3] With the exception of Iraq, Libya and Jordan, all Arab leaders attended, and endorsed Asad's proposed strategy: to strengthen Arab solidarity with Syria and Egypt; to liberate all territories occupied by Israel in 1967, including (Arab) Jerusalem, and not to give up any part of them; to recognize the PLO as the sole legitimate representative of the Palestinian Arab people and to recover the national rights of this people; and to continue the oil embargo against countries which support Israel.[4]

These decisions, which did not rule out a political settlement, were apparently designed by Asad to link Egypt to Syria in further interim agreements with Israel and to prevent Sadat from taking more unilateral steps towards Israel. This line was pursued by Asad throughout 1974 – in another Arab summit in Algeria on 13 and 14 February 1974 (with Asad, Sadat and the leaders of Saudi Arabia and Algeria) and in subsequent meetings with Sadat and other Arab leaders. In late October 1974 the seventh Arab summit meeting was convened in Rabat at the request of Asad and other Arab leaders. At this conference, Asad succeeded in mustering the support of the Arab states for a decision to oppose any Egyptian agreement with Israel regarding further withdrawal from the Sinai that was not also linked to a similar agreement in the Golan. (Or in the wording of the Rabat decisions: 'The conference rejects partial solutions or separate steps.') The Arab summit also approved a plan providing Egypt and Syria with US$1 billion each annually for four years (possibly to help keep Sadat within the Arab fold). No less significant was the unanimous declaration passed by the summit recognizing the PLO as the 'sole legitimate representative of the Palestinian people on any liberated Palestinian territory'.[5] Some six months later on 21 and 24 April 1975 Asad met Sadat and the Saudi King Khalid in Saudi Arabia for yet another summit conference. Both Asad and Sadat decided that 'the political action during the next stage requires close co-operation between Syria and Egypt . . . as a basis for the common Arab action against the common enemy'.[6]

But, of course, all these resolutions and other diplomatic actions taken by Asad did not prevent Sadat from signing a separate agreement with Israel in September 1975. It would appear that throughout the political process Asad suspected that Sadat was likely to deviate from his alliance with Syria if he could achieve a major Israeli withdrawal in Sinai. During 1974 and 1975 Asad went out of his way to obtain Sadat's commitments for a continued Egyptian–Syrian co-operation vis-à-vis Israel and the US. Asad also criticized and warned Sadat directly and indirectly against his tendency to strike a separate deal with Israel. Simultaneously Asad endeavoured to build an Arab consensus against such an Egyptian move during the Arab summit in Algeria in late November 1973 and the Rabat summit in late October 1974. Yet as a good strategist and a master manipulator, Asad took steps to establish an alternative alliance to his military–political axis with Egypt. This alliance, which might have also given Asad an effective leverage on Sadat, was designed initially to assist Syria in her confrontation with Israel. It was the so-called Eastern Front, to be composed of Syria, Lebanon, Jordan, Iraq and the PLO.

For many years Asad cherished the idea of establishing a Fertile Crescent alliance that would embrace those Arab nations. Although such an alliance had originally been an 'old imperialist' notion, conceived by the Hashemite rulers of Iraq, Asad was prepared to adopt it for the sake of Arab unity.[7] As early as September 1968, Asad, as Syrian defence minister, had supported the establishment of an Eastern Front Command (including Iraq, Syria and Jordan). And in March 1969 he forced the Ba'th regional congress to adopt a resolution, apparently in opposition to Salah Jadid, that 'new efforts should be made to establish the Eastern Command'. Simultaneously Asad admitted to Syria 6,000 Iraqi troops who subsequently held joint military manoeuvres with the Syrian army.[8] But about a year later these troops were evacuated by Iraq with the plea that they were needed to 'solidify the Iraqi revolution'. After seizing power in Damascus Asad tried to revive the Eastern Front, but the fierce rivalry between the two Ba'th regimes in Syria and Iraq nullified his efforts.[9] Yet during October 1973, upon Asad's request, Iraq sent two armoured divisions and one infantry division – the 'Saladin' force – to help Syria fight Israel in the Golan. This force, however, withdrew immediately after Syria accepted UN Resolution 338, whereupon Iraq labelled Damascus 'defeatist' and accused it of recognizing Israel.

Asad flew to Baghdad in an attempt to settle the differences between the two governments; he suggested the establishment of a union between the two countries but failed to convince the Iraqi leaders. After the Rabat conference Asad repeated his offer to unite the two countries,[10] and in early April 1975 he renewed his efforts to re-establish the Eastern Front Command with Iraqi participation.[11]

The Iraqi regime, however, again rejected Asad's offers while denouncing his readiness to 'make peace with the Zionist enemy', as had been reflected in his interview with *Newsweek* several weeks earlier.[12] In reaction to the Iraqi political warfare the Syrian Ba'thist institutions and media strongly attacked the rival Ba'th regime in Baghdad, depicting it as 'rightist', 'fascist', 'splitting Arab solidarity', 'betraying the problems of the Arab nation' and 'associating with imperialism'.[13] The conflict between the two rival Ba'th regimes was (and still is) deeply rooted and related to several important issues: an ideological contest regarding the authentic Ba'th doctrines; a political and strategic competition for predominance in the Fertile Crescent region; and a fierce personal enmity between Saddam Hussein, Iraq's strongman, and Asad. Apart from the propaganda warfare, each side has employed additional measures against the other. The Iraqis assisted various opposition groups operating against Asad's regime, and the Syrians backed the Kurdish rebels in northern Iraq. Syria has periodically blocked the Euphrates river water from flowing into Iraq, and has demanded high royalties for the flow of Iraqi oil through Syrian territory. Still, Asad himself offered several times to settle these differences, and refrained from personally attacking the Iraqi leaders, in an attempt to cultivate an Iraqi option in his Eastern Front strategy vis-à-vis Egypt and Israel. Nevertheless, it would seem after all that he has not been sincerely keen to unite with Iraq, lest Baghdad, the formidable Arab power, have the leading role in this venture. Neither has he been interested in having a large Iraqi force deployed in Syria for fear it would help his domestic opposition groups to topple him. Asad wished to have for himself the leadership of or a paramount influence in any form of union between the countries of the Eastern Front. This objective was easier to achieve with Lebanon, Jordan and the Palestinians – the nations comprising Greater Syria.

Asad's Greater Syria Strategy

The region of Greater Syria has been for centuries an historical–geographical term and periodically also has constituted a political–territorial unit. This was the case during the Muslim Arab Umayyad period (651–750) and the Muslim Mamluk era (1260–1516). In the mid-1860s this concept of a political entity was revived by a small group of Christian Lebanese intellectuals, and under the short rule of Amir (later King) Faysal in Syria (1918–20) the establishment of a Greater Syrian state was demanded by the Arab nationalist movement in Syria and Palestine.[14] In the 1930s the concept of Greater Syria was propagated by Antun Sa'adeh and his Syrian Nationalist Party (PPS), which was mostly composed of Lebanese and Syrian Christians; and in the early 1940s Amir (later King) Abdallah of Jordan designed a plan to unify Greater Syria under his rule. Although rejected by the Ba'th Party, which advocated pan-Arab unity, the notion of Greater Syria has been revived in a different guise by Asad. In a textbook for the Syrian school system published early in the 1980s, the term Bilad Ash-Sham (the Land of Syria) is cited as a geographical–historical term, as a region 'linking the two parts of the Arab homeland'. According to this textbook, Bilad Ash-Sham was divided after the First World War into four 'mini-states' (*duwaylat*), namely Syria, Lebanon, Jordan and Palestine; and in 1967 it lost territory to Israel.[15] Similarly the concept of Greater Syria was openly propagated over Damascus Radio and in the Ba'th daily *Al-Thawra* for several months (in 1976–7) by Shawqi Khayrallah, a leading figure of the Syrian Social Nationalist Party (SSNP – formerly the PPS). The party's leader, Ihsan Mahayri, stated in 1984 that Asad's regime is nationalist and that there were 'no contradictions between this regime and our ideology'.[16] Kamal Junblatt, the Lebanese Druze leader who met Asad frequently during the mid-1970s and dubbed him 'the Lion of Greater Syria', remarked in his memoirs:

> The rulers of Damascus . . . do not want the Palestinians to forget . . . the days which preceded the division of the Middle East in 1919, when the Lebanese, Palestinians, Jordanians and Syrians were one people – the people of historic Syria in its natural boundaries. . . . President Asad clearly emphasized this in the ears of Yasir Arafat . . . when he told him 'You do not represent Palestine more than we do. There is neither a Palestinian people, nor a Palestinian entity, there is only Syria, and you are an inseparable part of the Syrian people and Palestine is an inseparable part of Syria.'[17]

Regarding the notion that Palestine is an integral part of Syria, Asad said in a speech in March 1974: 'Palestine is not only a part of the Arab homeland, but constitutes the major part of southern Syria.'[18] (Asad's statement was made in reaction to the declaration of Israel's prime minister Golda Meir that the Golan was part of Israel.) Other Syrian leaders also stated on various occasions that Palestine was part of Syria.[19] By the same token Asad said in 1973: 'there are special relations between Lebanon and Syria and no regime in Syria or Lebanon can overlook these . . . historical–eternal relations'.[20]

Despite these statements, it is conceivable that Asad, the realistic and cautious politician, has been aware of the enormous difficulties involved in unifying the countries of Greater Syria under his leadership. It is more likely that his strategic goal has been (and still is) to achieve a (federal?) union of Syria, Lebanon, Jordan and the Palestinians under his leadership. Bearing in mind that Syria would be the biggest and strongest party in such a union, Damascus could manoeuvre among her partners and take the predominant role in shaping its political and military strategy. Indeed, it would seem that Asad's more concrete aim would be to establish a political–military structure of Greater Syria to serve his two interrelated goals of creating a new regional power centre, or sphere of influence, which can make its impact in intra-Arab politics vis-à-vis his two strong Arab rivals, Egypt and Iraq, and of co-ordinating the continued military and political struggle with Israel, both defensively and offensively, from Ras Naqura (in southern Lebanon) to Aqaba (southern Jordan).[21]

Asad's Bid to Influence Jordan

Yet even this relatively modest aim has been very difficult to achieve, even though Asad employed his remarkable skills as a strong leader and manipulator. Of the three potential partners for the Greater Syria alliance, Jordan was (and still is) perhaps the most important component, but also the hardest to tackle. Having the longest border with Israel among the Arab 'confrontation states' and the best-trained Arab army, Jordan constitutes an essential party in any Eastern Front military alliance. In particular the Jordanian army would have an important function in blocking an Israeli outflanking movement towards Damascus via northern Jordan. In addition, the pro-Western Hashemite kingdom may be useful in bringing US diplomatic pressure to bear on Israel to give up the West Bank, so rendering the Jewish state more vulnerable.

As far as Jordan's King Hussein is concerned, an alliance with Asad's Syria could provide important assets: in addition to the economic benefits stemming from having a Syrian outlet to the Mediterranean sea, Jordan is keen to avoid belligerent relations with her powerful Syrian neighbour. Further, Jordan could be in a position to require Syrian military assistance against possible attack by Israel. Likewise, Hussein would benefit politically from Asad's backing for his long-standing claim for the West Bank, against the PLO's demand for the same territory.

Yet the liabilities arising out of Syrian patronage seem to outweigh these assets. For notwithstanding the different or contradictory regimes in, and political orientations of, the two countries, Hussein has reason to fear that a political and military alliance with Asad might drastically diminish his manoeuvrability among the other major Arab states, and eventually even turn Jordan into a Syrian protectorate. Hussein might also be concerned that Asad would, in due course, prefer his alliance with the PLO, Jordan's enemy, or support its efforts to topple the Hashemite regime. Alternatively, Hussein might be greatly worried that his co-operation with Asad could provoke an Israeli military attack against his country, or force him to go to war with Israel; the outcome of either scenario could be an Israeli occupation of Jordan.

Fully aware of Hussein's strategic interests, which include peaceful relations with Israel, Asad nevertheless tried to integrate Jordan into his regional strategy, but the results were rather poor. As we have already seen, on the eve of his ascent to power in Damascus, Asad, as Syria's defence minister and air force commander, denied air cover to the Syrian troops which were dispatched by Jadid's government in September 1970 to help the PLO rebels in Jordan. Asad took this unusual step because he feared *inter alia* that the Syrian military intervention would severely alienate Hussein. Three years later, in preparation for the October war against Israel, Asad renewed diplomatic relations with Jordan (which he had severed in July 1971 following Hussein's further suppression of the PLO). Before the war started Asad urged Hussein to open a 'third front' (along the Jordan river) against Israel, adding, 'The road to Jerusalem is opened, why are you waiting? . . . you could rush to Jerusalem and liberate it, and thereby win a splendid and grand victory . . . but I did not succeed in convincing them. . . . I regret to say that Cairo pressured Jordan forcibly and emphatically not to participate in the war, being concerned over the fate of the East Bank . . . but . . . the King [nevertheless] . . . chose to send his forces [two brigades] to the Golan.'[22]

This modest Jordanian gesture helped to improve the relations between Asad and Hussein following the October war, despite certain mutual acts of defiance: Jordan's participation in the post-war Geneva conference (December 1973), and Asad's support for the PLO as the sole representative of the Palestinian people at both the first Algiers Arab summit (November 1973) and the Rabat summit (October 1974). Yet Asad assured Hussein that Syria did not fully share the PLO position against Jordan and would work to achieve a compromise between the two rivals. Accordingly, Asad refrained from putting the entire blame on Hussein for the September 1970 suppression of PLO guerrillas in Jordan: 'I said in the Rabat conference . . . that the responsibility concerning the September 1970 events was shared by King Hussein, the Palestinian resistance and other Arab countries. . . . But even if we assume that it was the responsibility of one party, must Arab history stop at that September? . . . our interests and the rules of life require us to overcome this complex and act to materialize the essential interests of our nation.'[23] While refraining also from either openly rejecting Jordan's claim for the West Bank or questioning her sovereignty in the East Bank, Asad suggested the establishment of a tripartite Syrian–Jordanian–Palestinian federation, or at least the co-ordination of his actions with both Jordan and the PLO.[24] As it was, a Syrian–Jordanian–Palestinian agreement was not feasible at that juncture, because of the fierce animosity between Hussein and Arafat. Asad then directed his efforts towards creating two parallel military–political alliances, one with Jordan and one with the PLO, putting his main thrust in the former alliance. Thus while offering (although he did not insist) in March 1975 to set up a joint military and political command with the PLO,[25] Asad endeavoured during 1975 (or even earlier, perhaps, since mid-1974)[26] to generate a Syrian–Jordanian union. The timing for such an initiative was ideal. Jordan had been isolated in the Arab world following the Rabat summit's decisions and Hussein was deeply disappointed in Sadat's attitude towards him. (In July 1974, in their meeting in Alexandria, Sadat and Hussein had publicly agreed that the PLO represented all the Palestinians, except those who were under Jordan's control. But at the Rabat conference Sadat withdrew from this pro-Jordanian formula in favour of the pro-PLO decisions. Sadat also signed in September 1975 the Sinai agreement with Israel without linking it to an Israeli withdrawal from the Jordan river, as Hussein had expected.)

Asad then took advantage of Jordan's predicament and suggested to Hussein in Damascus in April 1975 the establishment of a Joint Supreme Leadership Council (made up of Asad and Hussein). Subsequently in July 1975 Asad and Hussein also agreed to establish a Higher Jordanian–Syrian Joint Committee to prepare the integration (*takamul*) of the two countries in the political, military, economic, cultural and educational fields.[27] Earlier, on 11 June 1975, Asad had made a state visit to Amman, Jordan (it was the first visit in eighteen years by a Syrian head of state) and was hailed by the people as 'Asad Tishrin' (the 'Lion of October' [the 1973 war]). During his talks with Hussein Asad referred to Syria and Jordan as 'one people – one country' or 'one country – one people – one army'.[28] (Asad was careful not to say 'one people – one state' and so dispute the sovereignty of Jordan.) While a series of practical measures were subsequently taken to integrate the activities of Syria and Jordan in the economic and educational spheres, Asad persistently worked to promote military co-ordination[29] and political co-operation with Hussein, aiming at achieving 'one day a form of union or federation'.[30] Although such a day did not come, the integration steps as well as the military co-ordination and political co-operation between the two countries worked well for the next two years,[31] and Asad was able to secure Hussein's unstinting support for his intervention in

Lebanon in 1976 and beyond. Asad's success in incorporating Jordan into his strategic plan, as well as his initial achievements in Lebanon, led him in 1977 to reveal his long-term design: the creation of a federation under his leadership composed of Syria, Lebanon, Jordan and the West Bank.[32] (But even before he made such statements, Asad's achievements in Jordan and Lebanon provoked harsh criticisms from various Arab quarters. Egyptian and Palestinian papers, for example, argued that Asad was creating Greater Syria at the expense of the Palestinians, while Libyan leaders warned Asad against such intentions.)[33]

At that juncture, late in 1977, against the background of Sadat's historic visit to Jerusalem, Asad's relations with Hussein began to show signs of strain. Although Hussein rejected Sadat's initiative, he also refused, together with Saudi Arabia, to join the newly formed Tripoli Bloc initiated by Asad in December 1977 – with Libya, Algeria, PDRY (South Yemen) and the PLO – in order to co-ordinate an all-Arab political and military campaign against Israel, with the exclusion of Egypt. Concerned lest Hussein join the Egyptian–Israeli negotiations, Asad exercised pressure on Jordan, pressure which included the dispatch in mid-1978 of PLO commandos into Jordanian territory in order to carry out operations against Israel;[34] and late in 1978 Asad concluded a (short-lived) union with Iraq that carried a serious potential threat to Jordan. As a result of these pressures, and following the Egyptian–Israeli peace treaty (March 1979), the relations between Asad and Hussein were reinforced, but not for long. During 1979, Jordan allowed the Muslim Brothers, the most dangerous internal opposition to Asad, to operate in her territory, possibly as a potentially useful instrument against Asad's continued pressures on Jordan. As a further counterbalance to Asad's pervasive influence, Jordan became in 1980 the first Arab country explicitly to side with Iraq in its war against Iran, thus securing Iraqi amity but irritating Syria. These acts of defiance against Asad were taken by Hussein just as Syria was experiencing growing difficulties: she had serious domestic problems (the Muslim Brothers' opposition); she was increasingly isolated in the Arab world (the Tripoli Bloc was ineffective); and her continued involvement in Lebanon was becoming a grave liability. The close co-operation that had developed between Syria and the PLO following the Camp David accords, and the alleged Jordanian activities against the PLO in co-ordination with Israel, continued with the other developments to cause by late 1980 a serious rift between Syria and Jordan.[35] In an attempt to bring Hussein back under Damascus's influence, Asad demonstrated his muscles and resorted to subversion. In December 1980 he deployed his troops along the Jordanian border; then early in 1981 the Jordanian military attaché in Beirut was kidnapped, and a plot to assassinate Jordan's prime minister was uncovered. Jordan accused Rifat, Asad's brother, of initiating and organizing the murder attempt, and dispatched her troops to the border to counter the Syrian military build-up.[36]

So Hussein, himself a courageous and shrewd leader, showed that he would not be intimidated by Asad's threats. He put an end to Asad's systematic and painstaking efforts, which had been going on for some seven years, to bring Jordan into his sphere of influence, and thereby seriously undermined Asad's strategy of a military–political alliance within the framework of Greater Syria. For as we shall see presently, the other two partners in this alliance – the PLO and Lebanon – proved to be liabilities rather than assets to this strategy.

Asad and the PLO

Although, like most Syrians, Asad has been ideologically committed, perhaps more than any other Arab leader, to the Palestinian cause, he has essentially used this cause to advance his aims both domestically and externally. While in Syria his support for the Palestinians' aspirations has been used to strengthen his legitimacy as an Arab ruler, in the regional and international arenas the Palestinian issue and organizations served Asad in other ways: to achieve an all-Arab leadership in the struggle against Israel; to increase diplomatic pressure against Israel in the international community; to weaken Israel by periodic attrition warfare carried out by Palestinian guerrillas; and to score points in Syria's other regional struggles, notably vis-à-vis Egypt and Jordan.

Thus, while on numerous occasions he has proclaimed his and his country's adherence to the Palestinian cause, and has supported the PLO in various ways, Asad basically has sought to control the PLO and to make it an instrument of his policies. And as the PLO, despite its long strategic alliance with Syria, strove to preserve a substantial degree of independence (from Syria as well as from other Arab countries), Asad has periodically clashed with it by restricting its activities and even violently suppressing it.

Asad adopted such positions toward the Palestinian guerrilla organization long before he came to power in Damascus, and while the PLO and Fath (Al-Fatah) were two separate groups. As Syria's air force commander in 1964 and 1965, Asad, like his comrades, shared the aim of the newly established Fath organization: to wage an armed struggle against Israel. Initially, without the knowledge of the Syrian ruler, Amin al-Hafiz, Asad and the Syrian chief of military intelligence allocated to Fath two training bases and helped it obtain arms from China, via Algeria.[37] Syria then became for several years the major centre for military assistance and political support for the Fath, although there was occasional friction. Asad himself, serving also as defence minister in 1966, had a clash with Yasir Arafat, then a young Fath commander. He ordered the arrest of Arafat and other Fath leaders for allegedly killing Yusuf Urabi, a Syrian agent who had been planted among them. Although he went back on his decision to execute Arafat, Asad has developed a personal animosity to him since that time. Resenting his defiant conduct and suspecting him of being an Egyptian agent, Asad questioned Arafat's credibility as leader of the 'Palestinian revolution' (early in 1969 Arafat also became the PLO chairman).[38] Tightening his control over the PLO and its new leader, Asad issued in 1969 special orders strictly regulating its movements and activities in Syria.[39] A year later, just before he became Syria's leader, Asad acted in a way which severely harmed the PLO, but, as he saw it, it was in his personal interests as well as in the interests of Syria. As defence minister and air force commander Asad declined to give air cover to the Syrian forces which had invaded Jordan in September 1970 in order to rescue the rebellious PLO from the wrath of King Hussein. This move by Asad, which indirectly contributed to the destruction of the PLO presence in Jordan, had three purposes: to avoid antagonizing Hussein's Jordan, which was more important than the PLO in Asad's regional strategy; to save Syria from a possible débâcle had Israel and the US intervened on Jordan's side; to discredit his rival Jadid and facilitate his own ascendancy.

When he came to power late in 1970, Asad worked more systematically to employ the PLO as an instrument of his domestic and regional policies, notably his Greater Syria strategy. The transfer of the PLO headquarters and operations from Jordan to Lebanon, after September 1970, considerably helped Asad to extend his influence over the 'Palestinian resistance' movement. To achieve this goal Asad also used the remaining PLO bases in Syria, as well as the Syrian-controlled Palestinian organizations: the Saiqa and the Popular Front for the Liberation of Palestine (PFLP) – the General Command (Ahmad Jibril's group). As a rule, Asad has consistently endeavoured to demonstrate to his own public and to other Arab nations as well as to the international community that 'Syria is the lung from which Palestinian activity draws breath',[40] and that he himself has been the great champion of the Palestinian cause. In numerous speeches, interviews and public lectures, Asad has made the following points: that the liberation of Palestine and the rights of the Palestinians are the most important issues in the Arab world – even more important than the Golan;[41] that the PLO represents the Palestinian people and only it can define Palestinian rights and aspirations;[42] that Syria would do her utmost to fight for the Palestinians and help them to fight Israel;[43] that Syria has sacrificed much, more than any other Arab state, for the sake of the Palestinians. Asad presented his case by saying,

> Who has sacrificed for the resistance as much as Syria sacrificed? What Arab country other than Syria entered in warlike operations with another Arab country? . . . Syrian and Jordanian soldiers were killed . . . for the sake of the resistance. . . . why did we not enter into negotiations after the Sinai agreement and regain part of the Golan! . . . But for the sake of the Palestinian question . . . we refused to negotiate, despite the fact that such negotiation would have restored to us part of our occupied territory under acceptable conditions. . . . Syria's sacrifices are clear and bright. She is sacrificing her sons, economy, land and everything so that the Palestinian question may continue . . . and ultimately restore our occupied land and the rights of our displaced people.[44]

Asad indeed has continued for long periods of time to help the Palestinian organizations, notably the PLO, in various ways: providing training bases, supplying arms and intelligence, giving political, diplomatic and propaganda assistance both in the Arab world (for example, at the 1974 Rabat summit) and in the international community (the UN, the Third World and European countries). Yet he did all of this only when it served his own interests. Asad would naturally claim that his actions best served the genuine interests of the Arab nation and of the Palestinians themselves – that he was acting as the oracle who determined what these interests were. Thus, whenever the PLO threatened his policies, Asad would severely criticize it, restrict its activities and even fight it with arms. Asad told Arafat on one occasion, 'You do not represent Palestine more than we do.'[45] Asad also, of course, did not help the PLO in their 1970 predicament in Jordan, and subsequently criticized it for the way it had handled its relations with Jordan and for its slogan 'The road to Falastin passes via Amman'.[46] Later, as we have seen, Asad concluded a political and military alliance with Hussein, the so-called 'Butcher of the Palestinians'.

Almost all these of actions which damaged the PLO were carried out in accordance with Asad's regional strategy, notably his anti-Israel policy. In accordance with this, Asad for many years prohibited PLO operations against Israel from the Syrian border in order to avoid Israeli retaliation or a military conflict with Israel when Syria was not prepared. By contrast, Asad would organize the assassination of PLO representatives in Europe and the West Bank at times when the PLO adopted a more pragmatic political approach towards Israel.[47]

In sum, Asad's relations with the PLO have *not* been as they were once described by a PLO leader, 'a sort of Catholic marriage – although there are differences of opinion between the couple they must forever live together'.[48] It has been a bad marriage – one of exploitation on Syria's part – more like the relations between a master (Asad) holding his 'mule' (Arafat) on a short rein. Nonetheless this mule has not been always submissive and periodically has run off from his master to act independently, and has even kicked his master's leg when pushed. Asad's personal hatred for Arafat has led him to try to replace him, but without success.[49] This relationship was vividly and sharply manifested in the Lebanese civil war, during which Asad and the PLO were engaged in an open and violent conflict, basically because Arafat would not yield to Asad's dictates.

10 Asad's Lebanese Venture

As already pointed out, Lebanon has constituted the western part of Greater Syria. During the French mandate the Syrian Arab nationalist movement manifested its claim to Lebanon (which had been moulded as a separate state by the French in 1920) by including it on Syrian maps as part of Syria.[1] Similarly, successive national governments in Syria, as a sign of their refusal to accept it as a separate entity, did not establish diplomatic relations with the Lebanese state. But beyond this historical claim, Syrian leaders, notably Asad, regarded Lebanon as vital to their national and strategic interests in all aspects: military, political, economic and security. Much of Syria's trade passed through Beirut's sea port, part of her water supplies came from Lebanon, and remittances were sent home by the several thousand Syrian workers in Lebanon. More crucial, Lebanon's pluralist society and democratic, albeit weak, regime provided an antithesis to the Syrian system, notably to Asad's dictatorship, and Beirut became the main haven for Syrian opposition groups, who harshly attacked the Damascus rulers and plotted to overthrow them. Asad was obviously anxious to eliminate them. He wanted also, as we have seen, to control the various PLO groups which in late 1970 transferred their headquarters from Jordan to Beirut and their bases to southern Lebanon. This objective was part of the Greater Syria strategy in which Asad intended to employ the PLO as well as to use the Lebanese territory for both defensive and offensive purposes vis-à-vis Israel. Consequently, following his ascendancy late in 1970, Asad, within his Greater Syria policy, sought to extend his influence over Lebanon, if not to turn it into a Syrian protectorate. But unlike his militant predecessors, who during 1965–70 had endeavoured to undermine the conservative Christian pro-Western regime and replace it with a Muslim leftist system, the pragmatic Asad preferred to deal with that weak conservative regime. As it was, Asad had been on friendly terms with Lebanon's then president, Sulayman Franjiyya (Franjiyya and his family, fleeing from his enemies in north Lebanon, took refuge in the 1950s with Asad's family in Qardaha; Rifat Asad was a personal friend of Toni, the president's son). In addition, Asad apparently calculated that it would be easier to have his way with the current government than with its leftist alternative.

Apart from the chronic weakness of the Christian conservative regime, which he would be able to take advantage of, Asad was presumably concerned lest the destruction of this regime by the Muslim radicals provoke an Israeli intervention on the Christians' side and bring about a division of Lebanon.[2] Conversely, Asad might have been worried that a Muslim radical regime could become a serious constraint, if not a threat, to his policy of controlling Lebanon. These Muslim radical forces contained groups which had been critical of Syria (Kamal Junblatt) or were directed by her Arab rival Iraq (the pro-Iraqi Ba'th Party) or wished to be independent of Syrian dictation (most groups and also the PLO). Therefore, Asad's initial steps in the early 1970s were directed towards improving Syria's relations with the Lebanese conservative Christian government. While refraining from mentioning Syria's claim to Lebanon, Asad stated in 1971 and 1972 'there exist special historical relations between Lebanon and Syria, and no regime in Syria or in Lebanon can overlook this. . . . Syria and Lebanon are one land [not one state] and their two peoples are more than brothers.'[3] (But later, in 1976, Asad declared, 'Throughout history Syria and Lebanon have been one country and one people.')[4] Simultaneously Asad managed during these two years to involve, for the first time, the Lebanese government in some sort of military co-operation with Syria, although he failed in the early 1970s to obtain Lebanon's permission to deploy Syrian troops in the Arqub ('Fathland') region, near the Israeli border.[5]

Yet as a master manipulator Asad did not content himself with cultivating good relations with the Lebanese government only. He also developed significant links with other Lebanese forces outside the traditional establishment in order to diversify his options and increase his influence on Lebanese politics. One of these forces was the Shi'i community, the single largest community in Lebanon according to various estimates (there has not been a census in Lebanon since 1932). Building close ties with the new powerful Shi'i leader Imam Musa al-Sadr, Asad obtained from him significant help: Sadr acknowledged the

Lebanese Alawites as part of the Shi'i sect, thus assisting Asad both in strengthening his legitimacy in Syria and in mustering Shi'i support in Lebanon.[6] Asad also continued his strategic relations with the PLO in Lebanon, supplying them arms and giving them political backing in their attempts to establish a stronghold, particularly near the Israeli border. Drawing considerable leverage from his relations with the PLO and the Shi'is (as well as from pro-Syrian forces in Lebanon, like the Ba'th Party), and gaining high prestige from his role in the 1973 war, Asad became the most influential external factor in Lebanese politics in 1974 and 1975. Thus when he visited Lebanon in January 1975 (as was true of Jordan, no Syrian head of state had visited Lebanon for eighteen years) Asad was warmly welcomed by the public, the parliament and the cabinet. Depicted as the 'hero of the Golan in his second homeland, Lebanon', Asad discussed with the Lebanese leaders 'military co-operation' to defend both Syria and Lebanon against Israel.[7]

In the joint communiqué issued at the end of the talks it was stated: 'The two presidents surveyed the repeated Israeli acts of aggression against Lebanese territory. Asad announced that Syria will support Lebanon with her military, political and economic resources and is ready to give Lebanon all that she asks for, in order to enable her to withstand and act against the aggression, and to maintain her sovereignty and territorial integrity; and this on the basis of the common destiny vis-à-vis the common enemy.' There was no indication in the communiqué of how Franjiyya had reacted to Asad's statement or whether he agreed to it; but according to a senior PLO leader Asad and Franjiyya signed a secret agreement whereby Syria would send troops into Lebanon and train the Lebanese army.[8] Asad reportedly later told Arafat, 'You should know that he [Franjiyya] is the only Lebanese president who would immediately agree to sign a treaty unifying his country with Syria should I ask him to do so.'[9] Whether or not Asad agreed with Franjiyya on the terms for Syrian–Lebanese military and political co-operation, it would appear that his soaring prestige and Syria's strengthening position following the 1973 war motivated Asad to integrate Lebanon into his Greater Syria strategy at that juncture. But in this process it so happened that Asad's policies in Lebanon also indirectly contributed to the civil war in Lebanon in 1975. This in turn caused Asad to deepen his involvement in Lebanon, which has continued for more than a decade now. It is not intended in this chapter and the next to describe and examine the roots and developments of this war, but only to survey and analyse Asad's role in it and its impact on his regime as well as on his regional and international position.

On the eve of the civil war, owing to Asad's prestige and actions 'Damascus replaced Cairo as the external center of allegiance and guidance for Lebanese Muslims and acquired virtual veto power over major decisions concerning Lebanon's domestic and foreign policies.'[10] On the one hand, following the 1973 war Lebanese Muslims became more radicalized, owing partly to Asad's powerful stance, partly to Israel's declining political power but growing military actions in southern Lebanon, and partly to the weakening of Lebanon's Christian-dominated political system. Muslim radicals, led by the Druze leader Kamal Junblatt, also drew political encouragement and military support from the growing power of the PLO in Lebanon, which was in turn given Syrian arms and equipment. These Muslim radicals were organized in the Lebanese National Movement and aimed at overthrowing the traditional Lebanese regime. On the other hand, Christian Maronite groups, led by Pierre Jumayyil, the leader of the Phalangists, and Camille Chamoun, leader of the National Liberals, became increasingly worried lest the old status quo be shattered by the Muslim radicals and the PLO; thus they became more belligerent towards these anti-establishment forces. A single violent clash which started between Phalangist militiamen and Palestinian commandos of Ahmad Jibril's group on 13 April 1975 in a Christian quarter of Beirut soon developed into armed clashes in various parts of Lebanon between Christian militias and Muslim radicals, assisted by Palestinians from the 'rejectionist front' of the PLO.

It would appear that Asad's actions during that early stage of the conflict tended to encourage it. Either unaware of its depth, or inclined to use political manipulation, Asad then employed mediation in order to settle the military strife. While refraining from exerting strong pressure on the warring sides to reach an agreement, Asad continued on the one hand to support the existing regime and on the other to supply huge quantities of arms to the PLO – which were partly transferred to the radical Muslims; all of which did not discourage either side from continuing the civil war. Early in 1976 the Christian forces, motivated by strategic and political considerations, attacked for the first time Palestinian refugee camps in and around Beirut. Their attacks provoked the mainstream PLO, which until then had been only marginally involved in the war, to join forces openly with Kamal Junblatt and fight the Christians. Asad again failed to adopt a clear-cut and decisive policy, thus once more indirectly encouraging the warring parties. In January 1976 he ordered two battalions of the PLA (Palestinian Liberation Army, which was under his control) to cross into Lebanon, without the permission of President Franjiyya (who then protested) and help the PLO–Lebanese Muslim alliance against the Christians. Asad later admitted: 'we decided to go in [to Lebanon] under the name of the PLA . . . we had no choice but to intervene directly . . . and save the [Palestinian] resistance'.[11] But shortly afterwards, in February 1976, Asad and Franjiyya issued a 'constitutional document' which, despite certain changes, essentially preserved the status quo in the Lebanese government.[12]

This document became the official Syrian policy in Lebanon and was accepted by the Christian Maronites, who now regarded Asad as their strong ally (even Pierre Jumayyil reportedly reached a secret agreement with Asad in December 1975).[13] But the Lebanese radicals, notably Kamal Junblatt, fiercely rejected this document and challenged Asad's policy both verbally and by force of arms. Junblatt called Asad 'cunning, a genuine Alawite . . . he wants to dominate Lebanon to domesticate the Palestinians'. In his memoirs he cites his last conversation with Asad regarding his Maronite connection: 'President Asad expressed himself very frankly: "Listen," he said, "for me, this is an historic opportunity to re-orient the Maronites toward Syria, to win their trust, to make them realize that their source of protection is no longer France or the west." ' Later Junblatt added: 'circumstances and Syrian pigheadedness helped the Maronites against the parties of the Lebanese left, against the nationalist movement, against all those who opposed the Syrian plan to turn Lebanon into a satellite state without having to fight for it'.[14] Indeed, in the early summer of 1976 Asad was too much involved in his ambition to control Lebanon; and despite his public ideological commitments, he essentially sided with the Christian conservative establishment rather than with the Lebanese radicals and the PLO. He did this for five reasons.

First he wished to preserve the territorial integrity of Lebanon and integrate her within his Greater Syria strategy. Second, he was convinced that he could achieve this objective with the Christian conservative government ('President Sulayman Franjiyya . . . was loyal and patriotic . . . noble and honourable. We reached an agreement' [on the constitutional document]). Conversely, third, Asad was concerned lest a defeat of the conservative Christian establishment by the Muslim radicals should provoke an Israeli intervention and bring about the division of Lebanon and the creation of a 'second (Christian) Israel':

> A decisive military action [by Kamal Junblatt] . . . would open doors to every foreign intervention, particularly Israel's intervention. Let us all visualize the magnitude of the tragedy which might ensue if Israel were to intervene and save some Arabs [Christians] from other Arabs [Muslims]. . . . The partitioning of Lebanon is an old Zionist aim. . . . The partitioning of Lebanon would acquit Israel of the charge of racism. . . . When Lebanon is partitioned between Christians and Muslims, Israel will say, 'Where is racism! Israel is based on religion, and in Lebanon there would be states, or statelets, based on religion'. . . . [15]

Fourth, Asad was possibly also worried lest a victory of the Lebanese Muslims and the PLO, under the strong and charismatic leadership of Kamal Junblatt, might bring about a strong radical government in Lebanon which would be independent of his influence and might join with Iraq in an alliance against Syria. Fifth, Asad apparently wished to demonstrate to the West, notably the US, on the one hand, and to his own public on the other, that he was able to restore order and stability in Lebanon and bring it under his influence.

In the light of these calculations, Asad adopted tough military measures against the forces of the Muslim radicals and the PLO, while simultaneously trying to discredit their leaders Kamal Junblatt and Yasir Arafat, and to push a wedge between them. Thus the Syrian media depicted Junblatt as an 'American agent', 'a traitor' and 'a trader in revolution and progress'.[16] Asad himself described Junblatt as 'ambitious, adventurer and demagogue . . . he is not even an Arab . . .' (Junblatt's ancestors were Kurds); 'He has a thirst for power and blood.' Asad alleged that Junblatt fought the Christian Maronites not from ideological motives but 'in order to assume authority by force [together] with the Palestinians' . . . assistance. . . . The matter was one of vengeance, a matter of revenge which dates back 140 years' (when the Maronites in Lebanon defeated Bashir Junblatt, the Druze amir, and completed their control over Mount Lebanon).[17] Asad, however, was not content with verbal attacks only. On 27 May 1976, Kamal Junblatt's sister was assassinated by an unknown gunman; the leftist press in Beirut denounced the killing as the work of the Syrians.[18] Less than a year later, on 16 March 1977, Kamal Junblatt himself was assassinated, allegedly by Syrian agents, and his forces consequently disintegrated.[19] Earlier, in 1976, Asad had ordered the organization of a rival leftist front to oppose Junblatt's National

Movement. Simultaneously he put pressure on Arafat, warning him that he should 'stop intervening in domestic Lebanese politics' and that he had 'to choose between Syrian support or the support of Mr Junblatt'.[20] Arafat preferred his alliance with Junblatt, trusting that Asad 'would not permit a Syrian rifle to shoot the Palestinian masses'.[21] Arafat was wrong. Early in June 1976, Asad sent his regular army to fight the PLO and to impose Pax Syriana on Lebanon, calculating that the PLO would not resist the formidable Syrian army.[22] Asad was also wrong. The PLO–Lebanese radical alliance bravely fought back against the Syrian troops, blocking their advance and causing them severe losses. Asad was apparently deeply hurt by the PLO's so-called attempt to turn Lebanon into a 'second Vietnam' for Syria ('Asad's mean attempts to scare us [the PLO] will not succeed . . . we fear nobody but Allah and if Asad wants to try again – let him').[23]

Asad then changed his tactics: he stopped the direct military assault against the PLO and adopted diplomatic and propaganda measures accompanied by certain limited military actions in order to erode the PLO strength. Thus in an attempt to disgrace the PLO and Arafat, on 20 July 1976 Asad declared,

> The Palestinian resistance is currently fighting for the accomplishment of the objectives of others [Junblatt] and against the interests and goals of the Palestinian Arab people. . . . I cannot imagine what the connection is between the fighting of Palestinians in the highest mountains of Lebanon and the liberation of Palestine. . . . He [Arafat] wants to liberate Juniyya [the Maronite stronghold] and Tripoli and does not want to liberate Palestine, even if he so claims. This is what they used to say in 1970. Brothers, remember what was being said in Jordan in 1970. They raised slogans, such as 'all power for the resistance, all power for the revolution, and we will liberate Palestine through Amman'. In essence, the matter is being repeated in Lebanon. . . . They had also attacked the Syrian soldiers who had earlier gone there [Lebanon] to help them. They mercilessly attacked those soldiers . . . the gunmen of the organizations poured fire on our soldiers and the children and women [in Sidon] . . . killing whomever they could and destroying whatever they could.[24]

At the same time Asad ordered political negotiations with the PLO, during which Syrian troops and Christian forces carried out co-ordinated attacks on Palestinian camps and positions. Among these was the notorious Christian attack in early August 1976 on the refugee camp of Tal Za'tar, which was reportedly co-ordinated with the Syrian army.[25]

By October 1976, following direct Syrian military assaults, Asad succeeded in defeating the PLO militarily and bringing the civil war to an end. Yet Asad was still unable to dominate the PLO politically. Indeed, despite the virtually free hand he was granted at the Arab summit conferences in Riyadh and Cairo (October 1976) to control the PLO (and Lebanon), Asad was geared to make a rapprochement with Arafat (and with the Lebanese radicals led by Walid Junblatt, Kamal's son). For one thing, being harshly criticized in the Arab world as well as within Syria for his ill-treatment of the PLO, Asad wished to prove that he was still the guardian of the 'Palestinian resistance'.[26] More crucial was his need for PLO co-operation (and vice versa) against the common enemy, Israel. There were four reasons for this. First, Syria had been deterred by Israel from playing a direct role in southern Lebanon and therefore needed the PLO as a proxy in that area. Second, in late 1977 the right-wing Likud bloc came into power in Israel and was believed by both Syria and the PLO to harbour aggressive intentions. (Israel indeed invaded southern Lebanon in March 1978 [the Litani operation] and both Syria and the PLO anticipated bigger Israeli attacks in the future.) Third, Sadat's initiative late in 1977 and the subsequent Camp David accords in 1978 produced an Egyptian–Israeli peace; to fight it Asad needed to work closely with the PLO (Asad said at that juncture: 'It would not be logical to dislodge the Palestinian from his rifle when the Camp David accords threaten our future.')[27] Fourth, there was the growing military assistance of the Israeli Likud government to the Maronite militias in Lebanon.

Indeed, parallel to his rapprochement with Arafat, Asad's relations with the Maronite Lebanese Front deteriorated after about a year and a half of close co-operation. At its height, during 1976, the three principle Maronite leaders, Franjiyya, Jumayyil and Chamoun, not only accepted Asad's constitutional document but in May 1976 also agreed that Asad's candidate, Elias Sarkis, should be elected as Lebanon's new president. (Of these elections, which were 'organized' by the Syrians, a Christian oppositionist remarked, 'Elias Sarkis does not have any function in this big election farce, since the true winner … is President Asad.')[28] On the eve of Syria's direct military intervention in Lebanon most Christian Maronite leaders (but not the president) publicly called on Asad to intervene in the civil war and subsequently thanked him for doing so.[29]

Asad himself cited these requests as one of his considerations in sending his troops to Lebanon: 'we had received many … calls for help from many towns and villages in Lebanon, and after we had received such calls from several officials in Lebanon . . . we started and developed our political and then our military efforts'.[30] Pierre Jumayyil, the Phalangists' leader, later explained his own attitude to Asad's intervention: 'The Christians felt that their existence was in danger and tried to appeal again to the West. Asad's action motivated the Christians to relinquish the foreigner and to approach Syria. . . .'[31] Camille Chamoun, the leader of the National Liberals, who served as Lebanon's foreign minister in mid-1976, strongly supported Asad's policy in Lebanon in various dispatches he sent to the Arab League, to Arab leaders and to the UN.[32]

Asad, who needed this Christian backing in order to legitimize his *de facto* protectorate over Lebanon, courted the chief Maronite leaders while taking steps to avoid breaching the Christian autonomy. He continued his close ties with Franjiyya, praised Pierre Jumayyil as 'a patriotic and sincere person', and gave the new Lebanese president a 'warm and grand welcome' when Sarkis visited Damascus ('I felt for the first time that I am a president').[33] Asad particularly cultivated Sarkis, since he was nominally the commander of the Arab Deterrent Force (composed mostly of Syrian troops) which was assigned by the Riyadh summit conference to help Sarkis supervise the pacification of Lebanon and the restrictions imposed on the PLO. Through Sarkis Asad was able to assert his hegemony over most of Lebanon with the help of the various well-equipped militias, cultivated by him: the Shi'i Amal, the SSNP, the Franjiyya militia Fursan Al-Arab and the like. Nonetheless, the region of southern Lebanon was controlled by the PLO (except for the strip held by Israeli-backed Christian militia) and parts of Mount Lebanon, northern Lebanon and eastern Beirut were dominated by the Christian Maronite militias.

As it happened these Christian militias, which had helped the Syrian army in 1976 to fight the PLO, manifested during 1977 increasing disillusionment with their alliance with Asad. More and more Maronites became deeply concerned when he made his rapprochement with the PLO, their arch-enemy; and as time went on they suspected that he did not intend to evacuate his troops from, and relinquish his control over, Lebanon.[34] The leaders of this anti-Syrian current were Bashir Jumayyil, the younger son of Pierre Jumayyil and the commander of the Lebanese Forces (the Maronite militias), and Camille Chamoun, the veteran Maronite politician and head of the Lebanese Front (the Christian political establishment). Encouraged by the ascendancy of Menachem Begin in Israel (who was likely to help the Maronites more actively than his predecessor Prime Minister Yitzhak Rabin) and by the growing domestic problems and regional isolation of Asad, these Christian leaders decided, in early 1978, to liberate Lebanon from the Syrian occupation through an armed struggle. Yet the Lebanese Front, which led this struggle, did not represent the entire Maronite community (and certainly not the whole Christian population). Former President Franjiyya, Asad's friend, broke away from the Front and following the assassination of his son Toni in June 1978 (apparently by the Phalangists) he stepped up his previous activities to create (with Rashid Karami, the Muslim politician) a Christian–Muslim pro-Syrian bloc.

President Elias Sarkis found himself in an awkward position. He admired Asad as a person and a leader ('he [Asad] is a person who comprehends everything and is profound, profound, profound'), and was also aware of Asad's predominant position in Lebanon's destiny: ('Syria is the key for the solution [in Lebanon] and Asad is the game master').[35] Sarkis thus acted virtually according to Asad's dictate ('as an instrument of the Syrians')[36] until mid-1978 when the violent conflict between the Lebanese Forces and the Syrian army intensified and the latter was about to launch a massive attack on the Maronites.[37] Pressured by the Lebanese Front and dismayed by Asad's alleged intention to subjugate the Maronite community by force, Sarkis threatened to resign on 6 July 1978. Following diplomatic activities, a ceasefire was finally achieved in early October 1978. At that juncture the Maronite forces had been weakened, their territory had been eroded, and their community had suffered greatly; but they managed to sustain and subsequently to develop their political and military autonomy with Israeli assistance. Asad retained his hegemony over most of the country for several more years in an attempt to keep Lebanon (and the PLO) within his Greater Syria design.

The year 1977 seemed to mark the peak of Asad's success in his regional (and international) policies, notably the Greater Syria strategy. He managed during the second half of 1976 to split the wide intra-Arab coalition which had been formed following his invasion of Lebanon. By manoeuvring among the Arab states, Asad was able, in the Riyadh and Cairo summit conferences, to obtain an all-Arab (with the exception of Iraq) sanction or legitimization for his *de facto* control over Lebanon. Simultaneously relations between Sadat and Asad noticeably improved against the background of their common efforts to present a unified front to the incoming Carter administration in the US. Thus in press interviews late in 1976 and early in 1977 Asad stated, 'Regardless of any differences that might occur' (between him and Sadat) neither could 'forget that they were partners in the [1973] October war . . . we started with common efforts with our big sister Egypt to strengthen the co-ordination and links between the two countries. We decided to establish a joint political leadership. . . .'[38]

Within the framework of the Greater Syria region, Hussein of Jordan, while giving unstinting support to Syria over the Lebanese issue, continued his political and military alliance with Asad 'on the path of their cherished unity'. By early 1977 Asad was thus in a position to declare, 'We have taken big steps towards integration and co-ordination with Jordan. . . .'[39] Apparently as further steps in the unity of Greater Syria Asad was keen to 'bless any link between Jordan and the Palestinian state', and when asked about a federation between Syria, Jordan and the West Bank, Asad answered, 'I am not against anything that reinforces Arab unity.'[40]

Asad, as we have seen, had by 1977 established his virtual hegemony over most of Lebanon. With the help of 30,000 troops he directly dominated the eastern region of the country (the Biqa) and virtually controlled its other strategic regions. He revived his alliances with the PLO and the Lebanese Muslim radicals while still maintaining working relations with the Christian Maronite forces and giving orders to Lebanon's president.[41] At that juncture it is possible that Asad also contemplated legitimizing his protectorate over Lebanon through formal political and military treaties or a federal union with Syria and linking it then with Jordan. In one of Asad's media instruments, *Al-Thawra*, a Lebanese member of the SSNP was permitted (or encouraged?) to write early in 1977: 'We unionist Lebanese ask Syria, "Is it possible for Syria to unite with all the Arabs with the exception of Lebanon . . . is the union with Jordan useful and the union with Lebanon harmful?" '[42]

The Maronite leader, Camille Chamoun, also mentioned such an idea, albeit negatively. In one of his last visits to Damascus in the spring of 1977, he reportedly told the Syrian leaders that 'Lebanon is detached from the alliances and unions that are occasionally heard about, notably the union between Syria, Lebanon and Jordan.'[43] Karim Paqraduni, the young Phalangist leader who liaised between President Sarkis and Asad, suggested that 'special relations should exist between Lebanon and Syria, particularly in the following arenas: the establishment of a national security council with the participation of Jordan . . . ; the creation of a Lebanese–Jordanian–Syrian common market. . .'.[44] Still more significantly, in an interview in March 1977

Patrick Seale, a British journalist, observed that 'Asad saw Syria's immediate neighbours, Lebanon and Jordan, as a natural extension of its territory, vital to its defence. This three-nation grouping is already a fait accompli. . . . Asad now rules by proxy in Lebanon, while the progressive integration with Jordan is well advanced. If the Palestinians ever recover a West Bank homeland, they too will inevitably join this complex.'[45] Asad also outlined to Seale his international strategy: 'It is to forge an Arab bloc strong enough to become a regional power able to stand up to pressure from either of the superpowers.'[46] Indeed, it seemed for a while in 1977 that in addition to his remarkable achievements with his regional policies, Asad was the only Middle East leader capable of playing one superpower off against the other and drawing considerable benefits as a result.

11 Manoeuvring Between the US and the USSR

Employing tactics similar to those he had used during the post-1973 political process Asad continued during the Lebanese crisis his strategic alliance with the Soviet Union, asking for more arms and economic assistance. Yet he would not comply with a Soviet request to abandon his invasion of Lebanon and his fight against the PLO; at the same time he signalled to Moscow that he might diminish the Soviet presence in Syria and improve his relations with the US. On the other hand, while publicly attacking the US for her alleged hostile meddling in Lebanon, Asad would covertly seek American support and co-operation, hinting that this might help advance American interests in the Middle East. To be more specific, Asad improved his strained relations with the USSR following both the Syrian–Israeli disengagement agreement under US auspices and the renewal of Syrian–US relations in May–June 1974. Shortly afterwards, Asad described his relations with the Soviets as 'differences between friends', adding that Syria had a right to enter 'other friendships in the world'.[1] In early October 1974, while visiting Moscow, Asad issued a joint communiqué with Leonid Brezhnev, the Soviet leader, referring to the 'permanent character' of the USSR–Syrian friendship. Asad was then promised continued Soviet military and economic aid, and in return agreed to the resumption of the Geneva peace conference. Following the Egyptian–Israeli Sinai agreement (September 1975), which both Syria and the USSR opposed, Asad visited the USSR again in early October 1975 where he emphasized the importance of Syrian–Soviet relations, and obtained further promises of Soviet arms. But once again he refused to sign a friendship treaty with the USSR.[2]

During the first phase of the civil war, up until spring 1976, the

Soviets did not protest to Asad about his indirect venture in Lebanon, even though the PLO was bitterly complaining to Moscow of Syria's harsh measures against it.[3] Asad apparently had not consulted the Soviets about his decision to invade Lebanon. He decided to go ahead although on that very day Alexsei Kosygin, the Soviet prime minister, visited Damascus only hours after he had left Baghdad, where he and the Iraqi leaders had obliquely expressed their dissatisfaction with Syria's growing role in Lebanon. Reportedly, 'the Soviet prime minister had to wait two days in the Syrian capital before being granted an interview with President Asad'.[4]

As time went on and the Syrian army failed to defeat the PLO–Junblatt alliance, and the leaders of this alliance appealed for Soviet help, Moscow openly criticized Syria for her fight against her 'natural allies', and depicted this as a 'knife in their back'.[5] Brezhnev sent Asad a letter on 11 July 1976 (and possibly a second letter on 1 October 1976) requesting him to evacuate his army from Lebanon and stop his actions against the PLO and the Lebanese left.[6] Asad not only ignored the Soviet requests and pressures (Soviet arms supplies to Syria were reported to have slowed down) but, as we shall see presently, he continued his co-operation with the US over the Lebanese issue. Furthermore, while threatening early in 1977 to cancel port services to the Soviet navy in Tartus port, Asad responded favourably to the wooing by the new Carter administration, which aimed to integrate Syria in a new Middle East peace process. Unwilling to alienate their important Syrian ally further, and anxious to participate in a comprehensive political settlement for the Middle East, the Soviet Union had to comply with Asad's policies in Lebanon (by then Asad had also improved his relations with the PLO and the Lebanese left) and made a rapprochement with him. Thus from 18 to 22 April 1977, Asad visited Moscow to discuss bilateral relations, but on 9 May he met President Carter in Geneva, demonstrating both his independence and his ability to manoeuvre (for a while) between the two superpowers.

While sustaining his strategic alliance with the Soviet Union and trying to obtain from them more arms as well as economic aid and political support, Asad opted to maintain a good working dialogue with the US mainly as a potential instrument in his confrontation with Israel. Indeed, beyond his intention to use the US as a counterweight to Soviet demands and as a source of technological and economic assistance, Asad essentially endeavoured to weaken American support for Israel, or alternatively to use US influence over Israel to advance

Syrian interests. In return for such American help Asad signalled not only that was he not a Soviet client but that he could be an asset to US interests in the Middle East if he were to be properly acknowledged.

As we have seen, in 1974, with US help, Asad succeeded in winning back the territories he had lost in the 1973 war plus the town of Quneitra and part of the Hermon Mount, captured by Israel in 1967, thus undermining the 1967 ceasefire lines with Israel. Subsequently, in June 1974, Asad received President Nixon in Damascus and renewed his diplomatic relations with the US. Although he was unable to bring the US to link the Egyptian–Israeli Sinai agreement (September 1975) to a further Israeli withdrawal from the Golan, he continued to accept American economic aid (US$90 million annual development loans) and to sustain workable diplomatic relations with Washington. When the civil war in Lebanon erupted in 1975 and Syria began its involvement there, Asad sought American approval of this venture, and was particularly keen to obtain US help in preventing an Israeli military intervention in Lebanon against Syria. Initially, however, the US did not support the Syrian military involvement in Lebanon, fearing that this might lead to a new Israeli–Syrian armed conflict. Thus in a speech on 20 July 1976, Asad revealed that on 16 October 1975 the US ambassador to Damascus had told him that 'Israel will consider the intervention of foreign [Syrian] armed forces a very grave threat.'[7] Yet, although publicly Washington did not change its attitude towards Asad's Lebanese venture, later it virtually backed both his political and military measures in Lebanon. Asad himself confirmed this: 'the United States supports Syria's intervention in Lebanon, especially the armed intervention'.[8] The American support of Asad's policy in Lebanon was apparently based on a number of calculations. First, Asad was the only leader in the region able to stop the civil war and bring about a constructive and balanced solution to the Lebanese problem. Such a solution could be found in his constitutional document of February 1976, which the US supported. Second, the alternative to Asad's policy in Lebanon was much worse: the emergence of a Lebanese leftist–PLO regime in the country which would probably become a source of regional instability. Third, co-operation with Asad over the Lebanese issue might reduce Soviet influence in Damascus and might help reintegrate Syria in the political process with Israel.[9]

Apparently taking into account these American calculations, Asad managed to secure American support for his Lebanese venture, including US help in achieving a tacit Israeli–Syrian agreement over

Lebanon. Of course, Asad was aware of Israeli sensitivities and interests concerning Lebanon. His initial military actions in that country, for example, were conducted in a sporadic and indirect fashion apparently in order not to antagonize Israel. Similarly, his subsequent direct intervention on the Maronites' side and against the PLO was partly calculated to neutralize Israeli military action, as these Syrian moves were in line with Israel's interests. Yet, to be completely sure of Israeli neutrality, Asad agreed through US mediation to the Israeli so-called 'red line' conditions which basically entailed that Israel would agree to Syrian military intervention in Lebanon provided it was restricted to ground forces, and that these forces should not move south of the Sidon–Jezzin line (the red line) towards the Israeli border. In other words, in spring 1976, Israel agreed to give Asad a free hand in the major part of Lebanon in return for Asad's recognition of Israeli security interests in southern Lebanon. Significantly, the tacit understanding between Asad and Rabin was so extensive that Asad withdrew most of his offensive military power from the Golan ceasefire line and sent it to Lebanon and to Syria's troubled border with Iraq.[10]

It is also interesting to note that at that point, whereas the Syrian media (and Asad himself in his domestic speeches) fiercely attacked the US and Israel for allegedly inflaming the civil war in Lebanon,[11] Asad secretly negotiated with these two 'enemies'. Moreover in an interview with the American media Asad said that he was willing to resume negotiations in Geneva for a peaceful solution to the Middle East conflict. He stated that he was willing to sign a non-belligerency agreement with Israel (which he defined as a peace treaty) but without exchange of people or goods with Israel; this was provided Israel withdrew from all territories captured in 1967 and agreed to the creation of a Palestinian state in the West Bank and Gaza. Asad also implied that the US should have the major role in mediating a political settlement in the Middle East.[12]

It would seem that Asad's statements (late 1976 and early 1977) were directed mainly towards the newly elected Carter administration in Washington. After all, in October 1976 Asad had made a rapprochement with Sadat (with Saudi mediation) and anticipated a fresh American approach to the Arab–Israeli conflict. He might have been initially encouraged by Carter's reported belief that 'real peace between Arabs and Israelis could be achieved, and he clearly wanted to play a role in bringing that about if possible'.[13] During the first months of 1977 Asad was apparently encouraged by certain moves made by the new Carter administration. The first was a trip undertaken by Cyrus Vance, the new secretary of state, to the Middle East countries in February 1977 to explore the possibilities for reconvening the Geneva conference. Next the US decided not to approve the sale to Israel of a certain kind of cluster bomb, and this inevitably produced a strain in US–Israeli relations.[14] Then there was Carter's Clinton speech in March 1977 advocating the creation of a homeland for the Palestinians. Asad was further gratified by Carter's evident inclination to regard him as an important factor in Middle East politics and in Arab–Israeli relations.

Indeed, in March 1977 the Syrian press had begun a favourable examination of Carter's new Middle East policy. *Tishrin*, for example, cited British experts who concluded that Carter's policy was based on the Brookings Institution's report on the Middle East.[15] Other Syrian journalists were greatly impressed with the 'process of separation between the American–Israeli twins [effected by Carter, who] . . . tries to liberate American foreign policy from the Zionist dependency'.[16] Above all, the Syrian media elatedly reported that Carter acknowledged 'the important position President Asad fills in the Arab arena, and the big role he plays in the improvement of the Arab problem. . . . Carter did not hesitate to wander from the USA to Geneva in order to meet President Asad and listen to his unique opinion regarding the achievement of a just peace.'[17] In their meeting in Geneva on 9 May 1977 Carter and Asad 'seemed to get along remarkably well during their nearly seven hours together in talks and over dinner'. Both agreed that there was 'a need for progress in 1977'. Asad was apparently pleased when Carter 'reiterated publicly his support for a Palestinian homeland' but 'Asad proved himself to be wily and elusive' regarding the Palestinian question, 'showing the American side that it had nothing to teach him on this topic . . . he resolutely refused to state his own preferred outcome. He placed emphasis on the need to include something for the refugees outside the occupied territories. He was not necessarily opposed to the idea of a Jordanian–Palestinian federation, but he expressed skepticism, asking what would be in it for the Palestinians.' Regarding peace with Israel,

Asad said there must be full evacuation of occupied territory. Syria was ready to talk of peace but not if territory were to be lost. Asad added that he would agree to an end of the state of belligerency as well as to certain security measures, that was all that would be needed for peace. . . . Ending the state of belligerency would lead automatically to peace . . . [it] would solve many psychological problems. Security measures could be added to buy time. Economic development would help. But [he] would not say what else might take place in the future. Commerce required two partners, and no one in Syria would now be prepared to trade with Israel. In conclusion, he added that East Jerusalem would have to be returned to the Arabs, though the holy places could be given a neutral status.[18]

It would appear then that Asad's proposal for a solution to the Syrian–Israeli conflict in 1977 was similar to his position in 1975 (expressed in his interview with *Newsweek*) on the eve of Nixon's visit to Damascus: an Israeli evacuation of all territories occupied in 1967 in exchange for an end to the state of belligerency but without having full peace relations. On the Palestinian question Asad seemed less clear. Although he did not rule out a Palestinian–Jordanian federation he was inclined to leave the final decision to the PLO. Nonetheless, this remark, coupled with his proposals for East Jerusalem and for the Palestinian refugees outside the occupied territories (that they should be returned to Israel), indicated Asad's uncompromising attitude towards Israel. Carter himself wrote in his memoirs: 'I was troubled by his extremely antagonistic attitude toward Israel. He seemed quite convinced that the Israelis were international outlaws.'[19] Asad also seemed assured of his final victory if the Israelis would not comply with his requests: 'Otherwise [he said] the seeds of future conflict remain. Time was on Syria's side. . . .'[20] Although Asad's antagonism towards Israel in Carter's presence might have been genuine or no more than a bargaining position, it might also have reflected Asad's sense of power and achievement, perhaps euphoria.

Indeed, it would seem at that juncture that Asad not only managed to solve the Lebanese problem (for a while), but used it as a springboard for both his regional ascendancy and his international standing. Western media reports of his remarkable successes were proudly quoted by Syria's *Al-Thawra* paper: 'These successes [in Lebanon] turned Asad into the star of the Arab homeland, and made Damascus a new power centre. . . . Asad became popular every-where. . . . he is the spokesman of the Arabs. . . . Syria is a new dominant power in the Middle East – peace in this region must pass through Damascus. . . . Asad now rides on two horses [the Soviet and the American].'[21] President Carter was himself attracted by the light of the rising star (Asad) and overlooked the Syrian leader's refusal to meet him in Washington. The leader of the great superpower made an exception and went to meet Asad on neutral turf ('Sadat was reported to be resentful that Asad received such special treatment from the

American president'). Carter reportedly went to Asad's suite in the Geneva hotel where both leaders stayed, and his welcoming comments to Asad were 'particularly effusive'. Carter referred to Asad 'as the "great leader" of Syria and to his "close friendship" with him only minutes after the two leaders had met for the first time'.[22] Carter also reportedly told Asad that he expected to obtain from him advice and support. It is no wonder then that Asad was in his element. Carter obviously was deeply impressed with him: 'He was a brilliant and strong man, very confident of himself, somewhat autocratic in demeanor, but personable and cordial toward me.'[23]

Other Westerners who met Asad around that time were equally impressed by his ability 'independently [to] analyse the state of affairs. . . . there is no room for mistakes. . . . [those traits] make him a prominent person'.[24]

Of course, Asad did make mistakes in the various stages of his political career, notably with regard to his Lebanese policy, both before and after 1977. Yet during the Lebanese crisis he displayed great stamina, consistency and decisiveness in achieving his strategic goals in Lebanon and the Greater Syria region. Joseph Kraft, who interviewed Asad late in 1976, reported: 'He showed no signs of being cock-a-hoop about the outcome of the long-drawn-out Lebanese drama. Neither did he show strain from an enterprise that at times brought him into conflict with Russia, the United States, Israel, all the other Arab states, the Palestinians, and various communities in Lebanon. On the contrary, he was enough at ease to joke a couple of times about his poor English and his weakness in the classical Arabic spoken by his interpreter.'[25] Karim Paqraduni, the Lebanese politician, who met him several times during the Lebanese civil war, described Asad's conduct and actions regarding that crisis:

His eyes are small, radiating intelligence and firmness . . . he moves quietly and with a touch of loftiness. He speaks always with refinement and in a low voice . . . he never raises his voice. . . . He approaches his goal patiently and obstinately . . . he never hurries – he prefers to reach his goal quietly and smoothly, he employs the method of conviction before he moves to coercive measures. . . . He entered Lebanon, first in a political way, in 1975, then in a military way, in 1976. . . . he stopped after each blow and negotiated, examined and calculated then he gave the next blow, this is the policy of short and successive electric shocks. . . . [He said during the Lebanese crisis] if Syria could not establish peace in Lebanon no one could do it. There will not be adjustments and no acts of flattery [*mujamalat*]. We shall hit it with no leniency. . . .[26]

Kamal Junblatt, the Druze leader of the Lebanese left, in his memoirs perceptively portrayed Asad's complex personality:

President Asad's personality is a mixture of commonsense, honesty, loyalty to his friends (the Frangies), a sense of balance, stubbornness, skill in manipulating antagonisms and a certain natural benevolence, but there is also duplicity and hardness. The big stick is always in the background and is usually an essential factor in his regime's approach. Apart from the fact that he listens far too much to his four or five different intelligence services, he is a man who knows what he wants and how to get it, by guile if need be. During his intervention in Lebanon, he showed himself vindictive and compassionate by turns. . . . Ordinary human nature is complex enough, but when one is dealing with politicians, party leaders or a military junta, life gets even more complicated. Everything is jumbled together: sincerity, ambiguity, ambition, destiny, and above all, the quest for power. On top of which, just as there is always a trace of the Pharaoh in Egyptian rulers, one can always detect the *wali* [Turkish Ottoman governor] in Syrian chiefs. . . . For President Asad, as I see it, Lebanon was a diplomatic wager of the first importance, a trump card, an asset to be traded off in negotiations with the US, the USSR and Europe, with a view to securing a satisfactory settlement of the problem of Syria's frontiers and of the territories occupied by Israel.[27]

The Lebanese Liability

But Asad inevitably made mistakes in Lebanon. As we have seen, he reacted, for example, rather slowly to the outbreak of the civil war in 1975 and did not perceive at that point the depth of the conflict. He wasted precious time mediating between the Maronites and the PLO and consequently was taken by surprise by both parties: the Maronites attacked Palestinian refugee camps in the Beirut region, provoking counter-attacks by the PLO, and thus aggravating the conflict. Subsequently, the PLO was not deterred by the dispatch of regular Syrian troops and was able to block their advance – contrary to Asad's expectations. One explanation for Asad's mistakes is that, as well as being a slow mover, he personally and singlehandedly made the final decisions regarding the various political and military actions. (Asad: 'I never felt so lonely in my life' [during the Lebanese crisis].)[28] And it is likely that the information and evaluation given to him by his advisers were not always accurate. This is perhaps because his lieutenants were unable always to understand the complexity of the Lebanese situation or to withstand the pressure of the fast-changing developments.[29] Perhaps more crucial to the decisions taken by Asad were the serious external and domestic constraints: Israeli threats, Arab opposition, Russian pressures and, last but not least, the domestic ideological inhibitions. These last constraints, which affected Asad's actions as well as the positions taken by his aides, were particularly burdensome when he decided to support the Christian Maronites and to fight against the Muslim Lebanese and Palestinians. Significantly, Asad commissioned three of his Sunni Muslim assistants to deal with the Lebanese crisis on the official level: Abd al-Halim Khaddam, the foreign minister, Hikmat Shihabi, the chief of staff, and Naji Jamil, the deputy defence minister and air force commander. (Behind the scene, assignments were given to Asad's Alawite aides: his brother, Rifat; the chief of air force intelligence, Muhammad Khawli; and the chief of military intelligence, Ali Duba.)

It is true that despite his constraints, by late 1976 Asad had managed to pacify Lebanon and control most of its territory. He succeeded also in using these achievements as a springboard for his remarkable gains in both the regional and international arenas during 1977. But, as we shall see presently, most of these achievements, particularly those in Lebanon, proved to be rather superficial and by no means lasting.

The pacification of Lebanon did not last long mainly because the inherent problems of this country were not solved by Asad. His constitutional document of February 1976 was not implemented for several years. He could neither establish an effective central rule in the country which would carry out his dictates, nor succeed in legitimizing his control over Lebanon by means of a Syrian–Lebanese treaty or by a long-term sanction from the Arab League.[30] Moreover, not only was Asad unsuccessful in integrating Lebanon into his Greater Syria strategy, but the deployment of some 30,000 Syrian troops in Lebanon in fact weakened his military posture vis-à-vis Israel, in addition to draining his economic resources.

No less crucial was Asad's inability to dominate the two main power factors in Lebanon – the Lebanese Forces and the PLO – after weakening them in 1976. In fact, these two elements remained fairly independent of Syrian control in their respective regions – Mount Lebanon and southern Lebanon – thus creating a *de facto* partition of the country in defiance of both the ideological and the strategic notions of Asad. The PLO 'state within a state' in southern Lebanon was sealed off from the Syrians, ironically, by the Israeli 'red line'. Not only was Asad unable to master this PLO enclave, but as the political circumstances changed he made a rapprochement with Arafat and helped the PLO strengthen its military infrastructure in southern Lebanon. This he did in the aftermath of Sadat's visit to Jerusalem (November 1977) and following the Israeli invasion of southern Lebanon (March 1978). At that point Asad needed the co-operation of Arafat against the Sadat initiative and was anxious to prove to the PLO his commitment to assist it against a future Israeli assault. Another common interest which developed between Asad and Arafat in that period regarding the Lebanese scene was the growing challenge of the Maronite–Israeli alliance. The co-operation was gaining momentum following the election of Begin as Israeli prime minister, with Israel providing training and large quantities of arms to the Lebanese Forces under the command of Bashir Jumayyil.

Encouraged by Begin's assistance as well as by Asad's fresh regional isolation and severe domestic problems, the Lebanese Forces were determined by 1978 to liberate Lebanon from the Syrian occupation. Waging guerrilla warfare against Syrian troops throughout 1978, mainly in Beirut, Bashir calculated that his actions would undermine the Syrian presence in Lebanon, while the Syrian counter-measures would provoke an Israeli military intervention.[31] The Syrian army indeed retaliated harshly against the Lebanese Forces as well as against Maronite regions, conquering two districts in northern Lebanon, but avoiding the occupation of the Maronite heartland. In October 1978 a ceasefire was achieved, following intensive diplomatic activities. It lasted until 1980. The Maronite Phalangists provoked a fierce major clash with the Syrian army in spring 1981 by taking over Zahle, a Christian town situated in the strategically important Biqa valley, and by destroying a Syrian military unit. Determined to meet this Maronite challenge, even at the risk of a confrontation with Israel, Asad ordered his troops to crush the Phalangist militia and to shell Zahle's civilian population. And when Israel, in a warning signal, shot down two Syrian helicopters near Zahle, Asad ordered the deployment of ground-to-air missiles in that area.[32] This bold action by Asad, a violation of the 1976 Syrian–Israeli tacit understanding over Lebanon, was one of the causes of the 1982 Israeli–Syrian war, which for a while brought an end to the Syrian presence in most of Lebanon.

Asad's Camp David Trauma

Asad's confrontation with the Maronite–Israeli alliance, which caused him grave trouble in the late 1970s and led to his eviction from most of Lebanon in 1982, had been interrelated in certain ways with the Camp David agreement. This 1978 agreement between Egypt and Israel, under American auspices, dealt a severe blow to Asad's important strategic and regional ascendancy and to his new understanding with the US, both of which he had achieved in 1977. The deep rupture between him and Sadat, the fast deterioration of his relations with Carter, coupled with his domestic predicament, had thrown him into what was at the time perhaps the worst period in his political career. Thus Asad's brief regional (intra-Arab) leap following the October 1976 Riyadh summit meeting was seriously threatened by mid-1977, ironically by Carter's initiative to reconvene the Geneva peace conference (which Asad cautiously favoured). As it happened, distrusting Sadat because of his separate post-1973 agreement with Israel and his American orientation, Asad insisted on a single Arab delegation to Geneva as a way to reduce Sadat's room for 'manoeuvring'. Sadat for his part, having 'much contempt for President Hafiz al-Asad of Syria was obviously alarmed by the American emphasis on Geneva as a real venue for negotiation, fearing Asad would gain a veto power over his moves'.[33] Sadat possibly was also concerned about Asad's regional ascendancy, his misguided ambition for all-Arab leadership, his relations with the Soviet Union as well as his hard line regarding negotiations with Israel. Worried that Asad's position would foil the chances of a peace agreement with Israel, and having other important considerations, Sadat made his spectacular trip to Jerusalem in November 1977.[34] Asad reacted with great fury. On the day of Sadat's arrival in Jerusalem, 19 November, an official day of mourning was declared throughout Syria; Syrian official statements and the state-controlled media attacked Sadat as a 'traitor', 'trader of blood', and compared him with Nazi collaborators such as Pétain or Quisling, or with men such as Neville Chamberlain and Rudolf Hess.[35]

At first, still hoping that Sadat would not carry on his peace initiative with Israel, Asad refrained from attacking Sadat personally. Only after the Camp David accords did he declare that 'the enemies of the Arabs could not have achieved a greater victory'. '[Sadat] turned his back on the Arab and on Egypt's Arab history. . . . in the near or distant future Sadat will participate with Begin in conducting an offensive operation against us.'[36] Asad then endeavoured to repair the severe damage caused by Sadat to his regional and international stature, and with a 'singlemindedness reminiscent of Bismarck' he tried to form a new Arab bloc under his own leadership. Such an alliance should have made it possible for Asad to pursue a comprehensive political settlement under the new combined aegis of the two superpowers as well as to work for a new strategic balance rendering Asad a credible military option against Israel independently of Egypt. Yet as we have seen, Asad's previous attempts to create an Eastern Front–Fertile Crescent alliance or a Greater Syria union had not succeeded owing to Iraqi rejectionism, Jordan's independent tendency, the PLO's evasiveness and Lebanon's civil war. This time Asad failed to form a solid and credible Arab alliance mainly because of the negative attitude of Iraq (whose huge military force would have made her a highly important component in such an alliance). Despite Asad's strong urging, Iraq's president, Ahmad Hasan Bakr, undermined the creation of an effective anti-Sadat Arab bloc.

In the Tripoli Bloc meeting, convening early in December 1977 as a reaction to Sadat's initiative, the Iraqis demanded that Asad disavow UN Resolutions 242 and 338, withdraw from Lebanon and allow the PLO complete freedom of action through the Syrian border into Israel. When Asad replied that 'a rejection of Resolution 242 would necessarily mean war with Israel and such a decision could not be taken lightly', the Iraqis walked out of the conference.[37] The Front of Steadfastness and Liberation which was subsequently established by the Tripoli Bloc conference (comprised of Syria, Algeria, Libya, the PDRY and the PLO) reluctantly supported Asad's position regarding a 'just . . . lasting peace' (i.e. political settlement) and decided to increase the financial assistance to Syria, being the 'principal confrontation state' in the Front. Yet the Tripoli Bloc did not signify that Asad had become the leader of the new Front bloc, nor did this Front prove to be a cohesive or effective organization.

Algeria, Libya and the PDRY were geographically remote from Syria, and their financial support was pending future developments, including a war with Israel. The latter condition, made in the third conference of the Front in Damascus (September 1978), provoked an angry reaction from Asad: 'I tell you unequivocally that the Syrian people which have stood alone for thirty years will continue to stand firmly, even if nobody will help them with one *qirsh* [penny]. Our people will tighten its belt and we shall persist in our way, since this is our national duty.'[38]

A more promising alternative to the problematic Steadfastness Front was soon made available by the unexpected suggestion of Iraq early in October 1978 to work closely with Syria in foiling the Camp

David accords. By the end of October 1978 Asad and Bakr signed in Baghdad a Charter for Joint National Action, which provided for the 'closest form of unity ties' including 'complete military unity' as well as 'economic, political and cultural unification'. The Charter described 'this historical pan-Arab step' (an Iraqi term) as 'a serious search "for greater strength in confronting the present Zionist onslaught . . . against the Arab nation" '.[39] Asad expected Iraq to provide Syria with strategic depth to balance Egypt's defection, to help him convince Jordan to join a new Eastern Front against Israel, and to persuade Saudi Arabia to give Syria more financial assistance to buy Soviet arms. By contrast, however, Asad was presumably disturbed by the Iraqi intentions not only to use the new union for her own regional ascendancy, but also to dominate it, to lead the unified Ba'th Party, and, with the help of the troops Iraq insisted on sending to Syria, even to topple Asad's regime. Thus although giving the impression that he had initiated the unity talks, Asad rejected Iraqi demands for full merger between the states and for immediate deployment of Iraqi troops in Syria – advocating a step-by-step approach. Consequently, by summer 1979, the unity talks were suspended by Iraq after an alleged discovery of a foreign (Syrian) plot to overthrow Saddam Hussein, the newly self-appointed Iraqi president. Asad reacted coolly and condescendingly: 'Maybe it is necessary and advisable to let some time pass until our brothers in Iraq are ready to embark again on a common way. This is entirely up to the Iraqi leadership. We will do our part.'[40]

Subsequently, in 1980, after the alleged discovery of another Syrian plot in Baghdad, the Iraqi government expelled the Syrian ambassador, and Syria retaliated in the same fashion. With the eruption of the Iraqi–Iranian war a while later, Syrian–Iraqi relations sank to their lowest ebb. This setback was soon followed by King Hussein's decision finally to pull away from his association with Asad and move towards a close relationship with Iraq. Losing his last potential military ally against Israel, and an additional indirect link to the US, late in 1980 Asad moved several military divisions to the Jordanian border in an unsuccessful attempt to exert pressure on Hussein.

With the total collapse of his ambitious regional Arab strategy (except for close relations with the PLO), bogged down in the Lebanese quagmire, exposed to a growing Israeli threat, and alienated again from the US (following the Camp David accords), Asad finally agreed (or asked?) in October 1980 to sign a friendship and co-operation treaty with the Soviet Union. In return he apparently expected to

147

obtain massive Soviet military assistance which would enable him to create a strategic balance with Israel without the help of other Arab states. In addition to strengthening his ties with pro-Soviet regimes in Libya and the PDRY – his Tripoli Bloc allies – Asad might have calculated that closer relations with the USSR would also help bolster his own shaky position in Syria.[41]

Indeed, in 1980 the fierce domestic opposition to his regime, led by the Muslim Brothers, reached its highest peak since Asad had assumed power in 1970: anti-regime violence spread in the major Syrian cities, nearly reaching the dimensions of an armed rebellion and threatening the stability and legitimacy of Asad's rule in the country – and, for perhaps the first time, throwing Asad himself off balance.

12 The Islamic *Jihad* and the Hama Massacre

For generations prior to the Ba'th takeover, political life in Syria had been greatly influenced by the country's large Sunni Muslim conservative population and by its powerful Muslim religious leadership, the *ulama*. Drawing on the allegiance and support of their followers and sometimes resorting to violence, these leaders resisted government attempts at secularization and modernization which eroded the Islamic character of the state as well as the economic interests of those leaders.[1] Recruiting partly from the *ulama* and other religious functionaries and partly from the traditional Muslim urban middle and lower classes, the Muslim Brothers movement was established in Syria in the late 1930s. It was based on the model and teachings of the original Muslim Brothers movement in Egypt[2] and operated also under other names, like Shabab Muhammad (Muhammad's Youth). Among their leaders, all of whom came from *ulama* families, the most conspicuous were the first superintendent-general Mustafa al-Sibai (1945–61) and his successor, Isam al-Attar (1961–72).[3] Under their spiritual guidance the Brothers openly struggled against Syrian reformist or leftist rulers who attempted to change or weaken Islamic institutions and norms in the country.[4] Yet the Brothers' political views were also voiced by several independent politicians or by members of various nationalist parties. For example, in the 1947 national elections following Syria's independence three Muslim Brothers representatives and followers were elected to the parliament; in 1954 there were five; and following the 1961 elections ten Brothers and followers held seats in the parliament (out of 150). Significantly, among their members were General Nahlawi, the leader of the 1961 coup against the

Egyptian–Syrian union, and Dr Dawalibi, Syria's prime minister in the early 1960s.

With the ascendancy of the Ba'th regime in Syria in 1963, the Brothers were outlawed, and an era of fierce conflict was opened between the Muslim conservative forces and the new Ba'th rulers. The Ba'th regimes carried out for the first time from 1963 to 1970 a far-reaching policy aimed at decreasing the role of Islam in public life, and in effect separating Islam from the state. This bold and unprecedented secularist policy was manifested in diminishing the powers, duties and income of the various religious functionaries and reducing religious teachings in state schools. Second, the harsh socialistic measures of the Ba'th, i.e. nationalization of big farms and factories and strict government control of private commercial enterprise, seriously damaged the economic interests of the traditional Muslim urban middle classes. These classes were also dismayed by government development projects in the rural areas and minority regions, allegedly made at the expense of the big cities.[5] Third, large sections of the Sunni Muslim population were intensely antagonized by the ascendancy and rule of neo-Ba'thist Alawites (under Jadid's leadership since 1966), whom they regarded as socially inferior (former servants) and religiously heretical. Not only did these Alawite rulers carry on the secularist and socialist policies, they also permitted publication of anti-Islamic and atheistic expressions in the media, and in 1969 they erased the Islamic clauses from the Syrian constitution. Consequently a series of strikes, demonstrations and riots erupted in several Syrian cities during 1964, 1965 and 1967, against the 'Godless' Ba'thist regimes. These disturbances, involving thousands of conservative Muslims, were initiated by the Muslim Brothers, who had gone underground and were led by Marwan Hadid from his headquarters in Hama. All these uprisings were bloodily suppressed by the Syrian army and involved the shelling of the Great Mosque of Hama (in 1964) and the arrest of many religious leaders.[6]

Asad, serving as defence minister from 1966, apparently did not share the uncompromising doctrinaire attitude of Jadid, the regime's leader, towards these Muslim religious leaders. Characteristically, he sought their support on the eve of the 1967 war in a call for *jihad* against Israel and in mobilizing the population behind the regime.[7]

Following his ascent to power in 1970 Asad lifted many of the restrictions imposed by his predecessors on both the private economic sector and the religious institutions and made additional gestures towards the *ulama*. He raised 2,000 religious functionaries in rank, appointed an *alim* as minister of religious endowments, encouraged the construction of mosques and revived the Islamic formulation of the presidential oath in the Syrian constitution. While hailing the role of Islam and of the Muslim leaders in national life Asad endeavoured to underscore his public image as a faithful Muslim. Verified as an authentic Sunni Muslim by the Mufti of Damascus, Sheikh Ahmad Kaftaru, Asad participated in public prayers and other religious ceremonies, and made the minor *hajj* (*umra* or pilgrimage to Mecca at an irregular time).[8] In 1972 he published a special edition of the Koran with himself photographed in uniform on the first page (a gesture which the pious Muslims regarded as an insult to Islam). The October 1973 war gave Asad an opportunity to fulfil again the important Islamic commandment of *jihad*. As already described, Asad and the state media used various other Islamic and Koranic terms and notions in order to render a religious (as well as nationalist) colouring to the war, encourage the soldiers and mobilize the support of the population.[9] Parallel to these Islamic gestures Asad, in an attempt to blur the notion that the Alawites were heretics, had the Shi'i Imam of Lebanon, Musa al-Sadr, verify in 1973 that the Alawites were Shi'i Muslims.[10]

Consequently, these great endeavours, accompanied by strict inspection of the Brothers' activities, helped Asad neutralize for a time the Muslim opposition to his regime, although he by no means gained their acquiescence to his *de facto* non-Islamic Alawite-minority rule. Indeed, when early in 1973 he deleted from the draft of the permanent Syrian constitution the clause stipulating that Islam should be the religion of the president, fierce demonstrations erupted in most Syrian towns. These violent disturbances, which occurred intermittently for several months (February to May 1973), were organized and led by the Muslim Brothers and *ulama*, who called for *jihad* against Asad's atheist regime and labelled Asad the 'enemy of Allah'. They denounced the Alawites' domination of the state and the army, the creation of a new 'aristocratic' class, as well as the corruption of the regime and the collapse of the economy. These riots, however, were firmly put down by the army, and resulted in the deaths or arrests of many Muslim Brothers and *ulama*.[11] In addition, some forty Sunni Muslim officers were reportedly arrested and executed for allegedly attempting to assassinate Asad.[12] These rigorous actions, coupled with Asad's decision to reinstate the Islamic clause in the Syrian permanent constitution, served to offset further major outbreaks of Muslim resistance to Asad's regime until the summer of 1976. Asad's support of the Christian Maronites and his military actions against the Muslim radicals and the PLO in Lebanon provoked that summer a fresh cycle of violent actions by the Muslim Brothers in Syria.

Yet this new phase of Muslim opposition to Asad was now characterized by well-organized and effective urban guerrilla warfare directed against military, government and Ba'thist officials and institutions as well as against Russian advisers. Indeed, under the leadership of the new Hama-born superintendent-general, Adnan Sa'd al-Din (Marwan Hadid was arrested in 1976 and died in jail), the Muslim Brothers took a more militant course in their *jihad* against Asad. Adopting the term *mujahidun* (holy warriors), the Muslim commandos were well equipped, trained and financed. Reportedly, some of them received military training in the Ivory Coast and in Jordan as well as in Palestinian and Phalangist camps in Lebanon. Jordan and Iraq apparently also provided military equipment and financial aid during various periods, while allegedly the US, Israel, Saudi Arabia and Egypt assisted the *mujahidun* in other ways. Financial and propaganda support was also provided by various Muslim organizations in Europe, notably in Germany and England.[13] The new *mujahidun* were made up of several thousands of men in their twenties or early thirties, ardently attached to their beliefs, daring to the point of recklessness. Many were university students, school-teachers, engineers, physicians and the like.[14] Indeed, extending beyond the traditional urban middle classes, the Muslim Brothers also drew their members from the young intelligentsia and the professional classes.

In addition to their opposition to Asad's venture in Lebanon and to his minority Alawite rule, a large section of the urban population harboured grievances against the widespread corruption in the government, the deteriorating economic conditions as well as Asad's brutal suppression of civil liberties. A manifestation of these grievances was published by the Islamic Front, or the Islamic Revolution, which was formed in Syria in 1980 and was composed of broad sections of the population including both the left and the right.[15] In the Declaration and Programme (or manifesto) the Islamic Front stated:

> In Syria, the Islamic Revolution is, at present, bearing the greater share of the responsibility of Muslims to confront the enemies of God and man. . . . The great majority of our nation, due to poverty, ignorance, illness and autocracy, became a victim of a well-planned brainwashing operation. . . . Those leaders flattered Islam, kept a temporary truce with it and did not hesitate to use it to serve their aims and strengthen

their rule. . . . The experiment of the Ba'th Party in power was, and still is, a total disaster. On the internal level, the party squashed freedom, abolished political parties, nationalized the press, threw people into prisons and hanged those who dared to voice their disapproval. . . . the party exiled the honest ones and favoured the agents and corrupt ones in its orbit, an easy way of unlawful earning and illegal riches. . . . The image of democracy was also distorted by the party; the constitution became a lie, referendums changed to comedy acts, and the so-called people's organizations were a disgrace. Worst of all, the Syrian regions fell into the mire of sectarianism. . . . One of the mocking acts of this sectarianism was the promotion to the highest position of the minister of defence who was directly responsible for the defeat of 5 June 1967. . . . Hafiz Asad and his brother Rifat . . . with the help of certain sectarian elements took absolute control of power, with their autocratic rule they transgressed beyond bounds in the lands and heaped mischief on mischief. They enslaved the Muslims and stripped them of their wealth, deadened their hearts and spread corruption. . . . Despite the frantic efforts to strengthen the power of Hafiz Asad and praise his abilities, they failed terribly . . . and only helped to increase the people's hatred for him. Furthermore, 9 or 10 per cent of the population cannot be allowed to decimate the majority.[16]

In other publications of the Islamic Front, notably *Al-Nadhir* (read: *Al-Nazir*), other references were made to Asad as 'the tyrant of Syria and his puppet regime', the 'snake', 'the poisoned dagger imperialism employs', 'arch-villain', 'bloodthirsty dictator', 'guilty of *kufr*' (heresy); a 'Maronite', 'a Jew who hates Muslims' and 'Asad Lubnan wa-Arnab al-Jawlan' (the Lion in Lebanon and the Rabbit of the Golan).[17] Aiming to eliminate Asad and his regime and establish an Islamic state in Syria, the *mujahidun* confined themselves at first (until 1979) to 'persistent minor blows in the hope of provoking Syria's rulers, involving them in repressive policies, and estranging them further from the people'. They concentrated on hit-and-run attacks on senior Alawite functionaries and officers, army headquarters, intelligence offices and the like.[18] Among the several dozens of personalities who were killed by the *mujahidun* were close associates of Asad: the rector of Damascus University, Professor Muhammad al-Fadil, who served as Asad's adviser, and General Razuq, commander of the missile unit.[19]

The noticeable success of the *mujahidun* in committing these acts of terror also prompted other unsatisfied elements and opposition groups among the population to join forces with the Muslim Brothers or to operate separately in an attempt to topple Asad's regime. One of these groups was Palestinians residing in refugee camps near Damascus (especially at Yarmuk). Intensely antagonistic to Asad's military actions against the PLO in Lebanon (Abu Iyad: 'Personally I believe that the fall of President Asad's regime is necessary'), they demonstrated violently against the regime and carried out various subversive activities partly in league with the *mujahidun*.[20] Reportedly pro-Jadid leftist elements, including Alawites and backed by the hostile Iraqi regime, were also engaged in anti-Asad activities. So were Druze from Mount Houran who during 1976 protested against Asad's atttacks on the Lebanese Druze leader Kamal Junblatt.[21] And although Asad's security forces made many hundreds of arrests among civilians and soldiers alike, a state of unrest prevailed in the country, while Asad's regime remained just a gunshot away from collapse.

By mid-1979 the public's restlessness and opposition grew deeper, first because of the continued involvement in Lebanon which, costing Syria US$1 million a day, caused serious problems to the economy. Second, large sections of the Syrian population, already dissatisfied with their economic predicament – inflation, soaring prices, food shortages, and so on – were critical of Asad's regional policy, which practically isolated Syria in the Arab world. By contrast the successful Islamic revolution in Iran encouraged many Syrian Muslims, notably the *mujahidun*, to believe that they could likewise overthrow Asad's regime.[22] Indeed, becoming more daring and violent, the *mujahidun* struck spectacular blows against army barracks and police stations as well as government and party offices. In June 1979, for example, they attacked with grenades and machine-gun fire 200 Alawite cadets of the Artillery Academy of Aleppo, killing at least sixty of them and wounding many others.[23] Possibly encouraged by this operation, 'On November 2, 1979 the "Leadership of the Islamic Revolution in Syria proclaimed . . . that their Jihad was now entering a new phase of intensity that would ultimately lead to the fall of Hafiz Asad." '[24] Thus in early March 1980 the *mujahidun*'s violent actions provoked a series of violent popular disturbances and riots by various sections of the population, lasting several days in Aleppo, Homs and Hama, and in June an attempt was made to assassinate Asad. Armed clashes between the *mujahidun* and the security forces continued throughout the summer in most Syrian towns and by late 1980 reports coming from Syria pointed out that 'Asad faced a generalized rebellion . . . that threatened his rule'.[25] In December 1980 the Muslim commandos reportedly attacked the (temporary) headquarters of Rifat Asad in Aleppo as well as other government establishments, killing scores of soldiers and government officials.[26] In spring 1981 the *mujahidun* attacked Alawite villages near Latakia, and staged an open revolt in Hama; in the fall of 1981 they set off several car bombs in Damascus, destroying important intelligence and government centres while killing many military and civilian personnel.[27] Thus by late 1981 the conflict between the Muslim *mujahidun* and Asad reached a point of zero-sum struggle, as Asad reportedly said to his Alawite comrades: 'It is us or them.'[28] On the one hand the bold *mujahidun* were now backed by a unified Islamic Front which consisted of, or was supported by, large sections of the Syrian population. Not a few of these anti-Asad oppositionists indeed belonged to the same sections from which the ruling Ba'th Party had derived its membership in the 1950s and 1960s. These urban intellectuals and professionals were now part of this broad but loose popular coalition which longed for the victory of the Islamic *jihad* against Asad.

On the other hand, Asad, backed by his Alawite community, as well as by Muslim peasants and workers, fighting for his regime and perhaps for his own life, was by no means ready to give in. During the two stages of the Islamic revolt, he tried to isolate the Muslim Brothers from the population by discrediting them, at the same time presenting himself to the public as a devout Muslim. Thus, following his invasion of Lebanon in June 1976, in explaining his policies there he stated: 'Islam is for justice for all and against injustice to anyone. Islam has prohibited vengeance and revenge . . . because Islam is love and justice and not hatred and animosity. . . . Islam is the greatest revolution in the history of our Arab nation and of humanity . . . and I am a true Muslim with Allah's help.'[29] On another occasion, in 1979, while addressing *ulama* in Aleppo, Asad remarked: 'We have always worked to strengthen religious values in the citizens' hearts. We have stated that Islam is a religion of life and progress.'[30] And in 1981 Asad hailed Islam as 'the religion of progress and the progressives and not the religion of the reaction . . . the religion of the fighters for their bread and liberty and independence . . . the religion of labour and honour for the building of the homeland'.[31]

While reviving his former practice of participation in Muslim religious ceremonies together with the chief (pro-regime) *ulama*, Asad made them denounce the Muslim Brothers as deviants from and 'enemies of Islam' who merely 'hide behind the guise of religion and have nothing in common with [it]'.[32] In addition Asad apparently instructed the Syrian media to denounce the Brothers as 'criminals', 'plotters', 'terrorists', 'gangs of hatred', 'reactionaries', 'Muslim

traitors' who were working with the CIA, Israel and Arab reactionaries against 'national unity and progress' as well as against Arabism
and Islam.[33] Significantly Asad, while displaying in public places
photographs of Khumeini and other Iranian leaders, enlisted the
support of the fundamentalist Islamic regime in Teheran to discredit
the Muslim Brothers in Syria while hailing him and his regime. Thus,
equating the Syrian *mujahidun* with the anti-Khumeini Mujahidun-i
Khalq in Iran, senior Iranian leaders described the Brothers as 'gangs
carrying out the Camp David conspiracy against Syria in collusion
with Egypt, Israel and the United States'. These leaders also attacked
the Brothers' guerrilla activities in Syria as the 'work of pro-Israeli or
rightist elements', while wishing Asad 'success in serving the sacred
ideals of the people of Syria'.[34] Asad was in great need of this Iranian
support. He was no longer in the mood, as he had been in early 1977,
to enjoy Sarkis' funny remark that Asad was not admitted to the
mosques in Syria, since he was considered a 'Maronite' by the
ulama.[35]

Asad was now, perhaps for the first time in his political career,
shaken and furious at the success of the *mujahidun* in isolating him,
questioning his legitimacy and almost carrying out a general rebellion
against his rule. In a series of interviews and public speeches during
1980 and 1981 he fiercely and bitterly attacked the Muslim Brothers
while emphasizing again his adherence to true Islam:

> Syria was and still is the torch of Arab nationalism, and the banner of
> Islam will continue to be hoisted in our country. Those who wish to
> distort Islam will not succeed in achieving their aim, and distort the
> grand ideals embraced by Islam. . . . Islam is for achieving the nation's
> goals and whoever does not do it has the devil, while we have Islam.[36]

> We are proud of Islam. When Islam was in danger we came forward to
> defend it. But the voice of the murderers was not heard then, and they
> did nothing to defend Islam. Today they carry the banner of the defence
> of Islam and its values, and under this guise they do very ugly things. . . .
> I, as a Syrian citizen, have believed in Islam . . . for more than thirty
> years. I pray but they do not acknowledge my Islam. . . . our enemies
> will vanish, because they are the enemies of the homeland, the enemies
> of the people, the enemies of Islam, in which they trade . . . the enemies
> of revolution, Arabism and Islam. . . . we shall not make concessions to
> the murderers . . . they do not know any limits . . . they killed the grand
> *ulama* [in Aleppo].[37]

> In order to kill the revolution they will have to kill the people, and this is

impossible. They should know that Asad is no one but one of you. Every citizen in this country is Hafiz Asad.[38]

They have ties with colonialism. . . . They tried to assassinate Nasser because of his stand against colonialism. . . . They attempted to kill Syria because of her position against colonialism, imperialism and Zionism. . . .[39]

Alongside his persistent efforts to discredit the Muslim Brothers and undermine popular support for them, Asad took elaborate actions both personally and through his government to appease all classes of society and particularly to strengthen the allegiance of the peasants, workers, intelligentsia and youth to himself and his regime. Thus, in addition to stressing, time and again, his foreign-policy achievements – notably the struggle against Israel and for Arab unity – Asad put special emphasis on his domestic policies, pointing out the remarkable political stability and 'popular democracy' which had been accomplished in Syria during the first seven years of his rule. Asad indicated the continuing work in the economic, social and cultural spheres: the strengthening of both the public and private economic sectors, especially in respect of agriculture and the rural areas; the improvement of social conditions and civil liberties with an emphasis on the equality of women; the development of the educational system on all levels 'for the sake of future generations'.[40] Asad, however, was not content merely with stating his goals and citing the achievements of his regime. He and his ministers did not hesitate to admit that grave mistakes had been made by the government and that many problems remained unsolved.

Economic Difficulties and Corruption

The major crucial problems in the social and economic fields towards the end of the 1970s continued to be, even according to Syria's prime minister, General Khulayfawi: corruption and inefficiency in the government bureaucracy and public services, as well as in the public and private economic sectors; inflation, the high cost of living, and shortage of consumer goods, particularly agricultural products; the movement of productive peasants to unproductive jobs in the cities as well as the growing brain-drain of professionals; illiteracy, particularly in the rural areas, and a low level of educational standards.[41]

Yet, despite public commitments, actions and cabinet reshuffles made by Asad during his second term in office (from 1978) to repair the mistakes and to solve the problems, very little was changed by the early 1980s. For example, under Asad's directive a 'committee for the investigation of illegal profits' was established in August 1977 to combat corruption, but to no avail. Certain quarters in Syria who opposed the work of this committee argued that in view of the widespread involvement of high-ranking officials, uprooting corruption would weaken the whole structure of the regime.[42] One of the high-ranking officials was Asad's brother Rifat, who was notorious for his extensive corruption. He allegedly headed a large network of business rackets ranging from legitimate trading and contracting firms, casinos and nightclubs to the smuggling of hashish and luxury consumer goods in Lebanon. Yet ironically Rifat was assigned to lead a new anti-corruption drive by the Ba'th regional congress in 1979.[43] Significantly, one of the first to be sacked by Rifat was Muhammad Halabi, who had been appointed in 1977 as prime minister, with a mandate to fight corruption.

Thus, despite Asad's personal intervention to increase salaries to public employees, supply more consumer goods and tighten government inspection, corruption in its various manifestations remained in the early 1980s (and thereafter) widespread in the highest echelons of the new ruling elite. And despite the development projects in the rural areas, most of the major economic and social problems remained critically unabated.[44]

Even Syrian intellectual leaders and writers complained late in 1979 that 'As for the social problem, it starts with bread and ends in the issue of freedom. Neither the bread problem nor the freedom issue have been solved, nor [the issues] which are between these two problems.' Criticizing the lack of civil liberties and the alienation of the government from the public, these intellectuals also spoke about 'the disintegration of the regime's structure and its institutions, and the lack of trust in it [by the population]. The regime is remote from the people. . . . the reason for it is the lie nobody believes . . . not even the weather forecast which is broadcast on the radio. . . . The street is now in a state of corruption – bribery, commission fees, speculation, officers who associate with companies and assist smugglers to take booty from Lebanon. These acts have been committed also by people who are in the government.'[45]

Confirming this self-criticism, the foreign media reported late in 1979 and in the early 1980s that 'most of Syria's biggest smugglers are generals. The arrogant flaunting of wealth and power by the Alawite "new rich" is even more galling to the Syrian establishment because Alawites are such "low-class" people. . . . Inflation, shortage of food and other basic items and prevailing corruption in government offices are cited as the main reason for the growing discontent.'[46] Indeed, Asad, although personally uncorrupt and well intentioned, was practically unable to uproot corruption, which had infested his ruling elite; nor could he successfully implement his new reforms, because he was too slow and too late in introducing them. Thus a report published in April 1980 remarked: 'for the first time, too, it is the president himself who is being condemned. A few months ago . . . his critics claimed that whatever the state of Syria the president was a man of great personal integrity. Now they ask could an honourable man allow the state's corruption to spread into his own family?'[47]

Repression and Massacre

Consequently, facing what was almost a general opposition, Asad by early 1980 had to fall back on and draw support from the sections of population which had remained loyal to him – peasants, certain groups of workers, and students. While dissolving the councils of various professional associations who opposed him (doctors, lawyers and engineers), Asad initiated emergency meetings of Ba'th-affiliated organizations and encouraged them to take action for the sake of 'national unity' vis-à-vis the Muslim Brother 'criminals'. Most of these organizations announced in the media their total support for Asad, and the peasants' and workers' unions decided to form armed units to help the regime combat its enemies.[48] In at least one case, a group of teenage girls, the Daughters of the Revolution, apparently misinterpreted Asad's intentions: to his dismay, they ripped the *hijab* (traditional head cover) off Muslim women in Damascus streets.[49]

The most reliable, committed and efficient group that could ultimately support and help Asad were the members of his Alawite sect. As it happened, the Muslim Brothers approached the Alawite community with repeated appeals and warnings, requesting them to dissociate themselves from Asad:

> We hope that the followers of the Alawite sect, to which the people's affliction Hafiz Asad and his butcher playboy brother belong, will positively participate in preventing the tragedy from reaching its sad end. We also appeal to those attentive members in the sect to revise their accounts. We declare without deceit or intrigue that we shall be happy

to see them shake off the guardianship of the corrupt elements which drove them to this dangerous predicament.[50]

As early as March 1978 Asad started to tighten his Alawite security belt by appointing his close Alawite comrade Muhammad Khawli, chief of air force intelligence, as head of the National Security Bureau in charge of co-ordinating the work of the various security services. General Khawli replaced General Naji Jamil, a Sunni Muslim, who had failed to uncover and foil the Brothers' terrorist activities since 1976. Being a strong person Jamil may have been considered a potential threat to Asad's leadership as well as to Rifat's senior position in the regime.

As it happened Rifat was given a major role in the fight against the *mujahidun*. He was commander of the powerful Alawite-manned Defence Detachments. Mostly acting as a trouble-shooter dealing with rebellious outbreaks, Rifat's use of cruel measures possibly increased Muslim antagonism and enhanced the cycle of violence and counter-violence between the government forces and the *mujahidun*. Rifat was reportedly prepared to 'exterminate a million opposition forts and sacrifice a million fighters' in order to do away with the rebellious Brothers.[51]

Rifat as well as other army officers, Sunnis and Alawites alike (an unknown number of Sunni soldiers and officers refused to participate in the operations, or defected from their units),[52] employed brutal force unprecedented in modern Syrian history, against the *mujahidun* and those suspected as their followers. Apart from the direct military confrontations with the Brothers (in which the famous Sunni-manned 3rd Armoured Division was also involved) the various security forces assisted by hundreds of KGB advisers reportedly arrested several thousand suspects, tortured many of them, killed several hundred unarmed people (including prisoners) and caused the 'disappearance' of scores of suspects during the late 1970s and early 1980s.[53]

According to the 1983 report of Amnesty International (which refers also to previous years),

Syrian security forces are responsible for systematic violation of human rights, including torture and political killing. . . . [The report] cites overwhelming evidence that thousands of people have been arrested and wrongfully detained without chance of appeal and in some cases tortured and even killed by security forces. . . . [The report] lists 23 methods of ill-treatment and torture reported by former detainees, including electric shock, burning, whipping with braided steel cable, sexual violations and forcing detainees to watch relatives being tortured or sexually assaulted. . . .

The security forces are also believed to be responsible for political killings of selected individuals or groups and to have assassinated several opponents of the government abroad. . . . [It cites] six cases of mass political killings alleged to have been carried out by the authorities between March 1980 and February 1982. They include the reported killing on 27 June 1980 of between 600 and 1000 inmates of Palmyra prison suspected of belonging to the banned Muslim Brotherhood.[54]

In addition to these gross repressive measures, in further attempts to split and weaken the Muslim Brothers Asad passed in July 1980 Law no. 49 in the Syrian parliament stating:

Article 1. Any person belonging to the group of Muslim Brothers will be considered a criminal subject to death penalty.
Article 2. Any member of this group will be exempted from the penalty . . . if he declares his withdrawal from this group within one month of the implementation of this law.
Article 4. Any member of the Muslim Brothers will be exempted from the penalty for misdemeanours committed prior to the effective date of this Act . . . if he surrenders within one month. . . .[55]

Before the enactment of this law Asad ordered the release of more than 100 liberal and leftist political prisoners; and later he extended the period of amnesty to Brothers who surrendered.[56] Yet, although several hundred Muslim Brothers subsequently surrendered to the authorities, the Islamic *jihad* guerrilla warfare spread so much further that the Asad regime felt 'besieged . . . surrounded by a belt of enmity and conspiracy'.[57] Asad reacted for the first time, as noted above, in great fury and desperation. He was deeply hurt by the Islamic rebellion and by the attempt on his life. According to a report in April 1980, 'The president's recent speeches have gone down badly in Syria. Where once Assad addressed his people in careful, constructive language that avoided insult and rhetoric, he now attacks the state's presumed enemies with anger and bitterness. He sounds like a man in despair. By vilifying the Muslim Brotherhood he has given them credibility, and by his clumsy reaction to the Brotherhood's ruthless assassinations he has sapped his own credibility.'[58]

In late 1980 Asad reportedly 'took personal command of the repression . . . turning the security forces loose. . . . There is blood now between the regime and part of the population for the first time.'[59]

In March 1981 Patrick Seale, veteran Middle East correspondent for the London *Observer* and one of the foreign journalists most respected by Asad, reported with a certain personal agony:

So President Asad, the longest-serving ruler of independent Syria and an astute and reasonable man, now finds himself running a morally flawed regime practising gangster methods indistinguishable from those of his adversaries. To meet terror Asad has resorted to ferocious counter-terror, indiscriminate arrests, beating and torture, wholesale destruction of buildings thought to be sheltering suspects, reprisals against the families of the accused, shoot-outs and mass killings. . . . It is a sad come-down after the hopes and achievements of his early years. Apart from repression, another criticism which can be levelled against him is the narrow, essentially sectarian, basis of his authority. Little attempt is made to disguise the fact that this regime is run by and for the Alawite minority. . . .[60]

By the end of 1981 it seemed that Asad's fierce counter-measures had succeeded in suppressing the Muslim Brothers throughout Syria, with the conspicuous exception of Hama, the so-called 'head of the snake'.

The final showdown between Asad and the *mujahidun* was thus imminent, and both sides were apparently preparing for it. According to certain reports at the end of 1981 and the beginning of 1982, Rifat was assigned by his brother Asad to besiege Hama, the stronghold of the Islamic *jihad*, in preparation for a total purge. Twelve thousand soldiers conducted house-to-house searches, while committing acts of repression against the population, including the destruction of buildings and the killing of people ('the blood is flowing in Hama').[61] Another report claimed that the *mujahidun* in Hama were preparing a general uprising in the country during this period, calculating that the Sunni Muslim soldiers in the Syrian army would rebel against Asad when sent to quell the revolt.[62] Whether provoked by the security forces or not, some 500 *mujahidun* attacked after midnight of 2 February 1982 the main centres of the regime in Hama – government buildings, police stations, Ba'th Party and intelligence offices – killing some 250 people (mostly officials), including the governor. Taking control of the entire city for about ten days, the rebels called for a *jihad* against Asad's 'atheist' regime. Suppression of this rebellion by Asad's troops was very bloody and devastating: parts of the city, including mosques and churches, were destroyed by heavy artillery; between 10,000 and 30,000 people, including children, were indiscriminately killed; women were raped, and property was looted.[63] The terrible crushing of the Hama revolt not only broke the military backbone of the Muslim Brothers but also served as a vivid warning to them, as well as to other opposition groups, against further acts of disobedience. And although in recent years small groups of Muslim Brothers have occasionally conducted guerrilla attacks on army units, the *mujahidun* ceased for the time being to be a threat to Asad.[64]

So Asad managed to withstand the challenge of the Islamic opposition, but he had to pay a very high price. Although he succeeded in intimidating the Sunni Muslim majority population, he also further alienated them. Following the Hama massacre, 800,000 Syrians reportedly left the country, while discontented groups in Syria formed a new anti-Asad alliance: the so-called National Alliance for the Liberation of Syria, containing the Islamic Front, pro-Iraqi Ba'thists, Nasserites and socialists.[65]

13 Asad's Predicament; Terror and Strategic Balance

In the aftermath of the Hama massacre in February 1982 and for the following year or two, it seemed as if Asad and his regime were (or rather continued to be) in sharp decline. Asad's considerable achievements during the first decade of his rule in expanding the basis of his regime and gaining popular legitimacy suffered a severe setback. He was now greatly isolated, virtually running an Alawite military dictatorship which was feared and hated by large sections of the population. Even in his major power-base, the army, cracks started to show: a significant number of Sunni and Alawite officers (reportedly 140, among them a general and many colonels) and pilots had been involved in an attempted coup against Asad early in 1982 and were subsequently purged.[1] Several months later, in summer 1982, the Syrian army in Lebanon suffered heavy blows from the invading Israeli army, while Asad's beloved air force lost some ninety planes in dogfights.

These traumatic events, as well as other troubles in his domestic and foreign policies, may have undermined Asad's health, which reportedly had been deteriorating in 1980 during the *mujahidun* rebellion. In late 1983 Asad suffered a major heart attack, and as he lay seriously ill a struggle for power erupted early in 1984 between Rifat and Asad's other coterie members. Military units were also involved, and, subsequently, another plot to overthrow Asad was reportedly uncovered in the army, resulting in further purges of officers.[2]

Other signs of decline in Asad's regime were reflected in the economic situation, which went from bad to worse, despite continuing development projects, particularly in agriculture.[3] Corruption, smuggling, mismanagement and inefficiency continued to flourish, helping to diminish the real gross domestic product and to encourage inflation.[4]

The great increase of military expenditures and a sharp decrease in income from external sources, notably in foreign exchange, inflated the foreign trade deficit and drained the foreign currency reserves. (For example, while defence costs in 1984 had increased threefold since 1978, comprising in 1984 56 per cent of Syria's current accounts budget and 30 per cent of the total government budget, Arab aid had decreased by the same proportion.)[5]

Syria's crucial economic difficulties during 1982–4 and thereafter were in large part related not only to her growing military build-up vis-à-vis Israel, but also to Asad's increasing political isolation in the Arab world. Indeed, beyond the fact that the Gulf war caused a decrease in Syria's income from the Arab oil-producing states as well as from Syrian workers' remittances from abroad, Asad's co-operation with Iran against Iraq further diminished his foreign currency receipts. For example, his decision in April 1982 to cut the pipelines through which Iraqi oil was exported to the Mediterranean cost him US$600 million in annual transit fees.[6] Furthermore, in political terms, his 'unholy' alliance with Khumeini served to worsen his relations with his Arab neighbours and, in certain respects, diminished his status in the region.

Asad's association with the fundamentalist Islamic regime in Teheran since 1980 has been motivated essentially by his desire to weaken the rival Ba'th regime, Iraq, and gain a leading role in the Arab east. In addition to extorting more financial aid from Saudi Arabia, and obtaining cheap oil from Iran, Asad calculated that his close relations with the Islamic Shi'i regime in Iran could help him in his campaign against the Muslim Brothers in Syria, as well as in his relations with the Shi'is in Lebanon.[7]

Although gaining important benefits from his alliance with Iran, Asad, as we have seen, failed to make use of it in order to split his Islamic opposition. Similarly, his policies towards the Gulf war contributed to Jordan's decision to cool relations with Damascus and to favour a stronger link with Baghdad, to bring about a rapprochement between Iraq and Egypt, and, to some extent, to alienate from Syria the Arab Gulf states including Saudi Arabia. Indeed, despite the strong stance manifested by Asad towards the Arab summit meetings in Fez in 1981 and 1982 (regarding both his relations with Iran and the Saudi peace plan), Asad became, to a large extent, isolated in the Arab world in 1982 because of his failure to pacify Lebanon. With the exception of Libya and the PDRY, Asad was sharply assailed in various parts of the Arab world (although not always by the governments), not only for his alliance with Iran and his 1982 massacre at Hama, but also for his continuing military presence in Lebanon.[8]

Thus when in June 1982 Israel invaded Lebanon and attacked the Syrian army, the other Arab countries refrained from helping Asad to fight Israel, and most of them (with the exception of the Steadfastness Front) continued to criticize Syria for her Lebanese policy.[9]

Defeat in the 1982 War

As it happened, Israel, under the leadership of Prime Minister Begin and Defence Minister Ariel Sharon, while increasing her co-operation with the Phalangists, decided in early June 1982 to wage a war against the PLO and apparently also against the Syrian army in Lebanon.[10] Among the objectives pursued by Sharon, the architect of the 1982 war, was the dual-purpose plan: to push the Syrian army from Lebanon back to Syria and to help re-establish Maronite hegemony under the leadership of Bashir Jumayyil, the commander of the Lebanese Forces.

Without going into the details of the various phases of the war, it should be pointed out briefly that within the first week the IDF defeated the Syrian troops in the Biqa valley, while destroying its ground-to-air missile system in Lebanon, hitting the new T-72 tanks, and shooting down some ninety Syrian planes.[11] Subsequently the IDF drove the Syrian army (and later also the PLO) from Beirut and helped Bashir Jumayyil to be elected as Lebanon's president in September 1982. Asad, being unprepared to fight a full-scale war with Israel, did not employ his troops to prevent the IDF from defeating the PLO in southern Lebanon. But when he realized that the IDF was attacking his troops in the Biqa it was too late to prevent their defeat. And although in later stages the Syrian army fought fiercely against the IDF, its losses were rather humiliating for Asad, particularly in the air battles. His political predicament was equally distressing, as he was pushed out from large parts of Lebanon by the Israeli–Maronite alliance and was unable to prevent Amin Jumayyil, the new Lebanese president, from signing a political agreement with Israel on 17 May 1983.[12]

The Final Rift With Arafat?

Another important issue which severely damaged Asad's prestige and further isolated him in the Arab world was his new and very harsh treatment of the PLO. Indeed, Asad's rapprochement with Arafat following the Camp David accords (1978) had already started to erode in summer 1981 when Arafat accepted the initial plan of Saudi Arabia's King Fahd for a political settlement of the Arab–Israeli conflict. Asad, who rejected this plan, was likewise not pleased with Arafat's decision around that time to conclude a ceasefire agreement with Israel in southern Lebanon without first consulting Damascus. Reportedly Asad reproached Arafat, saying 'You act beyond your capacity.'[13] Nor did Asad approve of Arafat's inclination during that period to develop contacts with Syria's enemies Iraq, Egypt and Jordan, in order to diminish his dependency on Damascus.[14]

Nonetheless, in anticipation of a large Israeli offensive, in late April 1982 Asad and Arafat signed an agreement for joint strategic action vis-à-vis Israel.[15] But when Israel opened her military operation against the PLO on 6 June, the Syrian army, despite previous public commitments by Asad, did virtually nothing to 'defend the Palestinian existence'.[16] Furthermore, taking advantage of the PLO retreat into the Syrian-controlled Biqa valley, and the transfer of PLO commandos from Beirut to Syria, Asad sought to implement his long-standing aim – to put the PLO under his rule. Rejecting this, late in 1982, a PLO leader stated:

> Mr. Assad ... wants an Arafat who, while continuing to enjoy his prestige as the symbol of Palestinian nationalism, is nonetheless just an extension of Syria's will. ... if he thinks that he can reduce us to a carbon copy of himself, he will only push Arafat further into the arms of the Jordanians. ... We cannot have a husband–wife relationship in which the husband says 'You must stick with me but I cannot provide you with breakfast.'[17]

Yet at that juncture the rift between Asad and Arafat reached a crucial point. Arafat's subtle attempts to enter into the Middle East political process with Jordan (and Egypt) following President Reagan's peace initiative of September 1982 apparently finalized Asad's determination to depose Arafat as the PLO leader.

> But the last straw for Assad reportedly came in December 1983 [sic: 1982], when Syria found that Arafat had harbored more than fifty Moslem fundamentalists who had led a bloody religious uprising in

which eighty members of Assad's Alawite sect were killed. 'Assad was totally enraged. . . . He would forgive many things for political expediency, but never the murder of fellow Alawites. . . . Assad simply can't bear Arafat. . . . It's almost a physical revulsion.'[18]

Consequently, rejecting Arafat's repeated requests to meet him, and directing a media smear campaign against him, Asad promoted an internal rebellion within the Fath led by Colonel Abu Musa. By late June 1983 Arafat was deported from Damascus while the commandos loyal to him were besieged by the Syrian army in the Biqa valley. Subsequently these commandos were transferred to Tripoli (northern Lebanon), and late in 1983, under Syrian pressure, they and their leader Arafat were forced to go into exile in Tunis.[19]

Most Arab countries, including Algeria, which was a member of the Tripoli Bloc, decried Asad's repression of the PLO and his attempts to create an alternative leadership to Arafat's. While the oil-producing Arab states cut the financial aid to Syria, the Muslim mufti of Jerusalem, Sheikh Sa'd ad-Din al-Alami, in June 1983 issued a *fatwa* (religious opinion or ruling) calling for Asad to be killed because of his hostile actions against the PLO. In late July 1983 a similar *fatwa* was issued by a group of Iraqi *ulama*, stating:

> Hafiz al-Asad, the oppressive tyrant of Syria, bears the blame for the present state of the [Arab] nations' fate . . . particularly the fate of the Palestinian movement . . . because of the series of crimes he has committed against the Syrian people, the Palestinian people and the Iraqi people . . . in Tal Za'tar, in Hama, in Tadmur [Palmyra] prison . . . in the Biqa [and owing to] the material, moral and military aid he extends to the Khumeini regime together with Qaddafi and the criminal Zionists. . . .[20]

Added to Asad's growing alienation in the Arab world was the hostile attitude of the Reagan administration to his regime and policies. Both dimensions of Reagan's new Middle East policy – the 'strategic consensus' (1981) and his peace initiative (1982) – excluded Syria. And while Asad's formal ally, the USSR, initially stood by when the Syrian army was defeated by the IDF in Lebanon, the US tacitly backed Israel's invasion of Lebanon. Subsequently the US demanded the withdrawal of all 'foreign forces' (including Syrian troops) from Lebanon while helping to bring about the Lebanese–Israeli agreement of May 1983 without ever consulting Asad.[21]

As early as spring 1981 Asad was alleging:

The new administration in the US wants to frighten us from the outset. They started with arrogant threats. . . . The US is a superpower which adopts the ideas and actions of the racist movement [Zionism] and extends to it equipment, arms, money and political guarantees, without any limit . . . by means of the . . . so-called strategic co-operation . . . as a result of the Begin–Reagan agreement the US has moved into a position whereby it stands in a direct confrontation with us, the Arabs.

Accordingly Asad defined the Israeli invasion of Lebanon and the Lebanese–Israeli agreement of May 1983 as 'part of the American–Zionist plan to dominate' the Middle East and as 'worse than the Camp David accords'.[22] The US not only backed the Israeli venture in Lebanon and Israel's agreement with President Amin Jumayyil, but also committed a substantial military contingent to the Multinational Force with the aim of supporting the new regime of Amin Jumayyil. In the autumn and winter of 1983 US forces even went into military action against Jumayyil's enemies, which involved the bombing of Syrian artillery and missile-launchers by US navy and aircraft.

Decline and Recovery

At that point, when on the brink of military confrontation with the US and threatened by Israeli military deployment some eighteen miles from Damascus, Asad became seriously ill. On 13 November 1983, exactly thirteen years after he had assumed power in Syria by force of arms, he suffered a serious heart attack and was said to be almost in a coma.[23] Early in 1984, Asad, who is also diabetic, apparently suffered a relapse and was hospitalized again, whereupon a power struggle erupted in February among the members of his coterie. In a bid to succeed or perhaps even replace him, his brother Rifat displayed his military strength at key points in and around Damascus, while his photographs were widely displayed in public places. His opponents, both Sunni Muslim and Alawite political and military leaders, including Asad's relatives, tried to defeat his attempt to seize power. They confronted his Defence Detachments with their military forces in a series of stand-offs, and at one point shots were exchanged near the presidential palace between these warring factions.[24] Yet at that point, in March 1984, when it seemed that his regime was about to collapse, Asad recovered well enough to restore his personal authority, while taming Rifat by temporarily separating him from his military power-base and appointing him as one of three vice-presidents in charge of security affairs. But Asad has not fully recovered from his illness. Eyewitnesses reported in the mid-1980s that 'he's aged ten years', that occasionally 'he looks like hell', that his left arm was paralysed and his eyesight impaired.[25]

Yet he had a remarkable political resurrection which started at the end of 1982, a year before his heart attack and a short while after he had suffered a series of crucial setbacks in Lebanon, in his regional policies and in his relations with the superpowers. Indeed, Asad's traumatic experience during the 1982 war with Israel – his unprecedented isolation in the Arab world and his antagonistic relations with the US – apparently injected him with fresh ideas and vigour. With his back against the wall, Asad neither despaired nor gave up. Taking on this enormous challenge, exploiting his rivals' mistakes and using his unique qualities as a political tactician and military strategist, Asad completely turned the tables on his enemies and re-emerged as a major actor in both the regional and international arenas. He managed, through direct and indirect measures, to drive the American and Israeli forces out of Lebanon, to demolish the Lebanese–Israeli agreement of May 1983, and to reassert his singular influence, if not control, over the major parts of that country. By neutralizing the 1982 Reagan peace initiative, Asad forced the US to acknowledge his undeniable position in any political settlement of the Arab–Israeli dispute. Related to this achievement was Asad's success in weakening Arafat's PLO and preventing it from reaching an agreement with Jordan in 1983 and later. Last, but not least, while improving his regional position, Asad set out to challenge Israel with his reformed policy of 'strategic balance'. Indeed, as will be discussed later, this concept of strategic balance or military parity became the cornerstone of Asad's new strategy vis-à-vis Israel and the other Middle East actors. Yet, since this would be a long-term process, Asad chose to employ simultaneously a sub-strategy which would enable him to achieve both his interim and his long-term goals. This was manifested in a war of attrition, state-run terrorism and guerrilla warfare carried out by the army, by intelligence agents and by surrogates.

State-run Terrorism and Guerrilla Warfare

Asad's employment of guerrilla warfare and terrorist actions – assassinations, intimidation, sabotage and the like – to achieve his political and military objectives started, as we have seen, in the mid-

1960s when he served as Syria's air force commander and defence minister. Assisting the Fath organization with arms, training facilities and intelligence, Asad enabled or encouraged the Palestinian guerrillas to carry out subversive activities inside Israel. These activities constituted one of the factors leading to the June 1967 war.[26]

After coming to power in 1970, Asad continued to use the Palestinian guerrilla organizations against Israel, although not through the Syrian–Israeli ceasefire line. In addition to assisting the PLO, Asad employed the state-run (and partly Syrian-manned) Palestinian guerrilla organizations: the Saiqa, led by Zuhayr Muhsin, and the PFLP – General Command, led by Ahmad Jibril. Until the eruption of the 1975 Lebanese civil war these groups operated mainly against Israeli targets; for example, as mentioned above, in September 1973 Saiqa agents hijacked a train carrying Russian Jews in Austria, apparently as part of Asad's tactics to distract Israel from its preparations for the October 1973 war.

Following this war, while carrying out a war of attrition against the Israeli army in the Golan and during his negotiations with Kissinger, Asad refused to commit himself to prevent Syrian-based (Palestinian) guerrilla activities against Israel.[27] And although in practice he has not permitted such activities from the Syrian–Israeli ceasefire line since 1974, he did encourage and initiate (as will be discussed presently) guerrilla and terrorist actions against Israeli targets in Lebanon, Israel and Europe alike. But Israel has not been the only target for Asad's state-sponsored terrorism and guerrilla warfare. During most of the 1970s he periodically employed such methods in order to eliminate domestic and Arab adversaries (allegedly including General Muhammad Umran and Kamal Junblatt) as well as to advance certain political objectives.

Yet it would appear that by the late 1970s and the early 1980s, in response to the growing opposition to his regime both domestically and externally, Asad transformed his occasional usage of terrorism and guerrilla warfare into a highly organized and elaborate state-run affair. According to Jordanian definition, it consisted of 'special apparatuses for terrorism, assassination and crime'. And while a Turkish writer equated Asad's regime to the notorious Assassins of the Middle Ages (eleventh and twelfth centuries), Patrick Seale, a British journalist respected by Asad, wrote in 1981 (as we have seen) that 'to meet terror Asad has resorted to ferocious counter-terror. . . .'[28] These remarks refer to Asad's terror campaign against the Muslim Brothers in Syria during the early 1980s. In addition to the assassinations Asad's counter-terror reportedly included 'disappearances' and mass executions of many Muslim *mujahidun*, as well as more than twenty methods of brutal torture. The most notorious among these were allegedly:

> a Russian tool for ripping out finger nails, pincers and scissors for plucking flesh, and an apparatus called *al-'Abd al-Aswad* [the black slave] on which they force the torture victim to sit. When switched on, a very hot and sharp metal skewer enters the rear [anus] burning its way until it reached the intestines, then returns only to be reinserted.

(According to another version it is the *'khazuq*, a sharply pointed shaft', which 'enters the rectum and emerges through the upper body'.)[29] Asad's agents also hunted his domestic enemies abroad, be they Muslim Brothers or Ba'thist leaders. Thus in March 1981 Bahan al-Attar, the wife of Isam al-Attar, a Syrian Muslim Brother activist living in Aachen, West Germany, was assassinated by Syrian agents who intended to kill her husband.[30] A year earlier, in July 1980, Salah al-Din al-Bitar, one of the two founders and leaders of the Ba'th Party in Syria, and Asad's political opponent, was assassinated in Paris, presumably by Syrian agents too.[31]

In addition, Asad has reportedly employed political assassination and sabotage against his Arab enemies – Egyptians, Iraqis, Jordanians, Palestinians and Lebanese alike. For example, according to Egyptian sources, in an attempt to thwart the Israeli peace process Asad's regime planned to launch terrorist actions in Cairo in April 1979 by means of the Eagles of the Palestine Revolution, an offshoot of Saiqa. Cairo held the same group responsible for the attack on the Egyptian embassy in Ankara in mid-July 1979. Around the same time the Baghdad government reportedly uncovered a foreign (Syrian) plot against the Iraqi regime, allegedly aimed at foiling the Syrian–Iraqi unity talks which had been conducted against Asad's interests.[32] Subsequently Asad's regime employed terror and assassination in the early and mid-1980s in order to thwart the rapprochement between Jordan and Iraq as well as the agreements between Lebanon and Israel and between the PLO and Jordan. For example, in early 1981 while Amman was warming its relations with Baghdad, the Jordanian military attaché in Beirut was kidnapped and a plot to assassinate Jordan's prime minister was allegedly uncovered by Jordan; Amman accused Rifat Asad of initiating the murder attempt.[33] In 1985 while Arafat and Hussein were prepared to sign their confederation agreement on 11 February, gunmen (apparently Syrian agents) assassinated Fahd Qawasmi, a close ally of Arafat's and a former mayor of Hebron, who had just been elected to the PLO executive committee. Jordanian diplomats also became the targets of assassins in Europe and Asia and some were killed. A year later, on 2 March 1986, Zafir al-Masri, the newly elected mayor of Nablus (apparently under Jordanian–Israeli understanding) was murdered by agents of 'a Palestinian group in Syria, supported by Asad'.[34] Asad's terrorist methods served, alongside other important factors (which will be discussed below), to persuade King Hussein to drop his alliance with Arafat and draw closer to Syria. Most significantly 'the king went in December 1985 on a pilgrimage to Assad's capital, after making an extraordinary public confession', admitting to the charge Asad had been making for many years – that Amman had permitted the Muslim Brothers to operate from Jordan's territory against Asad's regime.[35]

Asad's sponsored terrorist actions and guerrilla warfare proved to be most effective in the Lebanese scene, not only vis-à-vis the Maronite-dominated government and Arafat's PLO, but also vis-à-vis the American and Israeli military presence. Asad of course has denied that he has employed terrorist measures but has praised acts of resistance against foreign occupiers (i.e. Israel and the US). Co-ordinated by Colonel Ghazi Kan'an, Syrian intelligence chief in Lebanon, Asad's terrorist and guerrilla operations were carried out mostly by non-Syrian surrogates, members of various organizations: Lebanese fundamentalist Shi'is from Hizballah and Amal groups, as well as secular socialists from the SSNP and Ba'th parties;[36] Palestinians from the various organizations of the newly established National Salvation Front (Saiqa, and the groups headed by Abu Musa, Jibril, George Habash and Naif Hawatma); and the Iranian Islamic Jihad group sent by the Khumeini regime.[37] The major operations carried out by members of these Syrian-dominated groups were: the assassination of Lebanon's president Bashir Jumayyil on 15 September 1982; the suicide attacks on the US Marine compound in Lebanon in 1983 (killing 241 Marines) and the US embassy in Beirut in 1984; and the long series of guerrilla and suicide attacks on Israeli military targets and units during 1983 and 1984.[38]

These and many other attacks, mostly directed by Syria, resulted in major gains for Asad. First, the newly elected Lebanese president Amin Jumayyil decided in February 1984 to abandon the May 1983 agreement with Israel and subsequently accepted Asad's reform plan for Lebanon[39] (but, as of November 1987, this plan has not been implemented). Second, the US withdrew its military forces from

Lebanon in February 1984 and subsequently had to acknowledge Asad's predominant influence in Lebanon as well as his ability to spoil a political settlement of the Arab–Israeli conflict. Third, Israel was at last forced in 1985 to evacuate its forces from southern Lebanon (with the exception of the six-mile security belt along its border with Lebanon) without retaining any political gains in Beirut.

It would appear that the success of these guerrilla and terrorist actions against Israel and the US encouraged Asad to initiate more terrorist operations against Israeli and US targets abroad, presumably in order to revenge his humiliation by these two countries and advance his political objectives. Reportedly, most of these 'operations were planned by a top official of Syria's air force intelligence network' (Muhammad Khawli, Asad's close aide?).[40] Thus the hijacking of the TWA 847 flight to Beirut in May 1984 by members of Hizballah was allegedly co-ordinated by Syria, and was aimed at deflecting attention from the peace process and at damaging US–Israeli relations.[41] On 27 December 1985, gunmen from Abu Nidal's group, reportedly coming from Syria, carried out co-ordinated attacks at both Vienna and Rome airports, killing 20 people (including five Americans) and wounding 110.[42] On 2 April 1986 a TWA airliner overflying Greece was bombed, killing four Americans. This terrorist act was said to have been carried out by a team 'operating under the guidance of the Syrian air force intelligence services'.[43] Then on 29 March 1986 a bombing attack was made in a West Berlin Arab club; on 17 April 1986 at London airport an attempt was made to place a bomb aboard an El-Al airliner carrying close to 400 passengers; and on 26 June 1986 an attempt was made to attack another El-Al plane in Madrid.[44] The Italian, Spanish, West German and British governments accused Syria of being linked to these terrorist actions. Britain decided to break off diplomatic relations with Syria in November 1986; the US, Canada, West Germany and Italy subsequently recalled their ambassadors from Damascus; while the US and the EEC imposed various sanctions on Syria.[45]

According to one evaluation, these (and other) Syrian-sponsored terrorist actions have been part of a global network of terrorism, directed by the Soviet Union and comprised of some twenty terrorist organizations in Europe, Asia, East Africa and the Middle East. Its aim has been to damage and undermine the political and economic interests of the West, notably the US and Israel.[46] Within this network there has existed, according to this evaluation, and to a US version, a significant co-ordination between Syria, Iran and Libya. For example, CIA director William Casey stated in May 1986:

> Libya, Syria and Iran use terrorism as an instrument of foreign policy. They hire and support established terrorist organizations. . . . These countries make their officials, their embassies, their diplomatic pouches, their communications channels and their territory as safe havens for these criminals to plan, direct and execute bombing, assassination, kidnapping and other terrorist operations. . . . Syria traditionally has regarded terrorism as a weapon to be used in precisely defined and coldly calculated ways to war against Israel and to intimidate or eliminate forces resisting Syrian President Hafiz Assad's drive to make Syria the dominant force in the Arab world . . . [but] Assad denies that he supports terrorism, except in the case of Israel, and has sought to conceal Syria's ties with terrorist groups (claiming for example that Abu Nidal has an office in Damascus which is engaged only in 'cultural and political' activities).[47]

Indeed, not only has Asad denied any link to the anti-US terrorist actions (claiming that Syria herself has been a victim of terrorism) but he has also successfully received credit for his helping in the release of the US and European hostages kidnapped by Shi'i groups associated with him. Regarding terrorist acts against Israel, Asad told the *Washington Post* in May 1986, following the attempt to bomb the El-Al airliner: 'Although we wish all kinds of disasters to befall Israel since we are enemies and in a state of war for 38 years – and the Israelis wish the same for us – we refuse to carry out such acts against civil aviation. We condemn the hijacking or exploding of civilian aircraft, such acts are cowardly.' But in the same interview Asad also remarked: 'We stick to the rule which says nobody can strike Syria and evade punishment. The past years have proved that Syria accepts no humiliation and fears no danger, however big it is, when it concerns its dignity and the dignity of the Arab nation.'[48] Asad was possibly alluding to the US and Israeli military operations against Syria in Lebanon in 1982–3 and also to the fact that Israel had forced a Libyan plane carrying senior Syrian officials to land in Israel in April 1986. (Following the latter event Ahmad Jibril, leader of the Syrian-run PFLP – General Command warned people 'not to travel on American or Israeli planes from now on'.)[49]

Regardless of whether or not he was involved in the El-Al bombing attempt, Asad has certainly been inspired by the success of the suicide operations in pushing the IDF from Lebanon and in 'breaking Israel's fighting spirit'.[50] Regarding it both as an heroic and an effective way to wage a war of attrition against Israel, Asad hailed the Muslim concept of *shahadah* (martyrdom) in some of his speeches during 1985–6 (and earlier). For example, in his address to the Eighth Regional Convention of the Ba'th Party (January 1985), Asad stated, 'Our people in Lebanon are teaching a lesson to all Arabs and paving the way for the destruction of Zionist arrogance by showing that the way to repulse and punish the enemy for the crime is first *shahadah*, second *shahadah* and third *shahadah*.'[51]

Several months later, addressing the Syrian students' union, Asad again praised *shahadah* as a manifestation of the highest values in life and said that sacrifice and martyrdom

> was my motive for volunteering among others to fight in Palestine in 1947 [possibly referring to the irregular forces, not the Syrian army]. I was then seventeen years old and to my disappointment . . . we were not taken to Palestine. . . . Then I joined the army and became an air force pilot. . . . I used to discuss with my comrades the necessity for the state to form a unit of *fidaiyyun* [fighters ready for self-sacrifice] from among the pilots. We used then the term 'suicidals' or 'Kamikaze', the well-known Japanese term . . . the *fidai* mission requires the pilot to pounce on the enemy target and strike enemy ships, airports and other targets by turning himself, his plane and the bomb into one single fireball. Such attacks are aimed at causing the enemy heavy losses . . . they are also spreading terror among enemy ranks on the one hand, and raising people's morale and enhancing their awareness of the importance of the spirit of sacrifice, on the other hand. Thus waves of popular *fidai* sacrifice will follow successively and the enemy will not be able to endure them. . . .

Asad later concluded, 'the battle against Zionism is a fatal battle – to be or not to be'.[52]

Asad's pronounced advocacy of *shahadah* and *fidai* – martyrdom and sacrifice – and of guerrilla warfare may raise the question whether or not he believes that these methods should be employed (or merely propagated) *instead* of a regular war against Israel, or *alongside* such a war. There has been no indication in his public utterances that he has ruled out a conventional war against Israel. On the contrary, he has never ceased to call for regular military action against Israel; and in both 1967 and 1973 he helped start such wars. Whether or not he intends to wage a conventional war against Israel in the future – this will be discussed later – one thing is crystal clear: Asad has systematically sought in the last several years to reach a 'strategic balance' or a 'military parity' with Israel. Terror and guerrilla warfare

are certainly important components in this strategy; they aim at weakening Israel's morale and social fabric while distracting her until Asad achieves his strategic parity.

Asad's Concept of Strategic Balance

Since coming to power, Asad has been gripped, perhaps obsessed, by the need to achieve a balance of power with Israel. Apart from his deep ideological animosity to the Zionist 'racist' state, his search for legitimacy as an Alawite ruler of Syria and his personal ambition to recover the Golan Heights (which he lost to Israel when serving as Syria's defence minister), Asad's attitude towards Israel has been largely based on his strategic thinking. Viewing the Jewish state as the predominant regional power bent on establishing a Greater Israel 'from the Nile to the Euphrates',[53] Asad has sought to counterbalance Israel's superiority, as a prerequisite for either a military or a political solution to the Arab–Israeli conflict. As he stated in 1981: 'If the military balance is needed to liberate the land and repel the aggression, it is needed equally to implement the just peace . . . peace could never be established between the strong and the weak.'[54]

Yet, although giving an important role to his country in the confrontation with Israel, Asad, until the late 1970s, regarded the power balance with Israel in pan-Arab terms. Indeed, until the mid-1970s Asad endeavoured to integrate Syria into a wide regional Arab alliance (such as the Federation of Arab Republics) under the leadership of Egypt, which he recognized as playing the major and decisive role in the confrontation with Israel. And although the 1973 war ended in an Arab military defeat, Asad viewed the intra-Arab military, political, economic and diplomatic co-operation (or 'solidarity') during the war as a model for the future Arab posture vis-à-vis Israel. Revealing for the first time during the 1974 Rabat summit the concept of 'strategic balance' with Israel (al-tawazun al-istratiji),[55] Asad visualized the Cairo–Damascus axis as the core of the new Arab strategy, which would employ military power as well as diplomatic and other measures in the struggle with Israel.[56] But when in 1975 Sadat unilaterally signed the Sinai agreement with Israel, Asad was greatly disturbed by the possible change in the Arab–Israeli power balance.[57]

Nevertheless, Asad subsequently sought to create an alternative Arab alliance, possibly seeing himself, for the first time, as the leader of the fresh Arab axis. He tried, as discussed above, to implement his previous plan for a Fertile Crescent alliance or an Eastern Front Command to be composed of Syria, Iraq, Jordan, Lebanon and the PLO. Yet, since Iraq rejected his use of political and diplomatic methods in the struggle against Israel, Asad was determined to create a union of Greater Syria (Syria, Jordan, Lebanon and the PLO) under his undisputed leadership.

However, although recording significant achievements during the years 1975–9 in his co-operation with Jordan (and to a lesser extent with Lebanon and with the PLO), by 1979 Asad had virtually failed to establish a Greater Syria alliance to confront the claimed Greater Israel policy of the new Israeli Likud government. Indeed, at that juncture, Asad almost singlehandedly faced a powerful and allegedly more aggressive Israel.[58] In March 1979 Sadat signed a peace treaty with Israel, thus taking the last step in offsetting the Arab–Israeli power balance, but also enabling Asad to fill the vacuum in the leadership of the pan-Arab struggle against Israel. Iraq, the second most powerful Arab state, had sought to fill this vacuum in 1978, following the Camp David accords, an ambition which Asad himself had helped to thwart by mid-1979. In the following year, Iraq started her long and bloody war with Iran, thus, in Asad's words, 'departing from the Arab–Israeli struggle for not a short period'.[59] And as Amman switched from its alliance with Syria to a close co-operation with Baghdad in 1980, Israel – encouraged by the sympathetic policy of the new Reagan administration – stepped up her military operations against the PLO in southern Lebanon while becoming more belligerent towards Syria by formally annexing the Golan in 1981. Parallel to these crucial regional developments, the growing challenge from the fundamentalist Muslim Brothers from 1979 provoked, as discussed above, a strong backlash from Asad, alienating large sectors of the Syrian population as well as more Arab states. Consequently Asad's regime became a 'besieged citadel both from within and from without'.[60]

In the face of the mounting Israeli military threat and his increasing domestic and regional isolation, Asad has developed since the late 1970s a new concept of 'strategic balance', which Syria should achieve by herself independently of other Arab countries. This concept, which has been mentioned or examined since the late 1970s in many articles in Syrian publications as well as in numerous speeches by Asad, relates mainly to the need to gain a Syrian 'military parity' with Israel.[61]

Nevertheless this grand strategy alludes also to Asad's objectives in both his regional and domestic arenas.

Concerning military parity with Israel, Syrian military analysts pointed out as early as 1978 that, as against '158,000 [Israeli] soldiers in addition to 450,000 reservists', Syria had in 1977 an 'army of 227,000 in addition to 212,000 reserve forces'.[62] Furthermore, whereas Israel, with its population of barely four million, has reached the limits of her army growth, Syria, drawing on her great human potential, could substantially increase her military power; as Asad stated in 1980, Syria could enlist 900,000 to one million soldiers.[63] And in February 1986, while referring to the Syrian population in the Israeli-annexed Golan Heights, Asad declared, 'be assured, for your homeland is in good condition. You should not fear for the Golan because 12 million Syrian citizens are capable of regaining the Golan.'[64] Asad has considerably expanded his armed forces in the last decade, particularly since the 1982 war: from about 230,000 in 1977 to some 350,000 regular troops in 1982, reaching half a million soldiers in active service in 1986, according to certain sources[65] (or about 350,000 regular troops, plus 450,000 reservists, according to other sources).[66] This huge army consists of ten divisions (three of them created since the 1982 war). Five are armoured with some 4,200 Soviet tanks, including 1,000 modern T-72s. The Syrian air force, the largest Arab air force, is equipped with more than 600 aircraft (in comparison with 440 aircraft in 1977 and 500 in 1982), among them the advanced Soviet-made MIG-29s in addition to some 160 AA batteries including SA-5 long-range anti-aircraft missiles. In recent years Syria has obtained shore-to-sea missiles with 300-kilometre range, and reportedly the very accurate SS-23 ground-to-ground missiles with 500-kilometre range (to supplement the SS-21s as well as the short-range and less accurate SCUD and FROG missiles).[67]

As can be gathered from these figures, this great military leap forward has been achieved with enormous Soviet help, which reportedly includes the supply of sophisticated arms that no other Arab country or even Warsaw Pact country has obtained; and it has been accompanied by up to 6,000 Soviet military advisers.[68] This unprecedented military assistance, granted on easy terms under the 1980 Soviet–Syrian treaty, has indeed represented Asad's countermove to what he regarded as the 1981 'Strategic Co-operation' agreement between Reagan and Begin which 'directly puts US forces and arsenals against us . . . and on the side of the Israeli forces'. Given the Israeli–American strategic alliance, the only answer could lie in a

Syrian alliance with the USSR, which according to Asad is 'an important factor in securing the strategic balance between us and Israel'.[69] It would appear that, like the Soviet leaders, Asad has regarded strategic or military parity with Israel primarily as a *sine qua non* for deterring Israel from attacking Syria. Hence the function of the long-range missiles, as Asad remarked in 1982: 'They [the Israelis] must remember that Israeli towns are within our artillery range, and most Israeli towns are within the range of other weapons of ours.'[70] A further deterrent factor versus Israel could possibly be the threat of Soviet military intervention in the event of an Israeli assault on Syria, as well as the recent acquisition of chemical weapons. Related to this is yet another important objective of Asad's military augmentation programme – the defence of his country against Israel, or as he put it: 'We bought these arms in order to use them in defending ourselves.'[71]

This dual purpose of defence and deterrent is accompanied by another significant dual aim of Asad's strategic balance – enabling Syria on the one hand to withstand diplomatic pressures from the US and its Arab allies (Egypt) and on the other hand to negotiate or impose a political settlement to the Arab–Israeli conflict from a position of strength.[72] Obviously such strength must stem essentially from a credible military power; but a sound economy, a cohesive society and a stable political regime are also crucially important components for Syria's strategic balance with Israel.[73] As Asad has remarked on several occasions: 'In the strategic balance there are many elements: political, military, cultural and economic';[74] '. . . Syria must be strong, of course, and its strength is based on the power and firmness of its people.'[75] Of course, Asad's remarks (as well as his actions) can be interpreted also as an attempt to use the issue of strategic balance, or the need to confront the Israeli threat, in order to mobilize the Syrian people behind his leadership, regain their allegiance and motivate them to make economic sacrifices for the national goals.[76]

Yet it would appear that beyond these crucial needs to strengthen his popular power-base and defend his country against the Israeli threat, Asad has sought (apparently without Soviet approval) to use the goal of military parity to advance his broader strategic objectives and political ambitions. First and foremost, depicting himself as a pan-Arab leader ('We in Syria look at matters from the pan-Arab angle'), Asad has perceived the strategic balance as a means to defend not only Syria but also the whole Arab world against alleged Israeli expansionism:

Israel does not want Syria alone but the entire Arab homeland. The Israelis want Jordan because it is part of Palestine, and this land – as they claim – is the land promised to them by God. . . . The Israelis want Iraq because their promised land should extend from the Nile to the Euphrates. . . . Israel wants also the Arabian peninsula because the Israelis were there long before Islam and Christianity. . . . Israel wants Egypt . . . Lebanon and Sudan . . . [therefore] if Syria collapses, the entire [Arab] region will follow [the same fate]. We see the danger as it is, but some of our brothers [Arab leaders] do not see that as we do. . . . Syria is the only hope of the Arab world.[77]

Therefore it is essential for Asad to organize and carry out a pan-Arab strategy against this formidable enemy. But since Asad's 'brothers', particularly in Egypt and Iraq, are not aware of this danger, Asad has the obligation to construct and lead a Greater Syria bloc and to assert his influence in the Arab east as well as in global affairs.[78] In other words, the strategic balance, namely a powerful Syrian army, is also required to foil both the Israeli–Lebanese and the Jordanian–PLO agreements, to exert Asad's leverage over Lebanon, Jordan and the Palestinians, and to withstand opposition from the two other Arab regional powers, Egypt and Iraq. Despite his grave setbacks in the late 1970s he has not relinquished his ambitions to control or influence Lebanon, Jordan and the Palestinians, as he implied in the mid-1980s: 'I must point out here that we and the Lebanese people are linked by the same history, language and interests. . . . These interests were exchanged throughout history and will remain as such now and in the future.'[79] 'The Lebanese people can never be separated from their Arab body . . . namely Syria . . . we support the Palestinian resistance because . . . historically we in Syria have always been concerned with the Palestinian question. Like any Palestinian, we consider it to be our cause. . . . None of the Palestinians can carry through a solution between them and Israel. This is because it is not a Palestinian–Israeli conflict [but an Arab–Israeli conflict].'[80] 'If we refuse to accept part of the Golan for the sake of the Palestinian cause, it means that we are the guardians of the Palestinian issue and of the PLO . . . we shall not acquiesce as long as the Aqsa mosque and the Holy Sepulchre are in the hands of the oppressors, as long as our beloved Jerusalem . . . and Palestine are in the hands of the invaders, occupiers.'[81]

This finally brings us back to the issue of the struggle against Israel which has undoubtedly remained the major strategic objective of Asad's concept of military parity. As already pointed out, this concept essentially provides for a military capability to defend Syria and impose a political settlement vis-à-vis Israel. Yet the intriguing question is whether or not this concept contains a dimension of military offensive: does it enable Syria to attack Israel? Judging from his speeches before and after June 1982,[82] the partial defeat of his army in the 1982 war did not significantly shake Asad's belief that the Syrian army will be able to defeat the IDF in due course. On the contrary, while becoming more convinced than ever before that Israel is likely to attack Syria without any provocation, Asad has apparently derived great encouragement from the performance of his army in that war. Although admitting the loss of his anti-aircraft missiles and the defeat of his air force (but remarking, 'The Israelis acknowledge the bravery of the Syrian pilot'), Asad took pride in the performance of his ground forces and their equipment:

> In these battles there was a demonstration of the high standard of the Syrian soldier with respect to training and bravery . . . despite the Israeli military superiority . . . the enemy did not achieve strategic victories and did not succeed in destroying any Syrian army unit or in damaging, even slightly, the morale of the Syrian fighters . . . the battles have proved that the T-72 tank is better than the Israeli tank. This is the best tank in the world . . . in short, our armoured corps is good.[83]

Furthermore, it would appear that not only has Asad been reassured by the good performance of his army, but he has also derived important and useful lessons from the 1982 war. The subsequent guerrilla warfare carried out against the IDF by his surrogates, coupled with his own army's war of attrition against the IDF in 1974, possibly convinced Asad of yet another advantage over Israel that his people have: Israel's high vulnerability to human losses and what he believes to be her lack of motivation to fight as against the high morale, endurance and stamina of the Syrian people and army.[84]

Possibly encouraged by such thinking and by his unprecedentedly huge military growth, and motivated by his ideological and strategic goal, Asad has made unusually militant speeches against Israel. Thus, while praising martyrdom and sacrifice as the highest values and the way to fight Israel,[85] Asad made specific references to his intention to wage a war against Israel and defeat her. For example, when asked late in 1982, 'Is it possible to fight Israel and defeat her?' Asad answered, 'Why not? . . . affairs of nations are measured in the long range. There are many examples, the Vietnamese, the Algerians . . . we should not despair because for several years we have not defeated Israel, which is equipped with American arms. Certainly we shall achieve a victory.'[86]

Then in mid-1983 Asad stated, 'time is on our side . . . the just solution for the big problem in this region [Israel] will be achieved only when a strategic balance between us and Israel is reached'.[87] Finally, in his address to the newly elected People's Assembly in Damascus on 27 February 1986, Asad said:

If the Israelis work to put the Golan within their borders, we will work to put the Golan in the middle of Syria and not on its borders. . . . The opening of fire by Israeli security men in your villages . . . will only increase our hatred for that historical enemy and augment our determination to fight it through to the end. History will record that the Golan was the climax of the disaster for the Israelis.[88]

These militant speeches, coupled with Asad's extraordinary efforts to reach military parity with Israel, pose several important questions concerning the prospects for Asad's concept of strategic balance. The first set of questions would be: Has Asad already reached a strategic balance or military parity with Israel? Is his army now able to deter Israel from attacking Syria and effectively to defend Syria against an IDF assault? What are the prospects for a war initiated by Asad against Israel? Or are perhaps Asad's belligerent speeches against Israel and his frequent references to the strategic-balance issue mere rhetoric, a form of psychological warfare against Israel, while consolidating the Syrian public's support for the Alawite minority regime?

Related to these queries would be a second set of questions: To what extent has Asad been able to achieve the domestic objectives of his strategic-balance policy, which at its face value would mean mobilizing Syrian people and resources for the 'war of liberation' by 'turning every home in Syria into a steadfast fort, the resources into fuel for the battle, the economy into a war economy . . . and every citizen into a *fidai* and warrior'?[89] Yet, beyond these heroic slogans, it should be asked to what extent has Asad been able to expand and consolidate the Syrian people's support for his regime through his protracted series of economic, social and political reforms.

Finally, the third set of queries should deal with the pan-Arab objectives of Asad's strategic consensus, i.e. what have been his achievements, and what are his prospects, in forging a Greater Syria unity, or alliance, while turning his country into a regional power and the new leader of the pan-Arab struggle against Israel and her strategic ally, the US?

14 Asad's Prospects

Military Parity with Israel

It may be concluded that the major achievement of Asad's strategies since he came to power in 1970 is a military parity with Israel. Indeed from the data cited above, it appears that *quantitatively* the Syrian army has reached in 1986, or is about to reach, military equality with Israel: the half-a-million-strong Syrian regular army has been largely modernized with new Soviet weapons and has significantly improved its training, organization, performance and command. While emphasizing the size, fire-power and quality of his armoured corps, mechanized divisions and commando units, Asad has also endeavoured to counterbalance Israeli air force superiority by improving his own air force and by building a strong and effective anti-aircraft system.[1] These significant military accomplishments coupled with Syria's long-range ground-to-ground missiles, her development of chemical weapons,[2] and the alleged Soviet commitment to her defence substantially serve to implement Asad's basic dual aim vis-à-vis Israel – to deter her from attacking Syria and to defend Syria effectively against an IDF assault.[3] As Abd al-Halim Khaddam, Syria's foreign minister, has explained: 'The Israelis are aware that their next war will by no means be a limited war, nor would it be a picnic. They are also aware of the heavy losses that they would suffer if they chose to have a military escalation.'[4] Israel's army still has considerable *qualitative* superiority over the Syrian army, particularly in the air force and the armoured corps, as well as in the soldiers' performance, and thus could defeat the Syrian army.[5]

Nevertheless, except in extreme cases, Israel is unlikely in the near future to attack Syria without a serious Syrian provocation, since she would wish to avoid fighting a non-vital war in foreign territory and so suffer heavy human casualties in addition to severe economic losses. Essentially an outcome of the 1982 war with Syria and its aftermath, these Israeli constraints represent a substantial achievement for Asad's military-balance doctrine in its deterrent and defensive components. By contrast, however, despite his military parity, Asad is, and will be in the foreseeable future, unable to defeat Israel in a comprehensive war for several reasons: in addition to her qualitative military edge and her deep psychological motivation to fight and win a vital war of defence, Israel is said to have a nuclear capability and 500-mile long-range missiles[6] which enable her to threaten the destruction of the Syrian military and economic infrastructures. Yet, even in conventional terms, Syria alone is still far from having military and strategic advantage over Israel; the prospects of a joint Syrian–Iraqi–Jordanian military offensive against Israel are still very remote.

Hypothetically, then, the military parity, or stalemate, between Syria and Israel could lead to a political settlement between these countries, which could be based on the return of the Golan to Syrian sovereignty and the creation of internationally supervised demilitarized zones along the border.

Yet the chances of such a settlement seem to be rather slim. For whereas Israel would perhaps be willing to trade *most* of the Golan for a *full peace treaty* with Syria, Asad might perhaps agree to sign only a *non-belligerency agreement* with Israel if he could recover the *entire* Golan and have a Palestinian state established in the West Bank, Gaza and East Jerusalem. While this discrepancy cannot be bridged in the near future, Asad is apparently convinced that Israel will never give up the Golan (as well as the West Bank, Gaza and East Jerusalem), unless she is forced to it by a Syrian military victory. In this respect it can be concluded that Asad's military parity with Israel does not enable him, without going to war, to impose a political solution to the Arab–Israeli conflict (the recovery of the Golan and other occupied Arab territories).

If this analysis is correct, Asad, in theory, is left with the following options to confront Israel militarily: First, he could provoke Israel to attack Syria and cause Israel's army heavy losses by a well-prepared Syrian defensive posture, possibly helped by the Soviet Union and several Arab nations. Second, Asad could carry out a war of attrition against Israel along the Golan ceasefire line, coupled with Syrian-run guerrilla warfare in southern Lebanon and the West Bank. Third, Syria could storm the Israeli-held Golan by a surprise attack and subsequently establish a firm defensive line, which, enforced with Soviet military presence and Syrian strategic weapons, might deter Israel from counterattacking Syria.

There have been indications that Asad may intend to try any one of these options or a combination of them. For example, the Syrian-sponsored attempt to blow up the El-Al aircraft in London on 17 April 1986 may point to the possibility that Asad was prepared to risk a massive Israeli attack had this aircraft exploded. Similarly Asad's high praise for the successful guerrilla warfare against the IDF in Lebanon in 1983–4, and for his effective war of attrition against the Israeli army in the Golan in 1974, might indicate that Asad intends to use such tactics in the future.

Yet, although such Syrian actions in pursuit of the first and second options might cause heavy casualties, put strain on the economy and damage morale in Israel, they are not likely to produce any political gains for Asad. On the contrary, not only would Israel refuse, under such pressures, to make any territorial concessions (in the Golan) but she might severely retaliate or wage a war against Syria, aiming at the collapse of Asad's regime.[7] True, such an Israeli reaction is also very likely to occur if Asad employs the third option (a recapture of the Golan or part of it in a surprise attack). Yet this high risk of a fierce Israeli counter-offensive can be offset by the fairly tangible chance that Asad could regain the Golan by both military and political actions. Indeed, according to military analysts, the Syrian army could in a very short time transform its powerful defensive build-up along the ceasefire line (five or six divisions) and launch a major offensive against the comparatively small Israeli forces in the Golan. Thus, while Syrian forces disrupted the Israeli air force operations and the mobilization of Israeli reservists, and fired long-range missiles at Israeli airfields, military headquarters and emergency depots, the Syrian armoured division could advance along the front line. Assisted by helicopter-borne commandos dropped behind Israeli fortifications Syria could quickly gain control of the Golan or part of it.[8] In making this bold and fast move, Asad might calculate that Israel would not retaliate for fear of incurring further human losses and perhaps of confronting Russian combat troops (which might be deployed around Damascus). In addition, according to such a scenario, Israel's possible employment of tactical nuclear warheads against Syria could be neutralized by Syrian threats to fire long-range missiles carrying chemical warheads and by Soviet threats to retaliate with nuclear weapons. Simultaneously, the Soviet Union or Syria would approach the US suggesting the arrangement of a ceasefire with Israel along the new military lines, while starting a political process to settle the Syrian–Israeli conflict.

Contrary to such a scenario, it can as plausibly be argued that the cool, realistic and cautious Asad would not opt to launch a military offensive in the Golan in the foreseeable future, for fear that the final outcome of such a war could involve further territorial, military and economic losses to Syria and even cause his own downfall. He would thus continue to use the Israeli issue as a way to consolidate his domestic support-base, while attempting to improve Syria's economic conditions and regional position.

Asad's final decision, it seems, would be founded on various important calculations such as the expected positions of the US, the USSR and various Arab countries, as well as the political and economic conditions in Syria. For example, how long could he retain such a huge army while Syria's economy deteriorates? Would the US encourage Israel to defeat Syria or to negotiate with her? No less crucial would be Asad's inner evaluation of his real strategic balance with Israel: Are Syria's economic, social and military infrastructures firm enough to sustain a critical war, or is there a national readiness in Israel to fight a very costly war over the Golan?

Finally, while it is impossible to predict Asad's intentions, it is worth pointing to a personal or psychological factor that might influence his decision. Having been seriously ill, and aware that he may die in the near future, how does he wish to be remembered in Syrian and Arab history? As a leader who had lost the Golan in 1967, failed to recover it in 1973, and lost more Syrian territory and lives in yet another war in the late 1980s? As a leader who, though losing the Golan, was able to transform Syria into a stable country and a regional power, and who, while preparing his army to defeat Israel in a not-too-distant future, had evicted the IDF from Lebanon, eroded the Israeli air force activities over the Biqa and spilled Israeli blood in various guerrilla actions? Or perhaps Asad would not be satisfied with such minor achievements, but wishes to leave a heroic legacy, if not of a new Saladin at least of a Lion of the Golan, who defeated the IDF while recovering this symbolically important territory.

Understandably, on this highly crucial issue of whether or not to storm the Golan, Asad remains an enigma, a sphinx. Indeed, such a posture is not only compatible with his practice of keeping his cards close to his chest; it could keep open the above-mentioned military (and political) options, while enabling him to present himself as the leader of the Arab struggle against Israel.

Yet this prestigious (or presumptuous) position, assumed for the first time by a Syrian leader, by no means implies that Asad has been able, or will be able in the foreseeable future, to lead the Arab world into a military crusade, or even into a diplomatic campaign, against Israel.

For, on this issue too, Asad is very far away from becoming a modern Saladin of the Arab world. Despite the growing military might which has turned his country into a regional power, Asad has completely failed to implement his official policy of convening 'an international Middle East peace conference . . . under the supervision and auspices of the UN' in order to achieve a 'just solution' to the Arab–Israeli conflict.[9] In other words, Asad has been unable so far to forge a pan-Arab consensus which would adopt his policy of pulling Egypt out of her peace agreement with Israel and, with Soviet backing, impose on Israel a Syrian-designed political settlement.

Nevertheless, Asad has been strong (and skilful) enough to sustain a veto power against any further 'separate' political initiatives or agreements which could isolate Syria or undermine her policy towards the Arab–Israeli dispute. Thus, casting a dark shadow all the way from Damascus, Asad helped to foil the Reagan peace initiative of September 1982 by systematically exercising diplomatic and military pressures, including the use of political assassination against fellow Arabs. The major target of Asad's subversive efforts was the protracted dialogue between Hussein and Arafat which started after the Reagan initiative and culminated in the Jordanian–PLO confederation agreement of 11 February 1985. Having been able, with the help of rejectionist Palestinians, to thwart the initial rapprochement between Hussein and Arafat in 1983, Asad succeeded in late 1985 and early 1986 in helping to put off the Jordanian–PLO agreement and replacing it with a series of Syrian–Jordanian co-operation agreements.[10] Earlier, in February 1984, Asad managed a more direct achievement. He forced Lebanon's President Amin Jumayyil to abandon the May 1983 Israeli–Lebanese agreement (which had been concluded with American backing), replacing it with Syrian-sponsored reform and security plans.[11]

The Greater Syria Rebuff

Despite these achievements, however, Asad, the master manipulator and the achiever of military parity, has not managed so far to influence Jordan or the PLO to the extent of integrating them into a Greater Syria alliance under his leadership. For example, Asad failed to detach Hussein from his close ties with Iraq, or prevent him from reviving his diplomatic relations with Egypt (both these countries being Asad's fierce rivals). Hussein's new association with Asad seems not to be of a strategic nature, but basically aims at protecting Jordan's threatened Syrian flank during a precarious period (i.e. while being denied American arms and while castigating Arafat's unreliable conduct). And even though Hussein may have committed himself to help defend Asad's Jordanian flank against a possible Israeli attack, presumably he is not likely to admit Syrian troops into Jordan or to join forces with Asad in a military offensive against Israel. Finally, although Asad stated in February 1986 that he and Hussein 'are in agreement on rejecting direct negotiations and separate solutions',[12] it appears that Hussein has by no means decided to dissociate himself completely from the Middle East political process and join Asad's militant rejectionist alliance.

Such may also be the position of Arafat, the PLO chief who commands the allegiance of most Palestinians in the West Bank, Gaza and Jordan. He is still adamant in refusing to relinquish to Asad the PLO's 'independence of decision' while depicting him in mid-1985 as an enemy of the Palestinians ('Hafiz al-Asad, the head of the Syrian regime, has planned new bloodbaths among the Palestinians').[13] Indeed, even though Asad succeeded in 1983 in splitting the PLO, and since then has inflicted successive blows on Arafat's followers in Lebanon, he has failed either to impose his guardianship on the PLO or to replace Arafat with another leader. And, unable to thwart the 1984 Palestinian National Council Meeting, which overwhelmingly supported Arafat, the Asad-sponsored National Salvation Front has remained a marginal group in the Palestinian movement.[14]

Nonetheless, Asad has been more successful in his attempt at imposing a strategic tutelage over Lebanon since 1984: directing her foreign policy and using her territory (mainly in the Biqa) to construct a military defensive infrastructure vis-à-vis Israel. For example, despite Israeli threats Asad deployed, early in 1986, ground-to-air missiles inside Lebanon, along its border with Syria. And while controlling or influencing most of the local militia – Shi'i, Druze and Christian – he has employed them, and will continue to do so, against his various foes, Lebanese and non-Lebanese alike. Moreover, he has been able partly to impose on the Lebanese regime his reform plan of

Muslim–Christian power-sharing, a new version in fact of his 1976 constitutional document. An important step towards implementing this plan was taken by the formation in July 1984 of 'a national unity government', largely dominated by Asad's allies, notably Rashid Karami, the Sunni prime minister, and Nabih Berri, the Shi'i leader of Amal (as minister of justice). This government, but not President Jumayyil, has been inclined to adopt the 'Syrian option' ('a special and distinctive relationship' with Damascus) and follow by and large Asad's guidelines (in the 1985 Damascus accord) regarding administrative reforms and the reconstruction of the Lebanese army and of the country's intelligence apparatus.[15]

Yet the deep schism in Lebanese society, manifested *inter alia* by the many rival militias, might in the foreseeable future weaken Asad's strategic position in Lebanon. For example, his skilful manipulation of the various forces in Lebanon (even within certain communities) – balancing alliances and playing one faction against the other in order to achieve a 'balance of weakness' – might 'deepen mutual intransigence and produce new explosions with uncertain rather than general prostration before the feet of Asad's regime'.[16] Asad's complex tactics in Lebanon have not always worked to his satisfaction. In addition to the vicious cycle of bloody car-bomb explosions in both West and East Beirut during 1985–6, which he was unable to prevent, Asad has failed so far to eliminate through his surrogates those groups which oppose his control over Lebanon: pro-Arafat PLO commandos in Palestinian refugee camps near Beirut and Sidon (in the 'war of camps'), Sheikh Sha'ban's Sunni fundamentalists in Tripoli, Maronite Lebanese forces in Mount Lebanon, as well as the Israeli-backed South Lebanese Army. Asad has also been unable (or unwilling) to tame Walid Junblatt, the Druze leader who dominates the Shuf and Kharrub regions, and for a while maintained connections with the PLO and Israel. Neither has Asad been fully in charge of the fundamentalist Iranian Revolutionary Guards or the Iranian-backed Shi'i Hizballah in the Biqa valley and in Beirut.[17]

Asad could tighten his grip over these unruly elements and eliminate most pockets of resistance if he decided greatly to increase his direct military involvement in Lebanon (which he has done in West Beirut since early 1987). Yet such a venture, requiring a large military force, might expose his army to various dangers while inflicting further strain on the Syrian economy. But on balance Asad's prospects of sustaining his strategic protectorate over Lebanon are good, even without getting directly involved in her internal strifes. Indeed, in late

July 1987 thirteen pro-Syrian groups in Lebanon, including Shi'is, Sunnis and Druze, established a 'Unification and Liberation Front' and declared they would seek to achieve integration between Lebanon and Syria, in opposition to President Amin Jumayyil.

To conclude this discussion of Asad's regional designs, it would appear that, with the exception of the Lebanese component, as of late 1987 he has not managed to advance his Greater Syria scheme to the same extent that he was able to do in the mid- to late 1970s with much weaker military forces than he has now. Indeed, Asad has been, and will possibly continue to be, unable to impose his hegemony over Hussein and Arafat as long as they refuse to accept his militant regional strategy and are backed by the other Middle East powers: Egypt, Iraq and (in Jordan's case) Israel. Nonetheless, Asad is powerful enough to spoil political processes within this region which are threatening to his vital national interests and devoid of a wide Middle East consensus. (But if by chance Jordan, the Palestinians and Israel agreed, with Egyptian and Iraqi backing, to a political settlement, it is highly doubtful whether Asad would be able to thwart it.)

Asad's Iranian Connection

Asad's disruptive capacity stems not only from his formidable military power and his calculated use of political assassination. Apart from his high prestige as the would-be leader of the all-Arab struggle against Israel, Asad, the master manipulator, has skilfully used the different interests or conflicting positions of various Middle East actors in order to benefit Syria and undermine undesired developments. The most conspicuous example has been Asad's odd relationship with Khumeini since 1980. Thus, while sustaining his alliance with the pan-Arab pro-Soviet radical Tripoli Bloc (Libya, Algeria and South Yemen), Asad has simultaneously developed close ties with the Iranian anti-Soviet Islamic fundamentalist regime in Teheran. Ideology aside, this strange alliance has indeed benefited Asad's regional, and to some extent domestic, interests.[18] In addition to a large quantity of free and discounted oil that Syria received from Iran, Asad has enjoyed a number of advantages from his association with Khumeini. Iraq, his powerful rival for the Fertile Crescent hegemony and for the Ba'th Party leadership, has been considerably weakened and kept out of the intra-Arab power game. Saudi Arabia, fearing a joint Iranian–Syrian pincer, has been geared to help Asad in some of his regional ventures –

controlling Lebanon and opposing both the Egyptian–Israeli accord and the Hussein–Arafat agreement; Riyadh has also granted Syria large amounts of financial aid. Asad successfully employed the Iranian Revolutionary Guards group as well as the Shi'i Hizballah in terrorist activities against his rivals in Lebanon, notably the US and Israel. And he has acquired a unique position as a potential mediator between Iran and the Arab world, notably Iraq, under various circumstances, or as the Arab leader who might save Iraq on the verge of collapse in the face of an Iranian assault.

It is true that Asad's ingenious alliance with Teheran carries certain slight risks for him. In addition to alienating the oil-producing Arab states further, Syria's strategic regional position might be threatened in the long run by new Shi'i fundamentalist regimes which may be established in Baghdad or Beirut, following an Iranian military victory in Iraq, or as the result of a massive Iranian influence in Lebanon. Yet in the foreseeable future these hazards seem to be remote; and, at any rate, Asad, if he is still around, is likely to anticipate the dangers and switch alliances before it is too late. For example, when the pro-Iranian Hizballah group worked against his security plan for West Beirut Asad sent his troops there in February 1987, inflicting a bloody blow on this unruly organization. And when, in early August 1987, violent strife erupted between Iran and Saudi Arabia over the Mecca killings on 31 July 1987, Asad, while trying to mediate between Iran and Saudi Arabia, reportedly warned Teheran that Syria would not stand idly by if the security of the Saudi government was threatened by Iran.

Another indication of Asad's ability to change his policy or tactics in the face of menacing developments can be seen in the way he reacted to the American and European sanctions against his alleged use of terrorist action. On the one hand he sharply criticized the US for its April 1986 air raid on Libya, and Britain for its anti-Syrian measures late in 1986. But, on the other hand, being sensitive to his international standing and eager to have open channels to the West, Asad took steps to repair his relations with the US and West European countries, notably Britain. The deployment of 7,000 Syrian troops in West Beirut in February 1987 was apparently a sign of Asad's constructive role in the attempts to curb the terrorism of Hizballah and gain the release of the American and European hostages held in Lebanon. Similarly, the closure of Abu Nidal's offices in Damascus in July 1987 served as another signal of Asad's dissociation with international terrorism. Consequently, since March 1987 various West European countries have gradually improved relations with Damascus, including the revival of full diplomatic links; the US also reopened a dialogue with Asad in summer 1987.

In sum, despite the obstacles and setbacks faced in his international and intra-Arab policies, Asad has succeeded since 1970 in remarkably improving Syria's regional and global position. Indeed, having in the 1950s and 1960s been subjected to pressures and encroachment on the part of neighbouring countries, Syria has been transformed by Asad into a regional power. Using his unique qualities – notably, as a good strategist, shrewd politician, tough negotiator and master manipulator – Asad has managed to put his country almost on the same footing as Egypt, Iraq and Israel. And while defying both Egypt's and Iraq's bids for pan-Arab leadership, Asad, by building a huge military force, is for the first time challenging Israel's military superiority and thus unequivocally assuming the leadership of the all-Arab struggle against the Jewish state. Neither Israel nor the US nor Europe can ignore Asad as a pivotal Arab player in the Middle East.

Asad: A Nation-Builder?

Turning now, finally, to a brief examination of the balance sheet of Asad's domestic policies, the following equation emerges. On one side there appears the remarkable transformation of Syria from a notoriously weak, shaky and divisive system in the 1950s and early 1960s into the strong, stable and highly centralized state which has been developed since the early 1970s. And while staying in power much longer than any previous post-independence leader, Asad has succeeded in advancing a political–social–economic upheaval in the country: completing the elimination of the old Sunni Muslim urban oligarchy, which for generations had dominated Syria's political and economic systems, Asad has replaced it with a new ruling elite, composed mainly of younger members of the lower and lower-middle classes, mostly from small towns and villages, with a predominance of Alawite military leaders. Simultaneously he has substantially improved economic conditions among the underprivileged rural population, as well as among the urban workers, while enormously expanding the state's educational system at its various levels and cultivating a new young generation (men and women alike) of Ba'th-oriented Syrian Arab patriots.[19] And endeavouring to create a new Syrian Arab national community, built on a wide consensus and on organs of 'popular democracy', Asad has systematically worked towards the modernization of the country's economic infrastructure. Big development projects, notably the Euphrates agro-industrial project, have enabled him to complete the 'electrification' of the countryside, increase the irrigation of arable lands, improve the communications system, create new jobs for industrial workers and advance their technological knowhow.[20]

The other side of Asad's balance sheet nonetheless looks rather bleak, partly because of certain chronic problems in the country which he inherited and has failed to solve, and partly as a result of his own miscalculations and failures.[21] To begin with, the public sector in industry, agriculture and services continues to be plagued with mismanagement, waste and inefficiency. While land reform has been sluggish, more and more farmers have moved to unproductive jobs in the cities. Agricultural production has drastically decreased to the extent of causing severe shortages of fruits and vegetables in this predominantly agricultural country. Rapid inflation has eroded the salaries of industrial workers and lower-level public employees; and whereas the brain-drain of professionals has continued, a new class of *nouveaux riches* has emerged. Composed of senior military officers and high government and party officials who associate with private entrepreneurs, this class has been engaged in black-marketeering and exploitation of the public sector, while spreading bribery and corruption to unprecedented levels. Alongside these unhealthy developments, the country's impressive economic improvement during the first six or seven years of Asad's rule came to a halt in 1977, and subsequently deteriorated steadily, reaching its lowest ebb in the mid-1980s. The Syrian involvement in Lebanon since 1976, coupled with the huge military expenditure since 1978 and the parallel sharp decrease in income from external sources, greatly inflated the foreign trade deficit and drained the foreign currency reserves.[22] During 1985, 1986 and 1987 the economic crisis reached grave dimensions and was manifested in a severe decrease in imported goods, including raw materials, increasing unemployment and inflation, and grave shortages of basic foodstuffs and commodities.[23]

This prolonged economic predicament, together with Asad's Lebanese venture, his brutal repression of the Muslim Brothers and the fierce suppression of human rights since 1979, have greatly contributed to the widespread resentment of their president among large sectors of the Syrian population. This popular opposition shows of course that Asad's impressive efforts during the 1970s to create a cohesive national community have largely failed. Indeed, since the early 1980s his regime has been perceived by many Syrians as a brutal Alawite military dictatorship. Yet it is interesting to note that among the membership of the newly established anti-Asad National Alliance for the Liberation of Syria, as well as among the Muslim Brothers there is a significant representation of Syrian Nasserites, socialists and above all former leaders and activists of the Ba'th Party.[24] Thus Asad has even lost the allegiance of certain groups among the very classes that had initially supported the Ba'th Party, and he has deeply antagonized not only the Sunni Muslim fundamentalists but also a growing number of modern urban professionals and intellectuals – lawyers, doctors, engineers and the like.[25]

It would seem that during the last several years, perhaps since the late 1970s, Asad has virtually (but not publicly) relinquished his attempts at integrating the various sections of the population – notably the urban Sunni Muslim traditional and modern middle classes – into his would-be cohesive national community. Facing the growing alienation and resentment of these classes, which stemmed initially from his secularist and rural-oriented policies, Asad has opted to rely more heavily on his true constituencies. Among them, first and foremost, are the Alawite members of his family, clan and sect whom he essentially wishes to protect and cultivate and use as the hard core of his military force and security apparatus.[26]

Next in loyalty come the several hundred thousand Ba'th members, Sunni and non-Sunni alike, many of them sharing Asad's resentment of the urban middle classes. While providing legitimacy to his regime, they have been mobilized to support his policies and to curb his domestic enemies. The largest sections are peasants, followed by elements of the working class, salaried middle class and the state bureaucracy. Mostly organized in the Ba'th Party, mass syndicates and trade unions, these sections, like most of the Alawites, many Christians, Ismailis and some Druze, have greatly benefited from Asad's policies and are consequently dependent on him or are ideologically identified with his regime.[27] Asad favoured these sections of the population by setting up development projects in the rural areas and by effecting his social policies, as well as by recruiting many of their members into state employment or mobilizing them into the local and national political arenas.

Last but not least, Asad has given special attention to young Syrians, immensely expanding the state-run educational system, organizing many youths in Ba'th-affiliated unions and paramilitary organizations. Simultaneously Asad has worked to educate or indoctrinate these young generations with his notions of pan-Arabism, Syrian patriotism and populist egalitarian etatism, as well as those of anti-'Zionism–imperialism' (US) and 'anti-reaction' (Arab).[28] Possibly visualizing these hundreds of thousands of university and secondary-school students and other young Ba'th Party members as a potential solid support-base for his regime, Asad has apparently sought to integrate them, along with his indoctrinated army and the state-favoured peasantry and salaried working classes, into a cohesive, non-sectarian modernized political community.

Conclusion: Asad's Personality and Leadership

It would appear that since his youth Asad has represented or has been tangled in various contradictions, which he has endeavoured to accommodate. For the first time in Syria's modern history, an Alawite has succeeded in ascending to the supreme position of president and leader. Yet he has accomplished this remarkable climb not through ordinary political processes but mainly by means of military force. It may appear that in this respect Asad has not been different from his predecessors, the various Syrian army officers who had seized control of the country by military force. Yet, unlike his predecessors, Asad managed to assume the reins of power within a relatively short period of time: carrying only the rank of captain in the 1963 Ba'th coup, he became in 1966 Syria's defence minister and co- leader, and in 1970 the unchallenged ruler of the country. Subsequently Asad has continued singlehandedly and successfully to control Syria for an unprecedentedly long time, establishing a centralized and powerful presidential regime.

Asad achieved these outstanding results, which his predecessors had tried but failed to accomplish, not only as a result of his more effective use of military force and of the security apparatus, but also owing to his unique combination of traits and skills as a person and a politician. Highly ambitious, singleminded, stubborn and in no doubt of what he wants, Asad systematically and patiently worked towards his objectives. And apparently, adhering to the notion that the end justifies the means, Asad shrewdly used manipulation, ambiguity and deceit, betrayed the allegiance of his superiors and employed brute force against both his rivals and his enemies, in order to assume power and hold on to it. Yet Asad has sought to become not only a ruler but also a leader-reformer, a state-builder as well as a nation-builder: to integrate his people into a more coherent Syrian-Arab national community based on popular consensus, while developing and modernizing his country's economic infrastructure and achieving for the first time a stable political entity.

Primarily, Asad has sought to accomplish these grand designs in order to mobilize a wide support-base for his rule, particularly in view of his heterodox Alawite minority origins, as well as his initial ascendency through a military coup. Indeed, crucially in search of legitimacy, Asad endeavoured to portray his regime as a non-sectarian, popular democratic, Syrian-Arab nationalist system.

Beyond these calculations, however, Asad seems sincerely to care for the well-being of his people as well as to feel a deep sense of mission on behalf of his nation. Stemming from his early nationalist education and his Ba'thist indoctrination, Asad's political and social ideals have apparently been interwoven with his basic skills as a strong leader, a pragmatic politician and an outstanding political strategist seeking to consolidate Syria as a cohesive nation-state and make her a regional power.

Indeed, employing these ideals and skills as well as using conviction and manipulation, intimidation and force, Asad has succeeded in turning Syria into an assertive military and political power in the Middle East.

Nevertheless, although creating a strong domestic regime and considerably developing and modernizing the economic infrastructure of the country, Asad has failed to become a nation-builder. This failure is essentially due to his inability to accommodate the dichotomy between, on the one hand, his Alawite military support-base, which in the short run was essential to his political survival, and on the other his long-term vision of creating a new non-sectarian national community, which would give legitimacy and popular backing to his leadership and regime. Possibly underestimating or miscalculating the depth of the urban Sunni population's Islamic faith, as well as their political and economic vested interests, Asad did a great deal to provoke their antagonism and resistance through several of his policies. In the domestic arena these included not only the Alawite military pre-dominance, but also the subtle introduction of secular-oriented constitutional measures, as well as the countryside-oriented economic reforms. Coupled with these were Asad's unpopular regional policies – siding with the Lebanese Maronites in 1976 against the Lebanese

Muslim radicals and the PLO, and the successive blows he inflicted against Arafat and his Palestinian supporters.

Faced with the growing opposition of the various urban sections of the population, and possibly harbouring the Alawite's deep-seated animosity to the Sunni Muslim urbanites, Asad resorted to the use of brute force against them. Indeed, lacking the qualities of a charismatic or spiritual leader, and devoid of the Western norms of democracy, Asad reacted within his own conceptual framework of power-politics. Apart from his grossly excessive suppression of the Muslim Brothers, Asad has behaved more or less as have other leaders of 'popular democracies' or dictatorship systems in several Arab countries, in the Communist bloc or in the Third World.

It would appear, in sum, that during nearly two decades of his rule, while taking advantage of his predeccessors' achievements and pursuing their economic reforms, Asad has indeed effected a new political community composed of Alawites, sections of other religious minorities, large numbers of Muslim peasants, workers and other lower-class people, as well as the growing young population of high-school pupils, university students and state-employed public officials and army officers from the various communities. Either benefiting from his social and economic favours, educated in his vast state-run educational system, identifying with his domestic and foreign policies, or enthusiastically participating in his country-wide personality cult – these various new forces within the Syrian population constitute the political backbone of Asad's regime. They are intended to protect this regime against the hostile old forces of predominantly Sunni Muslim urban traditional middle classes and modern professionals.

The pertinent question is, then, whether Asad can consolidate these new forces, and, through his nation-building institutions, enable them to sustain his regime and legacy after his death. For whoever succeeds him, whether it is his brother Rifat or one of the three Alawite Alis (army generals Ali Duba, Ali Aslan or Ali Haydar) or a collective Alawite–Sunni leadership with Tlas, Shihabi or Khaddam as a Sunni figurehead, one thing now appears to be clear: none of these leaders is of the same calibre as Asad. It is therefore doubtful whether his successor would be capable of sustaining Asad's remarkable achievements, particularly rendering Syria such an unprecedented stability, and making her, for the first time, a regional power in the Middle East.

Notes

Preface: The Sphinx of Damascus

1 Ghalib Kayali, *Hafiz Al-Asad Qaid wa-Risala* (Damascus, 1977); Lucien Bitterlin, *Hafez El-Assad: le parcours d'un combattant* (Paris, 1986).

Chapter 1: The Syrian Setting

1 See Albert Hourani, 'The Changing Face of the Fertile Crescent in the Eighteenth Century', in *Vision of History* (Beirut, 1961), pp. 40–1. See also Abd al-Karim Rafeq, *The Province of Damascus* (Beirut, 1966); Herbert Bodman, *Political Factions in Aleppo 1760–1826* (Chapel Hill, North Carolina, 1963); Amnon Cohen, *Palestine in the Eighteenth Century* (Jerusalem, 1973).
2 Isabel Burton, *The Inner Life of Syria* (London, 1875), pp. 105–6.
3 See pp. 20–3.
4 Moshe Ma'oz, *Ottoman Reform in Syria and Palestine* (Oxford, 1968), pp. 110–11.
5 See Ali Haydar Midhat, *The Life of Midhat Pasha* (London, 1903), p. 183.
6 Public Record Office, London, FO 195/ 194, Beirut, 21 March 1842.
7 Charles Issawi, *The Economic History of the Middle East* (Chicago, 1966), p. 269.

8 For more details and references, see Ma'oz, *Ottoman Reform*; Philip Khouri, *Urban Notable and Arab Nationalism* (Cambridge, 1984); Ruth Roded, 'Tradition and Change During the Last Decades of Ottoman Rule' (PhD thesis, Denver University, 1984).
9 For references and more details see Moshe Ma'oz, 'Attempts at Creating a Political Community in Modern Syria', *Middle East Journal*, 26(4), Autumn 1972, pp. 389–404. See also Albert Hourani, *Arabic Thought in the Liberal Age* (London, 1962), pp. 101, 274–5.
10 A. L. Tibawi, *A Modern History of Syria* (London, 1969), pp. 161–2.
11 John Murray, *A Handbook for Travellers in Syria and Palestine* (London, 1858), I, p. xlvi.
12 Yusuf al-Hakim, *Suriyya wa'l-ahd al-uthmani* (Syria and the Ottoman Period) (Beirut, 1966), pp. 98–100.
13 Public Record Office, London, FO 78/1389, Aleppo, 7 August 1858.
14 Cf. Ernst Dawn, 'The Rise of Arabism in Syria', *Middle East Journal*, 16(2), Spring 1962, p. 163; see also by the same author, *From Ottomanism to Arabism* (Urbana, Illinois, 1973).

15 See Hourani, *Arabic Thought*, pp. 186–7; see also Z. Zeine, *The Emergence of Arab Nationalism* (Beirut, 1966); George Antonius, *The Arab Awakening* (London, 1938).

16 On Syria under the French mandate see Albert Hourani, *Syria and Lebanon* (London, 1946); S. H. Longrigg, *Syria and Lebanon Under French Mandate* (London, 1958); Tibawi, *A Modern History of Syria*.

17 See Hourani, *Syria and Lebanon*, pp. 93–5.

18 League of Nations, Minutes of the Permanent Mandates Commission, Twenty-seventh session (Geneva, 1935).

19 Albert Hourani, *Minorities in the Arab World* (London, 1947), p. 77.

Chapter 2: Alawite Heritage and Arab Ideals

1 See R. Dussaud, *Histoire de la religion de Nosairis* (Paris, 1900), p. 30; I. Goldziher, *Lectures on Islam* (translation into Hebrew, Jerusalem, 1951), p. 180.

2 See F. Walpole, *The Ansayrii and the Assassins* (London, 1854), III, pp. 96, 115.

3 Hanna Batatu, 'Some Observations on the Social Roots of Syria's Ruling Military Group', *Middle East Journal*, 35, Summer 1981, p. 332; Batatu here cites local contemporary accounts.

4 S. Lyde, *The Asian Mystery: The Ansaireeh or Nusairis of Syria* (London, 1860), p. 219.

5 A. Toynbee, *Survey of International Affairs 1925* (London, 1927), part I, p. 359.

6 J. de la Roche, 'Notes sur les débuts de notre occupation du Territoire des Alaouites', *L'Asie française*, December 1931, p. 369, quoted by Alastair Drysdale, 'The Syrian Armed Forces in National Politics', in R. Kolkowicz and A. Korbanski (eds), *Soldiers, Peasants and Bureaucrats* (London, 1982), pp. 52–76.

7 *Ibid.*

8 Itamar Rabinovich, 'The Compact Minorities and the Syrian State 1918–1945', a paper presented to a conference on 'Christians and Jews in the Ottoman Empire', Princeton University, 1978.

9 *Ibid.*

10 *Ibid.*, quoting an Alawite source.

11 Ted Morgan, 'The Wild Men Become a Nation', *New York Times Magazine*, 18 May 1975.

12 See *The Principles of the Syrian Social Nationalist Party* (no publication place, no date); *Note of the Syrian National Party to the League of Nations*, 1936. For a detailed study see L. Z. Yamak, *The Syrian Social Nationalist Party* (Cambridge, Mass., 1966).

13 According to T. Petran, *Syria* (London, 1972), p. 74. On the League see also A. H. Hourani, *Syria and Lebanon* (London, 1946), pp. 197–8.

14 E. Rouleau, 'The Syrian Enigma: What is the Ba'th?', *New Left Review*, 45, 1967, pp. 53–67; cf. I. Rabinovich, *Syria Under the*

Ba'th, *1963–6* (Jerusalem, 1972), p. 7n.

15 For detailed studies on the Ba'th Party's history and ideology see K. S. Abu Jaber, *The Arab Ba'th Socialist Party* (Syracuse, NY, 1966); J. F. Devlin, *The Ba'th Party* (Stanford, 1976).

16 For an excellent study on Syria between 1945 and 1958 see Patrick Seale, *The Struggle for Syria* (London, 1965).

Chapter 3: A Soldier Climbs to Power

1 *The Times* (London), 13 March 1978, interview by Judith Listowel.

2 Seale, *Struggle for Syria,* p. 37; see also N. Van Dam, *The Struggle for Power in Syria* (London, 1979), p. 610; Drysdale, 'The Syrian Armed Forces'.

3 Quoted by Van Dam, *Struggle for Power,* p. 41.

4 *Al-Nahar* (Lebanon), 17 March 1971.

5 For detailed studies on this power struggle, see Van Dam, *Struggle for Power, passim,* and Rabinovich, *Syria Under the Ba'th.*

6 Petran, *Syria,* p. 182.

7 See Devlin, *The Ba'th Party,* p. 298, and Rabinovich, *Syria Under the Ba'th,* p. 167. For more details see Van Dam, *Struggle for Power,* ch. 4.

8 Petran, *Syria,* p. 240.

9 'Statement on the Results of the 9th Emergency Congress' (The Ba'th Information and Publication Office, Damascus, September 1967), p. 23.

10 *Al-Anwar* (Lebanon), 15 November 1970.

11 Damascus Radio, April 1969; Petran, *Syria,* p. 243.

Chapter 4: The Man and the Leader

1 Henry Kissinger, *Years of Upheaval* (London, 1982), p. 781.

2 See article by Kati Marton, *Middle East Insight* (Washington, DC, 1986), 4(6), p. 15; Karim Paqraduni, *As-salam al-mafqud* (Beirut, 1984), pp. 83ff.; Jimmy Carter, *Keeping Faith* (London, 1982), p. 280; *The Blood of Abraham* (Boston, 1985), pp. 68ff.; Kissinger, *Years of Upheaval,* pp. 779ff., 1097–9.

3 See for example Karim Shaybani, *Hafiz al-Asad* (Beirut, 1972), pp. 15–17; David Hirst, *Guardian* (London), 21 December 1982.

4 Asad's address to the convention of Syrian students, Damascus Radio, 4 May 1985.

5 *Al-Hawadith* (Lebanon), 11 December 1970.

6 Carter, *Blood of Abraham,* p. 81.

7 Kissinger, *Years of Upheaval,* p. 779.

8 Cf. for example Asad's addresses in Shaybani, *Hafiz al-Asad,* pp. 10, 13; *Al-Nahar* (Lebanon), 17 March 1971; Damascus Radio, 9 June 1973, 16 April 1972; Kayali, *Hafiz Al-Asad,* pp. 23, 31; *Al-Nahar,* 8 March 1978.

9 Cf. Asad's public speeches: *Al-Anwar* (Lebanon), 15 November 1970; Damascus Radio, 29 October 1973, 6 October 1975, 5 January 1985. See also *Al-Majalla* (Saudi Arabia), 23 July 1983.

10 Kayali, *Hafiz Al-Asad*, pp. 31–3.
11 *Majmuat Khutab Hafiz al-Asad* (Damascus, 1972), II, p. 6; *Jaysh Al-Sha'b* (Syria), 11 November 1970; an interview with Aliyya al-Sulh, *Al-Nahar* (Lebanon), 17 March 1971.
12 Damascus Radio, 8 March 1972.
13 Hafiz al-Asad, *Khutab wa-Kalimat wa-tasrihat* (Damascus, 1981), p. 32.
14 See the Permanent Constitution of the Syrian Arab Republic, Damascus, 31 January 1973.
15 *Al-Nahar* (Lebanon), 17 March 1971.
16 Cf. Itamar Rabinovich, 'Syria', *Middle East Contemporary Survey*, henceforth referred to as *MECS* (Tel-Aviv University), I, p. 608.
17 Alastair Drysdale, 'The Succession Question in Syria', *Middle East Journal*, 39(2), Spring 1985, pp. 246ff.
18 *Ha'aretz* (Tel-Aviv), 31 July 1985.
19 Cf. Batatu, 'Some Observations', pp. 331–3.

Chapter 5: Relying on the Army

1 Asad's speech at a public rally, Damascus Radio, 5 December 1970, and Asad's address on 8 March 1972 on Damascus Radio.
2 Asad's speech in Tripoli, Libya on 9 December 1970; Damascus Radio, 9 December 1970; *Financial Times* (London), 22 February 1980; *New York Times Magazine*, 19 February 1984.
3 G. Michaud in *Merip Report*, no. 112, November–December 1982; *Bamachane* (IDF), 22 October 1975; *Ha'aretz* (Tel-Aviv), 1 November 1980; *Ma'ariv* (Tel-Aviv), 16 August 1974; cf. *Al-'usbu Al-Arabi* (Lebanon), 30 September 1974; *Al-Mustaqbal* (Paris), 15 April 1980; *Middle East Economic Digest (MEED)* (London), 5 April 1986, p. 25.
4 *MEED*, 5–11 April 1986; p. 25, *Ha'aretz* (Tel-Aviv), 25 November 1984, 28 May 1985, 17 October 1985, 1 November 1985; *New York Times*, 25 May 1986.
5 Asad's speech at the teachers' emergency conference, Damascus Radio, 15 March 1980.
6 Cf. article by Al-Naqri in *Jaysh Al-Sha'b* (Syria), 19 August 1985; Asad letter to his army, Damascus Radio, 1 August 1985.
7 See *Al-Anwar* (Lebanon), 15 November 1970; *Al-Hawadith* (Lebanon), 13 November 1970.
8 Statements of the Regional Command of the Ba'th Arab Socialist Party on results of the party's special regional congress, 10–17 March 1966 (Damascus, Ministry of Information, SAR, 1966), p. 34. Van Dam, *Struggle for Power*, appendix C; Moshe Ma'oz, 'Alawi Military Officers in Syrian Politics, 1966–1974', in H. Z. Schiffrin (ed.), *Military and State in Modern Asia* (Jerusalem, 1976), pp. 288–9.
9 See 'Internal Guidelines to the Ba'th Party Organization in the Army', no. 39, 19 September 1972, captured by the IDF in the

1973 war, document 278/1. Cf. Asad's speeches, *Jaysh Al-Sha'b* (Syria), 6 March 1973.

10 See for example *Jaysh Al-Sha'b* (Syria), 1 April 1975, article by Issa Salum; *Al-Ba'th* (Syria), 24 December 1979; *Jaysh Al-Sha'b*, 1 January 1984.

11 *New York Times Magazine*, 19 February 1984.

12 Petran, *Syria*, p. 235.

13 Alastair Drysdale, 'Ethnicity in the Syria Officer Corps', *Civilisations*, 29, 1979, p. 368.

14 Batatu, 'Some Observations', pp. 331–3; Van Dam, *Struggle for Power*, pp. 100–2. Drysdale, 'Ethnicity', pp. 246ff. From testimonies of Syrian war prisoners in Israel after the 1967 and 1973 wars.

15 See Van Dam, *Struggle for Power*, pp. 331–3; *Al-Musawwar* (Egypt), 11 March 1966.

16 Van Dam, *Struggle for Power*, p. 90; *Al-Hawadith* (Lebanon), 14 July 1971.

17 *Al-Hawadith* (Lebanon), 7 and 20 July 1972; UPI, 7 December 1972; *Al-Hayat* (Lebanon), 8 December 1972; *Al-Nahar* (Lebanon), 8 December 1972.

18 Cf. *Al-Hawadith* (Lebanon), 20 November 1970.

19 Drysdale, 'Ethnicity', p. 371.

Chapter 6: The Ba'th Instrument

1 *Al-Hayat* and *Al-Anwar* (Lebanon), 15 November 1970; *Statement by Baath Arab Socialist Party Leadership*, the 11th Pan-Arab Congress, 5 September 1971, p. 5.

2 *Statement by Baath Arab Socialist Party Leadership*, p. 5; *Ruz Al-Yusuf* (Egypt), 23 November 1970.

3 Cf. Y. M. Sadowski in *Merip Report*, no. 134, July–August 1985, p. 3; Damascus Radio, 15 and 16 November 1975.

4 *Merip Report*, no. 112, November–December 1982, p. 23.

5 *Al-Dustur* (London), 4 March 1985.

6 *Merip Report*, no. 112, November–December 1982, p. 21; *Al-Hayat* (Lebanon), 8 December 1972; Amman Radio, 19 August 1972.

7 Asad's speech, Damascus Radio, 5 December 1970. Cf. R. A. Hinnebusch, 'Syria Under the Ba'th', *Arab Studies Quarterly*, no. 3, 1982, pp. 193ff.

8 *Merip Report*, no. 112, November–December 1982, p. 23.

9 Richard Johns and Alain Cass, *Financial Times* (London), 24 February 1982 and 10 March 1975, respectively.

10 Hinnebusch, 'Syria', pp. 185–6.

11 *The Times* (London), 11 March 1980.

12 Van Dam, *Struggle for Power*, pp. 100–1, Table 2–5.

Chapter 7: The Six Good Years (1970–1976)

1 Cf. Asad's speeches. Radio Damascus, 5 December 1970, 7 January 1971, 8 March 1972, 7 and 16 April 1972.

2 Malcolm Kerr, 'Hafiz Asad and

the Changing Patterns of Syrian Politics', *International Journal*, 28(4), 1975, p. 701; cf. Kayali, *Hafiz Al-Asad*, pp. 10–12.

3 *Jaysh Al-Sha'b* (Syria), 31 December 1974.

4 See Asad's speech, Radio Damascus, 8 March 1972; cf. Petran, *Syria*, pp. 251–2; Hinnebusch, 'Syria', pp. 190–1; *Al-Hayat* (Lebanon), 15 November 1970.

5 For more details see Asad's speech, Damascus Radio, 8 March 1972; Petran, *Syria*, pp. 205–9; R. A. Hinnebusch, 'Local Politics in Syria: Organization and Mobilization in Four Village Cases', *Middle East Journal*, 30(1), Winter 1976, pp. 1–24.

6 Cf. *Al-Ma'rifa* (Syria), September 1973, no. 139, article by Ibrahim Bakri; see *Al-Ma'rifa*, May 1971, no. 111, article by Abu Ali Yasin.

7 For more details see Y. M. Sadowski, 'Ba'thist Ethics and the Spirit of State Capitalism', unpublished paper, University of California (Berkeley), October 1984.

8 See Asad's speech, Radio Damascus, 8 March 1972; Petran, *Syria*, pp. 210ff.; *Area Handbook Series: Syria*, American University (Washington, DC, 1979), pp. 95–149; *Syrie et le monde Arabe*, no. 24, December 1977.

9 Asad's speech, Radio Damascus, 8 March 1972; see also other references in note 8.

10 *Jaysh Al-Sha'b* (Syria), 20 January 1976.

11 Asad's speech, Radio Damascus, 8 March 1972. For details see Petran, *Syria*, pp. 218–29. Also

Al-Thawra (Syria), 15 March 1972; *Jaysh Al-Sha'b* (Syria), 31 December 1974.

12 From Asad's speech before the 12th session of the Ba'th National (pan-Arab) Congress.

13 Petran, *Syria*, p. 224.

14 *Nidal Al-Fallahin* (Syria), 21 August 1984; *Al-Thawra* (Syria), 20 September 1974.

15 *Al-Thawra* (Syria), 4 September 1974; *Al-Ba'th* (Syria), 20 April 1972; *Tishrin* (Syria), 18 November 1977.

16 *Al-Ba'th* (Syria), 20 April 1972, 17 September 1974; cf. *Nidal Al-Fallahin* (Syria), 4 September 1974.

17 *Nidal Al-Fallahin* (Syria), 2 October 1974; cf. interview with Syria's prime minister in *Tishrin* (Syria), 18 November 1977.

18 *Tishrin* (Syria), 18 November 1977.

19 *Jaysh Al-Sha'b* (Syria) 19 November 1974; *Al-Thawra* (Syria), 17 June 1972; Hinnebusch, 'Syria', pp. 189–92; Alastair Drysdale, 'The Asad Regime and Its Troubles', *Merip Report*, no. 112, November–December 1982, pp. 5–7; J. Pincus, 'Syria: Captive Economy,' *Middle East Review*, 12(1), Fall 1979, pp. 49–57; D. Carr, 'Capital Flows and Development in Syria', *Middle East Journal*, 34(4) Autumn 1980, pp. 455–67; cf. Petran, *Syria*, pp. 205ff.

20 Stanley Reed, 'Syria's Asad: His Power and His Plan', *New York Times Magazine*, 19 February 1984; *Ha'aretz* (Tel-Aviv), 4 July 1983, quoting *Le Monde* (Paris).

21 Morgan, 'The Wild Men'; Stanley Reed, 'Dateline Syria – Fin de Régime!' *Foreign Policy*, 39, Summer 1980, p. 179.

Chapter 8: Preparing an Arab Crusade Against Israel

1 For example *Al-Thawra* (Syria), 23 January 1978.
2 Cf. *Tishrin* (Syria), 10 January 1978; *Flash* (Syria), February 1978.
3 *Al-Anwar* (Lebanon), 15 November 1970.
4 Middle East News Agency, Cairo, 28 December 1970; Asad's speech, Damascus Radio, 21 February and 30 August 1971; Shaybani, *Hafiz al-Asad*, p. 10; Ghalib Kayali quoted in *Tishrin* (Syria), 8 and 10 January 1978.
5 Asad's speeches, Damascus Radio, 16 and 24 July 1972.
6 Asad's speeches, Damascus Radio, 9 December 1970, 17 December 1971, 9 June 1973. *Jaysh Al-Sha'b* (Syria), 15 December 1970.
7 Asad's interview with *Al-Nahar* (Lebanon), 17 March 1971; Damascus Radio, 8 March and 19 December 1972; Kayali quoted in *Tishrin* (Syria), 8 and 10 January 1978; *Financial Times* (London), 10 March 1975.
8 *Al-Nahar* (Lebanon), 17 March 1971; cf. Asad's interview with foreign journalists, Damascus Radio, 2 April 1971, 19 December 1972.
9 Middle East News Agency, Cairo, 8 November 1972; also *Al-Nahar* (Lebanon), 17 March 1971; Damascus Radio, 9 December 1970, 22 February 1971, 30 August 1971, 9 June 1973; *Al-Ma'rifa* (Syria), April 1972, no. 122, p. 7; October 1972, no. 130, pp. 127–8 (article by General Tlas); September 1973, no. 140, p. 43; *Al-Ba'th* (Syria), 3 and 4 October 1983.
10 Galia Golan, *Yom Kippur and After* (Cambridge, 1977), p. 29.
11 See discussion on this question in *ibid.*, pp. 56ff.
12 See Tlas's interview in *Al-Ba'th* and *Al-Thawra* (Syria), 5 and 6 October 1975; see also Mahmoud Riad, *The Struggle for Peace in the Middle East* (London, 1981), p. 176.
13 Radio Damascus, 19 December 1972. Cf. Asad interview with *Al-Nahar* (Lebanon), 17 March 1971.
14 Chaim Herzog, *The War of Atonement* (Boston, 1975), p. 28.
15 *Ibid.*, pp. 30–1; Zeev Schiff, *October Earthquake* (Tel-Aviv, 1974), p. 11.
16 *Jaysh Al-Sha'b* (Syria), 28 August 1973.
17 Cited in *Ma'ariv* (Tel-Aviv), 17 March 1973. See also *Ha'aretz* (Tel-Aviv), 9 March 1973.
18 Schiff, *October Earthquake*, p. 8.
19 See Damascus Radio, 2 August and 6 September 1973. See also Damascus Radio, 4 and 5 August, 16 and 25 September 1973.
20 Schiff, *October Earthquake*, pp.

2–4, 14–15. For detailed accounts of the war see *ibid.*, *passim*, and Herzog, *War of Atonement*.

21 Schiff, *October Earthquake*, p. 18; cf. Herzog, *War of Atonement*, p. 49.

22 Schiff, *October Earthquake*, p. 20.

23 *Ibid.*, pp. 1, 66; Herzog, *War of Atonement*, pp. 63, 76, 77; Mohamed Heikal, *The Road to Ramadan* (New York, 1975), p. 213.

24 Schiff, *October Earthquake*, p. 24.

25 See *Near East Report*, xxx (9), 3 March, 1986, p. 36.

26 Schiff, *October Earthquake*, pp. 24–5; Golan, *Yom Kippur*, pp. 64–6.

27 *Al-Ma'rifa* (Syria), October 1973, no. 141; Damascus Radio, 16, 20 and 21 October 1973; also Kayali, *Hafiz Al-Asad*, p. 47.

28 Damascus Radio, 29 October 1973; cf. Golan, *Yom Kippur*, p. 136, and Heikal, *The Road*, p. 213, giving another version.

29 *Jaysh Al-Sha'b* (Syria), 19 March 1974; Damascus Radio, 8 March 1974.

30 Kissinger, *Years of Upheaval*, pp. 782–4.

31 See for example *Ha'aretz* (Tel-Aviv), 8 February 1974, quoting *Le Monde* (Paris).

32 Kissinger, *Years of Upheaval*, pp. 781, 1088–9, 1097–8.

33 Tlas's speech, Damascus Radio, 10 March 1974.

34 Cf. *Tishrin* (Syria), 22 November 1976.

35 Quoted in *Ha'aretz* (Tel-Aviv), 11 March 1974.

36 Kissinger, *Years of Upheaval*, p. 1133.

37 *Newsweek*, 3 March 1975. Cf. *Ha'aretz* (Tel-Aviv), 25 August 1975.

38 Kissinger, *Years of Upheaval*, p. 1134.

39 *The Memoirs of Richard Nixon* (New York, 1978), pp. 1013–14.

40 Tad Szulc, *The Illusion of Peace* (New York, 1978), p. 783; cf. Kissinger, *Years of Upheaval*, p. 1135.

41 Cf. Asad's interview with *Rus Al-Yusuf* (Egypt), 25 November 1974.

42 Asad's interview with *Al-Ahram* (Egypt), 5 July 1974; *Jaysh Al-Sha'b* (Syria), 1 July 1975.

43 *Middle East Journal*, 29(1), Winter 1975, p. 104.

44 Cf. Asad's interview with French television, Damascus Radio, 20 March 1975; Asad's interview with the *Washington Post*, Damascus Radio, 5 March 1975.

45 *Newsweek*, 22 September, 1975.

46 *Middle East Journal* 29(3), Summer 1975, pp. 329–30.

47 See Asad's interview with the *Washington Post*, 5 March 1975; with French television, Damascus Radio, 20 March 1975; and with BBC television, Damascus Radio, 8 September 1975.

48 See interviews in *Rus Al-Yusuf* (Egypt), 25 November 1974, and *Al-Ahram* (Egypt), 5 July 1974.

49 See for example speech by Mustafa Tlas, Syria's defence minister, UPI, Damascus, 10 March 1974.

50 Asad's speech in Libya, *Jaysh Al-Sha'b* (Syria), 1 April 1975.

51 Damascus Radio, 2 August 1975.
52 Asad's interview with BBC television, Damascus Radio, 8 September 1975; Asad's interview with *Newsweek*, 22 September 1975; Damascus Radio, 6 October 1975, 8 March 1976.
53 Damascus Radio, 6 October 1971.
54 Asad's speech to the Islamic Congress, Pakistan, 22 February 1974.
55 From an interview with an Indian journalist, *Jaysh Al-Sha'b* (Syria), 20 January 1976; and from Asad's address at Damascus University, Damascus Radio, 8 March 1975; cf. Asad's address, *Al-Thawra* (Syria), 16 November 1975.
56 Interview with *Rus Al-Yusuf* (Egypt), 25 November 1974; see also Asad's speech at the Rabat conference, to Middle East News Agency, Cairo, 30 October 1974.
57 Asad's speech at Damascus University, Damascus Radio, 8 March 1975; *Al-Ray Al-'Am* (Kuwait), 18 October 1975.
58 Kissinger, *Years of Upheaval*, p. 1067.
59 Thomas Kiernan, *The Arabs* (Boston, 1975), pp. 303–10; cf. Asad's interview with BBC television, Damascus Radio, 8 September 1975.
60 Cf. Statement by the Ba'th National Command, *Al-Ba'th* (Syria), 16 November 1975; statement by the Ba'th Regional Command, Damascus Radio, 20 April 1975.
61 Cf. 'Syria', in *MECS*, 5, p. 613; *Al-Ma'rifa* (Syria), no. 148, March 1974, pp. 27–9, and no. 153, October 1974, p. 18.
62 Cf. Rifat Asad in *Al-Ba'th* (Syria), 22 September 1975; Hafiz al-Asad in *Jaysh Al-Sha'b* (Syria), 4 November 1975; statement by the Ba'th Regional Command, Damascus Radio, 20 April 1975; *Financial Times* (London), 26 November 1974.
63 Kissinger, *Years of Upheaval*, p. 780.
64 See interview with Syrian vice-president and foreign minister Abd al-Halim Khaddam, *Al-Mustaqbal* (Lebanon), 17 May 1986, p. 17.
65 See Asad's interview with *Al-Ahram* (Egypt), 5 July 1974.
66 For example, Damascus Radio, 21 June 1976.
67 See Asad's interview with *Al-Sayyad* (Lebanon), 7 March 1974; cf. interview with Haytham al-Ayyubi, a Syrian strategist, in *Al-Thawra* (Syria), 8 October 1975.

Chapter 9: The Lion of Greater Syria

1 Kayali, *Hafiz Al-Asad*, p. 31; also quoted in *Tishrin* (Syria), 8 and 10 January 1978; Kiernan, *The Arabs*, pp. 299, 301.
2 Asad's interview with *Al-Sayyad* (Lebanon), 7 March 1974; Tlas interviews with *Al-Ba'th* and *Al-Thawra* (Syria), 5 and 6 October 1975.
3 *Middle East Journal*, 28(1), Winter 1974, p. 40.
4 Cf. *Middle East Journal*, 28(2), Spring 1974, p. 156; interview

with Syria's information minister, *Al-Jumhur* (Lebanon), 28 February 1974.

5 *Middle East Journal* 29(1), Winter 1975, p. 67.

6 *Jaysh Al-Sha'b* (Syria), 29 April 1975.

7 Kayali, *Hafiz Al-Asad*, pp. 31–3.

8 *Al-Anwar* and *Al-Hayat* (Lebanon), 9 March 1969; *Al-Difa* (Jordan), 10 March 1969, quoted in A. Baram, 'National Integration and Exclusiveness in Political Thought and Practice in Iraq Under the Ba'th 1968–1982', PhD thesis, in Hebrew (Hebrew University, Jerusalem, 1986), pp. 199–200.

9 See *Al-Hawadith* (Lebanon), 29 January 1971; *Nida Al-Watan* (Lebanon), 16 November 1971; cf. Reuters dispatch from Damascus, 4 June 1971.

10 Asad's interview with *Al-Hawadith* (Lebanon), 26 June 1975; see also *Al-Nahar* (Lebanon), 27 March 1974.

11 *Al-Sayyad* (Lebanon), quoted in *Ha'aretz* (Tel-Aviv), 10 April 1975.

12 *Ha'aretz* (Tel-Aviv), 13 April 1975.

13 Damascus Radio, 9 April 1975; *Jaysh Al-Sha'b* (Syria), 3 April 1975; 22 April 1975; 20 May 1975; 10 June 1975; 8 July 1975; 19 August 1975.

14 For references and details see Hourani, *Arabic Thought in the Liberal Age*, pp. 101, 274–5; Antonius, *The Arab Awakening*, p. 24; Moshe Ma'oz, 'Attempts at Creating a Political Community in Syria', *Middle East Journal*, 26(4), Autumn 1972, pp. 389–404.

15 *The Geography of the Arab Homeland*, in Arabic (Ministry of Education, 1980–1), pp. 58–9, 104, 107, 180, cited in R. Avi-Ran, *The Syrian–Palestian Conflict in Lebanon*, in Hebrew (Dayan Center, Tel-Aviv University, 1985), pp. 2, 7.

16 Elizabeth Picard, 'The Recent Evolution of the SSNP', *Maghreb-Machrek*, 78, 1977, pp. 74–6; *Monday Morning* (Beirut), 1–7 October 1984, cited in Avi-Ran, *Syrian–Palestinian Conflict*, p. 8.

17 Kamal Junblatt, *This Is My Legacy*, in Arabic (Paris, 1978), p. 105. Cf. Kamal Junblatt, *I Speak for Lebanon* (London, 1982), p. 78.

18 Damascus Radio, 8 March 1974.

19 Avi-Ran, *Syrian–Palestinian Conflict*, pp. 6–7.

20 See *Jaysh Al Sha'b* (Syria) 28 August 1973; cf. *Al-Nahar* (Lebanon), 17 March 1971.

21 Cf. Damascus Radio, 21 June 1976.

22 See respectively Asad's interviews with *Al-Sayyad* (Lebanon), 7 March 1974, and with *Al-Ray Al-'Am* (Kuwait), 18 October 1975.

23 Asad's interview with *Al-Hawadith* (Lebanon), 26 June 1975.

24 Asad's address, Damascus Radio, 30 July 1975; Asad's interviews with the BBC, 5 September 1975, and with *Al-Hawadith* (Lebanon), 20 June 1975. See also *Ma'ariv* (Tel-Aviv), 4 April 1975.

25 Damascus Radio, 8 March 1975; *Jaysh Al-Sha'b* (Syria), 11 March 1975.

26 *Ma'ariv* (Tel-Aviv), 29 July 1974.

27 *Ma'ariv* (Tel-Aviv), 4 April 1975; Amman Radio, 28 July 1975; *Jaysh Al-Sha'b* (Syria), 10 June 1975, 22 July 1975 and 20 August 1975. For more details see *MECS*, I, p. 154.

28 *Los Angeles Times*, quoted in *Ma'ariv* (Tel-Aviv), 11 June 1975; *MECS*, I, p. 154.

29 Cf. Asad's interview with *Newsweek*, 15 September 1975; *Al-Nahar Arab Report*, 16 June 1975, no. 24; *Jaysh Al-Sha'b* (Syria), 12 August 1975 and 26 August 1975. See also *Tishrin* (Syria), 12 September 1975.

30 *MECS*, I, p. 155; *New York Times*, 8 December 1976. See Asad's interview with Joseph Kraft, *Washington Post*, 29 November 1976 (a copy of the transcript is in my possession).

31 *Tishrin* (Syria), 21 January 1977.

32 See Itamar Rabinovich, in *Skira Hodshit* (IDF monthly in Hebrew), February 1978, p. 27.

33 *Ahir Sa'ah* (Egypt), 10 March 1976; *Al-Ahram* (Egypt), 9 June 1975; *Al-Quds* (Jerusalem), 21 June 1976; cf. D. Dishon's article in *Skira Hodshit*, September 1976, p. 10.

34 See *MECS*, II, p. 738.

35 *Al-Hadaf* (PFLP), 1 March 1980; *Al-Bayraq* (Lebanon), 14 May 1980; *Al-Ba'th* (Syria), 24–5 November 1980, Damascus Radio, 22 and 23 January 1981.

36 See Joseph Nevo, 'Syria and Jordan: The Politics of Subversion', in Moshe Ma'oz and Avner Yaniv (eds), *Syria Under Assad* (London and New York, 1986), p. 145.

37 Abu Iyad, *Filastini bila Hawiyya* (Kuwait, no date), pp. 84–6.

38 Abu Iyad quoted in *Ma'ariv* (Tel-Aviv), 20 September 1985.

39 Moshe Shemesh, 'Political Representation of the Palestinians Among the Arabs: 1964–1971', PhD thesis (University of London, 1983), pp. 268–9.

40 *Al-Nahar* (Lebanon), 17 March 1971; for more references see Shemesh, 'Political Representation', p. 437, n. 27.

41 *Al-Sayyad* (Lebanon), 13 December 1973; Damascus Radio, 25 February 1975; *Jaysh Al-Sha'b* (Syria), 25 March and 4 November 1975.

42 Interviews with *Newsweek*, 1 June 1974; Damascus Radio, 25 February 1975; *Jaysh Al-Sha'b* (Syria), 25 March 1975; *Washington Post*, 5 March 1975; French television, 20 March 1975.

43 Asad's interviews with French television, 20 March 1975; Damascus Radio, 8 March 1975; *Jaysh Al-Sha'b* (Syria), 3 June 1975; *Newsweek*, 22 September 1975.

44 Asad's speech, Damascus Radio, 20 July 1976.

45 Damascus Radio, 8 March 1974; Junblatt, *This Is My Legacy*, p. 105.

46 Shemesh, 'Political Representation', pp. 451–2.

47 Abu Iyad to *Monday Morning* (Lebanon), 5–11 October 1981.

48 *Al-Watan* (Kuwait), 26 April 1977, cited in Shemesh, 'Political Representation', p. 437. For details of Asad's restrictions on PLO activities see Shemesh, *ibid.*, pp. 462ff.

49 Junblatt, *This Is My Legacy*, p. 105.

Chapter 10: Asad's Lebanese Venture

1 *Al-Hayat* (Lebanon), 5 November 1953, quoted in R. Erlich, 'Syria and the Lebanese Crisis: 1975–1978', MA thesis, in Hebrew (Tel-Aviv University, 1980), p. 3.

2 Cf. Asad's major speech on Lebanon, Damascus Radio, 20 July 1976.

3 See respectively Asad's interviews with *Al-Nahar* (Lebanon), 17 March 1971, and *Al-Anwar* (Lebanon), 10 August 1972.

4 Damascus Radio, 20 July 1976; see also *Jaysh Al-Sha'b* (Syria), 28 August 1973.

5 Erlich, 'Syria', p. 8.

6 See *Al-Hayat* (Lebanon), 24 February 1973, and Itamar Rabinovich, *The War for Lebanon* (Cornell, 1984), p. 37. On Musa al-Sadr, see Fuad Ajami, *The Vanished Imam* (Cornell, 1986).

7 Sa'ib Salam, a Muslim leader, to Damascus Radio, 6 January 1975; Beirut Radio, 3 and 5 January 1975; *Al-Yawm* (Lebanon), 5 January 1975.

8 *Ha'aretz* (Tel-Aviv), 9 June 1976, quoting *Le Monde* (Paris).

9 Junblatt, *I Speak for Lebanon*, p. 11.

10 Rabinovich, *The War for Lebanon*, p. 37. For other works on the civil war see K. Salibi, *Crossroads to Civil War* (New York, 1976); W. Khalidi, *Conflict and Violence in Lebanon* (Cambridge, Mass., 1979); M. Deeb, *The Lebanese Civil War* (New York, 1980); A. Dawisha, *Syria and the Lebanese Crisis* (London, 1980); I. Harik, *Lebanon, Anatomy of Conflict* (Hanover, 1981).

11 Asad's speech, Damascus Radio, 20 July 1976.

12 Junblatt, *I Speak for Lebanon*, p. 16; *Al-Nahar* (Lebanon), 15 February 1976; Beirut Radio, 14 February 1976; and Asad's speech, 20 July 1976.

13 *Ha'aretz* (Tel-Aviv), 9 June 1976, quoting *Le Monde* (Paris); *Al-Anwar* (Lebanon), 1 November 1976.

14 See respectively *Ha'aretz, Le Monde, ibid.*; and Junblatt, *I Speak for Lebanon*, pp. 81–2, 86.

15 All the above quotations are taken from Asad's speech of 20 July 1976; see also Asad's interview with an Iranian journalist, *Jaysh Al-Sha'b* (Syria), 30 December 1975; and Junblatt, *I Speak for Lebanon*, p. 17.

16 Abu Iyad, quoted in Erlich, 'Syria', pp. 19–20.

17 *Ha'aretz* (Tel-Aviv), 9 June 1976, quoting *Le Monde* (Paris); Paqraduni, *As-salam*, pp. 19, 36; Damascus Radio, 20 July 1976.

18 *Merip Report*, no. 11, October 1976, p. 4.

19 Baghdad Radio, 18 March 1977.

20 *Ha'aretz* (Tel-Aviv), 14 May 1976, quoting *Le Monde* (Paris); Paqraduni, *As-salam*, p. 37.

21 *Falastin Al-Thawra* (Lebanon), 13 April 1976, quoted in Avi-Ran, *Syrian–Palestinian Conflict*, p. 20.

22 *Ha'aretz* (Tel-Aviv), 13 June 1976, quoting *Le Monde* (Paris).

23 Faruq Qaddumi, PLO leader, to *Monday Morning* (Lebanon), 7 June 1976, quoted in Avi-Ran, *Syrian–Palestinian Conflict*, p. 21; and PLO Radio, 20 July 1976.

24 Asad's speech, Damascus Radio, 20 July 1976.

25 *Al-Muharrar* (Lebanon), 16 August 1976, quoted in Avi-Ran, *Syrian–Palestinian Conflict*, p. 23.

26 See Asad's interview in Riyadh, *Jaysh Al-Sha'b* (Syria), 26 October 1976.

27 Paqraduni, *As-salam*, p. 213.

28 *Ha'aretz* (Tel-Aviv), 14 May 1976, quoting *Le Monde* (Paris); see also *Merip Report*, October 1976.

29 Beirut Radio, 23 and 25 May 1976; Damascus Radio, 31 May 1976; *Al-Ba'th* (Syria), 1 June 1976; *Al-Thawra* and *Jaysh Al-Sha'b* (Syria), 2 June 1976.

30 Transcript of Asad's interview with Joseph Kraft, *Washington Post*, 29 November 1976, p. 6.

31 Interview with *Al-Sayyad* (Lebanon), 21 March 1977, quoted in Erlich, 'Syria', p. 41.

32 Beirut Radio, 2 and 3 July 1976, cited in Erlich, 'Syria', p. 44.

33 Paqraduni, *As-salam*, p. 34.

34 *Al-Nahar Al-Arabi* (Paris), 10 July 1977; *Time*, 22 November 1976; Erlich, 'Syria', pp. 81–2.

35 Paqraduni, *As-salam*, pp. 31, 37.

36 *Al-Dustur* (London), 12 September 1977; *Ma'ariv* (Tel-Aviv), 18 May 1977, quoting the *Washington Post*.

37 BBC, 6 July 1978; *Ma'ariv* (Tel-Aviv), 29 August 1978; Erlich, 'Syria', p. 90.

38 *MECS*, I, p. 148; Damascus Radio, 20 January 1977.

39 See *MECS* I, p. 155; Damascus Radio, 20 January 1977.

40 Asad's interview with *Time*; Damascus Radio, 17 January 1977; *MECS*, I, p. 157, cf. *Ma'ariv* (Tel-Aviv), 18 May 1977, quoting the *Washington Post*.

41 See *Al-Dustur* (London), 12 September 1977.

42 *Al-Thawra* (Syria), 18 January 1977.

43 *Al-Nahar Al-Arabi* (Paris), 10 July 1977; cf. Junblatt, *I Speak for Lebanon*, p. 12.

44 *Al-Anwar* (Lebanon), 5 September 1977.

45 *MECS*, I, p. 616.

46 *Observer* (London), 6 March 1977.

Chapter 11: Manoeuvring Between the US and the USSR

1 G. Golan, *The Soviet Union and Syria Since the Yom Kippur War*, Research Paper No. 21 (Hebrew University, Jerusalem, 1977), p. 13.

2 *Ibid.*, pp. 21–2; see also TASS (Moscow), 28 October 1975; *Pravda* (Moscow), 14 October 1975.

3 On this phase see Ilana Kass, *The Lebanon Civil War, 1975–77* (Jerusalem, 1979).

4 Junblatt, *I Speak for Lebanon*, p. 17; Baghdad Radio, 1 June 1976; Golan, *The Soviet Union*, p. 28.

5 Golan, *The Soviet Union*, p. 31. See there also a discussion of Soviet calculations vis-à-vis Syria and the Middle East.

6 Erlich, 'Syria', p. 58, citing *Le Monde* (Paris), 20 July 1976; Asad interview with *Al-Hawadith* (Lebanon), 1 October 1976; *Al-Safir* (Lebanon), 3 October 1976.

7 Damascus Radio, 20 July 1976. Regarding US objections to the Syrian intervention see also Y. Evron, 'Washington, Damascus and the Lebanese Crisis', in Ma'oz and Yaniv, *Syria Under Assad*, p. 211.

8 Asad's speech, Damascus Radio, 20 July 1976.

9 See R. Stookey, 'The United States', cited in Erlich, 'Syria', p. 47; cf. *Ha'aretz* (Tel-Aviv), 7 June 1976, quoting *Le Monde* (Paris); Erlich, 'Syria', p. 49, Evron, 'Washington, Damascus', p. 212.

10 *Time*, 13 September 1976; I. Rabin, *Pinkas Sherut* (Tel-Aviv, 1979), p. 503; Rabin interview with *Ma'ariv* (Tel-Aviv), 14 April 1976; *Ha'aretz* (Tel-Aviv), 7 June 1976, quoting *Le Monde* (Paris).

11 Asad's speech, Damascus Radio, 20 July 1976; *Jaysh Al-Sha'b* (Syria), 5 October 1976.

12 Asad's interviews with Joseph Kraft, *Washington Post*, 2

December 1976, and with *Time*, 17 January 1977.

13 William B. Quandt, *Camp David: Peacemaking and Politics* (Brookings Institution, Washington, DC, 1986), p. 30.

14 *Ibid.*, pp. 40–2; *Al-Ba'th* (Syria), 17 March 1977; *Tishrin* (Syria), 4 May 1977.

15 *Tishrin* (Syria), 22 March 1977.

16 *Tishrin* (Syria), 4 May 1977.

17 *Al-Thawra* (Syria), 14 May 1977.

18 Quandt, *Camp David*, pp. 56–8; cf. Carter, *Blood of Abraham*, p. 72.

19 Carter, *Keeping Faith*, p. 286.

20 Quandt, *Camp David*, p. 57; cf. Asad interview with *New York Times*, Damascus Radio, 30 August 1977.

21 *Al-Thawra* (Syria), 23 June 1977, quoting articles from *The Times* (London), *Le Quotidien de Paris* and *U.S. News and World Report*.

22 Quandt, *Camp David*, p. 50.

23 Carter, *Keeping Faith*, p. 286.

24 *The Times* (London), 19 May 1977.

25 *Washington Post*, 2 December 1976.

26 Paqraduni, *As-salam*, pp. 88, 21.

27 Junblatt, *I Speak for Lebanon*, p. 75.

28 *Ha'aretz* (Tel-Aviv), 22 April 1979, quoting *Le Monde* (Paris).

29 On the Syrian decision-making process in Lebanon's civil war see Dawisha, *Syria*.

30 See *Ma'ariv* (Tel-Aviv), 17 February 1978.

31 Erlich, 'Syria', p. 83, quoting Rabin and General Gur, the Israeli chief of staff in 1978.

32 On the Zahle event see Rabino-vich, *The War for Lebanon*, pp. 114–20.

33 Quandt, *Camp David*, pp. 52, 97; cf. *MECS*, I, pp. 152–3.

34 For Sadat's initiative and his motivations, see Quandt, *Camp David*, pp. 135–9; for Sadat's attitude to Asad, see *Al-Mustaqbal* (Paris), 7 January 1978.

35 *MECS*, II, pp. 159, 733; for more details see A. Dawisha, 'Syria and the Sadat Initiative', *The World Today*, 34, May 1978, pp. 192–8.

36 *MECS*, II, p. 162.

37 *New York Times*, 5 December 1977; *MECS*, II, p. 736; A. Baram, 'Ideology and Power Politics in Syrian–Iraqi Relations 1968–84', in Ma'oz and Yaniv, *Syria Under Assad*, p. 133.

38 *Al-Safir* (Lebanon), 26 September 1978.

39 *MECS*, III, pp. 236.

40 *MECS*, III, p. 816; cf. Baram, 'Ideology and Power Politics', in *Syria Under Assad*, pp. 135–6.

41 J. F. Devlin, 'Syria: Problems and Prospects', paper submitted to the Wilson Center, Washington, DC, January 1981, p. 14. For text of the Soviet–Syrian treaty see *Survival*, 23, 1981, pp. 43–4.

Chapter 12: The Islamic *Jihad* and the Hama Massacre

1 See Ma'oz, *Ottoman Reform*, ch. 5; and 'The Ulama and the Process of Modernization in Syria', *Asian and African Studies*, 7, 1971, pp. 77–88.

2 For a comprehensive and excellent study of this movement see R. P. Mitchell, *The Society of the Muslim Brothers* (London, 1969); see also Ishaq Musa al-Husaini, *The Moslem Brethren* (Beirut, 1956).

3 See U. I. Abdallah, *The Islamic Struggle in Syria* (Berkeley, 1983), pp. 96–102; Hanna Batatu, 'Syria's Muslim Brethren', *Merip Report*, no. 110/11, November–December 1982, p. 14.

4 On this movement between 1947 and 1952 see S. Rissner, *Ideologie und Politik der Muslimbruder Seriens* (Freiburg, 1980); see also Patrick Seale, *Struggle for Syria*, p. 121.

5 For details see Batatu, 'Syria's Muslim Brethren', pp. 15–16.

6 See M. Ma'oz, 'The Role of Islam in Syria', *New Outlook*, May 1973, pp. 13–18; on Marwan Hadid see Abdallah, *Islamic Struggle*, pp. 103–7.

7 *Al-Ba'th* (Syria), 22 May 1967.

8 Abdallah, *Islamic Struggle*, p. 111; *Al-Nahar* (Lebanon), 17 March 1971, 24 December 1972; Damascus Radio, 20 December 1970, 25 October 1971, 10 November 1971.

9 For example Damascus Radio, 6, 10, 12, 21, 22, 23, 26 October 1973.

10 Abdallah, *Islamic Struggle*, p. 271, n. 63; *Al-Hayat* (Lebanon), 24 February 1973.

11 Agence France Presse, 24 and 28 February, 1 and 7 March 1973; *Al-Hayat* (Lebanon), 25 February 1973; *Ha'aretz* (Tel-

Aviv), 25 and 28 February, 2 March 1973; *Ma'ariv* (Tel-Aviv), 18 April 1973.

12 *New York Times*, 30 August 1973.

13 Thomas Mayer, 'The Islamic Opposition in Syria, 1963–1982', *Orient* 1983, 4, pp. 595–6; *Observer* (London), 9 September 1979; *Jaysh Al-Sha'b* (Syria), 1 November 1980; *Ahir Sa'ah* (Egypt), 12 and 19 September 1979.

14 Batatu, 'Syria's Muslim Brethren', p. 20; see also F. H. Lawson, 'Social Bases for the Hamah Revolts', *Merip Report*, no. 110/11, November–December 1982, pp. 24ff.

15 Cf. *Tishrin* (Syria), 5 April 1980.

16 See the Manifesto in Abdallah, *Islamic Struggle*, pp. 201ff., and *Declaration and Program of the Islamic Revolution in Syria* (Damascus, 1980), p. 59; cf. interview with Amin al-Hafiz, former Ba'th leader, *Al-Dustur* (London), 19 May 1986.

17 A memo to the heads of states . . . attending the Islamic Summit at Taif, Damascus, 15 January 1981; *New York Times Magazine*, 15 August 1976; *Financial Times* (London), 19 March 1980; *Ma'ariv* (Tel-Aviv), 26 December 1980, article by T. Friedman.

18 Batatu, 'Syria's Muslim Brethren', p. 20; *Rus Al-Yusuf* (Egypt), 13 September 1976; M. Tannenbaum in *New Leader*, October 1977, p. 11.

19 *Business Week*, 2 May 1977; Reuters, 21 June 1977; Phalangist Radio (Lebanon), 2 September 1979.

20 *Merip Report*, October 1976, pp. 8–9; *Ma'ariv* (Tel-Aviv), 17 May 1976.

21 *Al-Anba* (Kuwait), 18 June 1976; *Ma'ariv* (Tel-Aviv), 21 May 1976; *Business Week*, 2 May 1977; cf. *Jaysh Al-Sha'b* (Syria), 1 November 1980.

22 Abdallah, *Islamic Struggle*, p. 187; cf. Helena Cobban, *Middle East International* (England), 14 September 1979; Patrick Seale, *Observer* (London), 9 September 1979. See also *Al-Ba'th* (Syria), 28 December 1979, article about economic difficulties.

23 Batatu, 'Syria's Muslim Brethren', p. 20; Patrick Seale, *Observer* (London), 9 September 1979.

24 Abdallah, *Islamic Struggle*, pp. 109–110.

25 *New York Times*, 28 November 1980; cf. *Daily Telegraph* (London), 31 December 1980; *Al-Ahram* (Egypt), 30 March 1980; *Guardian* (London), 12 March 1980; *The Times* (London), 27 March 1980; *Al-Yamama* (Saudi Arabia), 19 April 1980; *Al-Nadhir*, 28 September 1980, no. 23; 21 November 1980, no. 26.

26 *Le Matin* (France), 26 December 1980.

27 'The Islamic Opposition', p. 604; Abdallah, *Islamic Struggle*, p. 189; *Al-Nadhir*, 1 May 1981, no. 13; 17 June 1981, no. 35; 21 October 1981, no. 39; 9 November 1981, no. 40.

28 *Al-Nadhir*, 9 November 1981, no. 40.

29 Radio Damascus, 20 July 1976.
30 *MECS*, III, p. 811.
31 Asad, *Khutab wa-Kalimat wa-tasrihat* (Damascus, 1981), p. 9.
32 *MECS*, III, p. 810; *Tishrin* (Syria), 12 September 1976; Damascus Radio, 8 June 1980.
33 Damascus Radio, 12 October 1979; *Al-Thawra* (Syria), 6 April 1980: *Tishrin* (Syria), 9 November 1981; *Al-Ba'th* (Syria), 1 December 1981.
34 Abdallah, *Islamic Struggle*, pp. 10, 11, 14, 183.
35 Paqraduni, *As-salam*, p. 34.
36 Interview with *Al-Ray Al-'Am* (Kuwait), 9 March 1980; Asad, *Khutab*, p. 9.
37 Asad's address on the B'ath Revolution Day, *Al-Thawra* (Syria), 9 March 1980.
38 Damascus Radio, 11 March 1980.
39 Asad, *Khutab*, pp. 32–3.
40 Asad's addresses, *Al-Nahar* (Lebanon), 7 March 1977; Damascus Radio, 20 January 1977; *Al-Thawra* (Syria), 9 March 1980, 21 July 1981; *Al-Ba'th* (Syria), 23 July 1981.
41 Interview with Prime Minister Khulayfawi, *Tishrin* (Syria), 18 November 1977.
42 *Al-Ba'th* (Syria), 3 October 1977, quoted in *MECS*, II, p. 726.
43 Reed, 'Dateline Syria', 179–86; *Al-Hawadith* (Lebanon), 25 January 1980; *Guardian* (London), 4 September 1982.
44 See for example *Pravda* (USSR), 17 April 1980; *Al-Jarida Al-Rasmiyya* (Syria), 11 September 1980.
45 *Al-Hawadith* (Lebanon), 7 December 1979; see also *Al-Hawadith*, 25 January 1980; *Al-Jarida Al-Rasmiyya* (Syria), 11 September 1980, p. 17.
46 *Scotsman* (Britain), 18 December 1979; *Guardian* (London), 17 January 1980; *New York Times*, 11 January 1980; *Financial Times* (London), 18 February 1982.
47 Robert Fisk, *The Times* (London), 2 April 1980.
48 See for example Damascus Radio, 9, 11 and 12 March 1980; *Al-Ba'th* (Syria), 26 March 1980; *Al-Safir* (Lebanon), 30 March 1980; cf. Alastair Drysdale, 'The Asad Regime and Its Troubles', *Merip Report*, no. 110/11, November–December 1982, p. 3.
49 Asad's address, *Al-Masira* (Syria), 2 October 1981; Abdallah, *Islamic Struggle*, p. 189; *Financial Times* (London), 24 February 1982.
50 From the 1981 Manifesto of the Islamic Revolution, Abdallah, *Islamic Struggle*, p. 211.
51 *Al-Watan Al-Arabi* (Lebanon), 12 July 1980.
52 *Daily Telegraph* (London), 18 March 1980; *Guardian* (London), 5 January 1981; *Al-Nadhir*, 27 February 1981, no. 44; *International Herald Tribune*, 25 March 1981.
53 *Al-Hawadith* (Lebanon), 7 December 1979; *Al-Akhbar* (Egypt), 10 March 1980, 18 January 1981; *Daily Telegraph* (London), 18 March 1980.
54 Amnesty International press release, 16 November 1983, and

Report from Amnesty International to the Government of the Syrian Arab Republic (London, 1983); cf. Batatu, 'Syria's Muslim Brethren', p. 20; Daily Telegraph (London), 26 July 1980; International Herald Tribune, 18 February 1980.

55 Jaysh Al-Sha'b (Syria), 15 July 1980.

56 International Herald Tribune, 18 February 1980; Dawn (Britain), 9 August 1980.

57 Guardian (London), 2 August 1980; Al-Watan Al-Arabi (Lebanon), 12 July 1980.

58 The Times (London), 2 April 1980.

59 New York Times, 28 November 1980.

60 Observer (London), 22 March 1981.

61 Abdallah, Islamic Struggle, pp. 191–2; Al-Nadhir, 8 January 1982, no. 42.

62 Observer (London), 14 February 1982; cf. Guardian (London), 5 February 1982; Ha'aretz (Tel-Aviv), 5 July 1983, quoting Le Monde (Paris).

63 Observer (London), 9 May 1982; Ha'aretz (Tel-Aviv), 5 July 1983, quoting Le Monde (Paris); Report from Amnesty International, pp. 36–7; Abdallah, Islamic Struggle, pp. 192–3.

64 The Middle East (London), May 1983; International Herald Tribune, 20 December 1983; Ma'ariv (Tel-Aviv), 29 February 1984; Phalangist Radio (Lebanon), 12 March 1984; Hadashot (Tel-Aviv), 14 March 1986; Washington Times, 12 May 1986.

65 Observer (London), 4 May 1982; Al-Dustur (Lebanon), 15 August 1983; Egyptian Gazette, 23 March 1982; International Herald Tribune, 5 April and 8 May 1982; Al-Dustur (London), 4 March 1985, 19 May 1986.

Chapter 13: Asad's Predicament; Terror and Strategic Balance

1 Financial Times (London), 24 February 1982; International Herald Tribune, 25 March 1982; Al-Nadhir, 27 February 1982, no. 44; Daily Telegraph (London), 6 January 1981.

2 Al-Jumhuriyya (Iraq), 3 January 1984; Iraqi News Agency, 2 March 1984; Ha'aretz (Tel-Aviv), 14 September 1984.

3 Ann Milnes Roberts, 'Why Syrian Agriculture Is a Top Priority', The Middle East (London), July 1984, pp. 28–9.

4 Elizabeth Tamper, 'Problems at a Prestige Project', The Middle East (London), July 1984, pp. 29–30; Ha'aretz (Tel-Aviv), 4 July 1983, quoting Le Monde (Paris); Al-Thawra (Syria), 21 December 1983; MEED, 26 April 1986, p. 37.

5 Maggie Ford, 'Syrian Economy Faces Shortage of Foreign Currency', Financial Times (London), 24 December 1985.

6 Ford, 'Syrian Economy'.

7 For a detailed analysis of Asad's motivations see Y. Hirschfeld, 'The Odd Couple: Ba'thist Syria and Khomeini's Iran', in Ma'oz and Yaniv, Syria Under Assad, pp. 105ff.

8 Patrick Seale in the *Observer* News Service, 23 February 1982; *Al-Ahram* (Egypt), March 1980.

9 *Al-Ba'th* (Syria), 13 and 25 October 1982; *Tishrin* (Syria), 28 August 1982.

10 Rabinovich, *The War for Lebanon*, pp. 122ff. For a detailed analysis of the Israeli decision-making process, see also Z. Schiff and E. Ya'ari, *Milhemet Sholal*, in Hebrew (Tel-Aviv, 1984).

11 For a detailed account of the war, see Schiff and Ya'ari, *Milhemet Sholal*.

12 Eric Rouleau in *Le Monde* (Paris), 30 April 1983.

13 *Al-Watan Al-Arabi* (Lebanon), 4 October 1981; *Al-Dustur* (London), 28 September 1981.

14 *Al-Watan Al-Arabi* (Lebanon), 4 October 1981; *Al-Dustur* (London), 28 September 1981; Damascus Radio, 8 May 1982.

15 *Al-Nahar* (Lebanon), 29 April 1982; Damascus Radio, 28 April 1982.

16 *Tishrin* (Syria), 11 May 1982; Damascus Radio, 8 May 1982, 20 June 1982.

17 David Hirst in the *Guardian* (London), 23 December 1982.

18 Judith Miller, 'The PLO in Exile', *New York Times Magazine*, 13 August 1985; cf. *Al-Ahali* (Egypt), 15 December 1982.

19 *Tishrin* (Syria), 9 July 1983; *Al-Musawwar* (Egypt), 1 July 1983; *Al-Thawra* (Syria), 1 December 1984; Avi-Ran, *Syrian–Palestinian Conflict*, pp. 28–30.

20 See *Financial Times* (London), 24 December 1985; *Al-Quds* (Jerusalem), June 1983; Iraqi newspapers, 22 July 1983.

21 Evron, 'Washington, Damascus', pp. 216–21. For Syrian criticism of the US policies see *Al-Thawra* and *Tishrin* (Syria), 1 November 1981 and 1 August 1983; *Al-Ba'th* (Syria), 28 October 1981, 25 October 1982, 17 February 1983.

22 See Asad's addresses on Damascus Radio, 11 April 1981, 17 September 1981, 1 August 1983.

23 *International Herald Tribune*, 23 December 1983; *Time*, 19 December 1983.

24 For details see A. Drysdale, 'The Succession Question in Syria', pp. 246ff.; *International Herald Tribune*, 9 March 1983; *Financial Times* (London), 8 March 1984; *The Times* (London), 9 April 1984; *Al-Majalla* (Saudi Arabia), 24 March 1984.

25 *International Herald Tribune*, 24 May 1984; *Washington Post*, 18 December 1985; *Le Point* (France), 26 December 1983, 1 May 1984.

26 Ma'oz and Yaniv, *Syria Under Assad*, p. 194.

27 Cf. Asad's interview with French television, 20 March 1975; Damascus Radio, 8 March 1975.

28 See respectively Amman Radio, 25 July 1985; *Al-Nadhir*, 1 September 1984, no. 72; Patrick Seale, 'Why Syrian Assassins Hunt Assad's Enemies in Exile', *Observer* (London), 22 March 1981; on the Middle Ages' Assassins, see P. Hitti, *Syria: A Short History* (New York, 1961), pp. 176–7.

29 See *Report from Amnesty International*, pp. 27, 30; Abdallah, *Islamic Struggle*, pp. 32–83.
30 *Observer* (London), 22 March 1981.
31 *New York Times*, 26 July 1980.
32 *MECS*, III, pp. 238, 813.
33 Nevo, 'Syria and Jordan', p. 145.
34 S. MacLeod, 'How Asad Was Won', *New York Times Magazine*, 8 May 1986, p. 34.
35 *Ibid.*
36 *Tishrin* (Syria), 17 September 1985.
37 Zeev Schiff in *Ha'aretz* (Tel-Aviv), 12 July 1985; MacLeod, 'How Asad Was Won', p. 35; *Newsweek*, 3 February 1986.
38 *Time*, 19 December 1983.
39 W. Harris, 'Syria in Lebanon', *Merip Report*, no. 134, July–August 1985, pp. 9–11; *New York Times*, 16 October 1985.
40 *Newsweek*, 7 April 1986; *Washington Times*, 2 July 1985.
41 H. Goodman in *The Washington Institute Policy Forum*, 16 July 1985.
42 *New York Times*, 29 May and 25 June 1986.
43 *Jerusalem Post*, 11 April 1986.
44 *Ibid.*
45 *Washington Post*, 8 May 1986; *New York Times*, 9 and 11 May 1986, 31 March 1987.
46 D. Pipes, 'Syria: The Cuba of the Middle East', *Commentary*, July 1986, pp. 15–18; *Hadashot* (Tel-Aviv), 3 June 1986; *Newsweek*, 7 April 1986; cf. Asad's interview with French television, 20 March 1975, regarding Syrian help to the Eritrean rebels.
47 *Washington Post*, 22 May 1986;

cf. *Washington Times*, 2 July 1985, 5 December 1986.
48 *Washington Post*, 18 May 1986.
49 *Newsweek*, 7 April 1986.
50 *Washington Times*, 2 July 1985.
51 *Al-Thawra* (Syria), 6 January 1985; *Jaysh Al-Sha'b* (Syria), 15 January 1985. See also Asad's address, Damascus Radio, 12 March 1986.
52 Damascus Radio, 4 May 1985; *Al-Ba'th* (Syria), 5 May 1985.
53 See for example Asad's speeches, Damascus Radio, 3 February and 30 August 1971; Shaybani, *Hafiz al-Asad*, p. 10.
54 Asad's address to the Revolutionary Youth, 1 October 1981; *Al-Ba'th* (Syria), 3 February 1985.
55 Khaddam to *Al-Mustaqbal* (Lebanon), 17 May 1986, p. 17.
56 Asad's interview with French television, 20 March 1975.
57 Cf. Asad's interview with *Le Monde* (Paris), *Jaysh Al-Sha'b* (Syria), 23 March 1976; Damascus Radio, 18 March 1976.
58 Cf. *Tishrin* (Syria), 20 June 1976; Asad on Damascus Radio, 1 February 1984.
59 Damascus Radio, 7 November 1980.
60 *The Middle East* (London), 6 June 1981; cf. *Al-Ahram* (Egypt), 30 March 1980.
61 Cf. Al-Asali in *Tishrin* (Syria), 25 February 1978; *Tishrin*, 7 October 1972; Al-Ayyubi in *Tishrin*, 9 August 1981, 30 May and 10 October 1981.
62 *Tishrin* (Syria), 25 February 1978; cf. *Al-Safir* (Lebanon), 23 April 1980.

63 Asad's address to the teachers' emergency convention, Damascus Radio, 15 March 1980.

64 Asad's address to the newly elected People's Assembly, Damascus Radio, 27 February 1986.

65 *New York Times*, 19 May 1986; *Ma'ariv* (Tel-Aviv), 16 May 1986.

66 *Al-Majalla* (Saudi Arabia), 16 October 1985; *Ma'ariv* (Tel-Aviv), 20 April 1985.

67 *MEED*, 5–11 April 1986, p. 25; Z. Schiff, 'A Confrontation With Syria', *Midstream*, June–July 1986, p. 5; *New York Times*, 25 May 1986; *Ma'ariv* (Tel-Aviv), 16 May 1986; *Al-Majalla* (Saudi Arabia), 16 October 1985.

68 *Al-Majalla* (Saudi Arabia), 16 October 1985; *Ha'aretz* (Tel-Aviv), 20 May 1985.

69 Asad's interview and speech, Damascus Radio, 9 March 1981, 17 September 1981. See also Damascus Radio, 17 September 1982.

70 Damascus Radio, 20 September 1982.

71 Damascus Radio, 15 November 1985; cf. Abu Dhabi Radio, 3 April 1986: *Al-Ray* (Jordan), 7 April 1980; *Ha'aretz* (Tel-Aviv), 30 April 1985; *Tishrin* (Syria), 19 May 1980.

72 Asad's interview with Soviet television, Damascus Radio, 27 April 1986; *Al-Ba'th* (Syria), 23 October 1985; *Tishrin* (Syria), 23 September 1985.

73 *Al-Iqtisad* (Syria), July 1980; *Al-Mustaqbal* (Lebanon), 6 February 1982; *Al-Thawra* (Syria), 13 November 1985.

74 Asad's interviews with Italian television, Damascus Radio, 25 February 1982; and with the *Observer*, Damascus Radio, 7 March 1982.

75 Interview with Soviet television, Damascus Radio, 27 April 1986; cf. *Al-Ba'th* (Syria), 22 October 1985.

76 Cf. Asad addresses, *Al-Ba'th* (Syria), 19 July 1981; Damascus Radio, 3 March 1980; and also see *Al-Munadil* (Syria), March 1985.

77 See Asad's speeches, Damacus television, 1 October 1983; Patrick Seale's article in *Al-Majalla* (Saudi Arabia), 23 July 1983; French television, Damascus Radio, 18 November 1984; Damascus Radio, 20 January 1985.

78 Cf. Seale in *Al-Majalla* (Saudi Arabia), 23 July 1983; *Al-Ba'th* (Syria), 10 October 1985; *Tishrin* (Syria), 16 November 1985.

79 Asad's interview with ABC, Damascus television, 25 April 1984.

80 Asad's interview with *Le Monde* (Paris), Damascus Radio, 1 August 1984.

81 Asad's address to the Palestinian National Council, Damascus Radio, 11 April 1981; cf. *Tishrin* (Syria), 23 September 1985.

82 Cf. Asad's address to the PNC, Damascus Radio, 11 April 1981; his interview with *Al-Nahar Al-Arabi*, Damascus Radio, 30 October 1982; Khaddam's interview with *Al-Sharq Al-Awsat* (Saudi Arabia), 6 January 1982.

83 Asad's interview with *Al-Nahar Al-Arabi*, Damascus Radio, 30 October 1982; see also Schiff, 'A Confrontation With Syria', p. 5.

84 Cf. *Jaysh Al-Sha'b* (Syria), 1 July 1985; *Al-Thawra* (Syria), 6 October 1985, article by Faiz Ismail; *Tishrin* (Syria), 25 February 1978, article by Bassam Al-Asali, and 7 October 1978.

85 Asad's speech, Damascus Radio, 8 March 1986.

86 Asad's interview with *Al-Nahar Al-Arabi*, Damascus Radio, 30 October 1982.

87 Asad's interview, Damascus Radio, 23 June 1983.

88 Asad's speech to newly elected People's Assembly, Damascus Radio, 27 February 1986.

89 *Al-Ba'th* (Syria), 3 October 1983.

Chapter 14: Asad's Prospects

1 Interview with General Barak, Israeli chief of military intelligence, *Ma'ariv* (Tel-Aviv), 9 December 1983; *Al-Majalla* (Saudi Arabia), 16 October 1985; *Ma'ariv*, 16 May 1986. Cf. A. H. Cordesman, *The Arab–Israeli Military Balance* (Washington, DC, 1986), pp. 45–9.

2 *Near East Report*, 16 June 1986.

3 Cf. interview with Talcot Seelye, former US ambassador to Syria, *Al-Majalla* (Saudi Arabia), 6 August 1983; *New York Times*, 19 May 1986.

4 Interview with Saudi media, Damascus Radio, 10 May 1983.

5 Cf. Defence Minister Rabin, *Ha'aretz* (Tel-Aviv), 11 September 1985. Cf. Cordesman, *Arab–Israeli Military Balance*, pp. 39–45.

6 *Tishrin* (Syria), 19 September 1985; cf. Cordesman, *Arab–Israeli Military Balance*, p. 47; *New York Times*, 29 October 1986 and 27 July 1987.

7 Z. Schiff in *Ha'aretz* (Tel-Aviv), 19 March 1986.

8 *New York Times*, 19 May 1986; Schiff, 'A Confrontation With Syria', pp. 4–6; cf. *Ha'aretz* (Tel-Aviv), 13 February 1985; *Al-Majalla* (Saudi Arabia), 10 October 1985; Amos Gilboa, *Ma'ariv* (Tel-Aviv), 16 May 1986; Cordesman, *Arab–Israeli Military Balance*, p. 50.

9 Cf. Asad's statement, *New York Times*, 8 September 1986.

10 *International Herald Tribune*, 18 September 1985; *Middle East International*, 10 January 1986; *New York Times*, 6 May 1986.

11 *New York Times*, 16 October 1985; *Financial Times* (London), 31 May and 27 December 1985; for details see Harris, 'Syria in Lebanon'.

12 *Near East Report*, 3 March 1986.

13 Arafat's interview with *Der Spiegel*, cited in *Ha'aretz* (Tel-Aviv), 19 July 1985.

14 Cf. *New York Times*, 25 August 1980: *Financial Times* (London), 31 May 1985.

15 *Time*, 19 August 1985; cf. *New York Times*, 3 September 1986.

16 Harris, 'Syria in Lebanon', p. 13. Harris gives an excellent analysis of Syria's position in Lebanon.

Notes

17 *New York Times*, 18 May and 5 August 1986; Asad's interview, *Washington Post*, 18 May 1986; cf. *Near East Report*, 3 March 1986, p. 35; *Middle East International*, 3 May 1985, pp. 3–5; Joyce Starr in *International Herald Tribune*, 13 February 1984.

18 For a detailed discussion of that issue see Hirschfeld, 'The Odd Couple', pp. 105ff.

19 Cf. *Al-Ba'th* (Syria), 27 November 1980; Asad's address to the Syrian students' union, *Al-Ba'th*, 5 May 1985; and his speech to the People's Assembly, Damascus Radio, 27 February 1980.

20 Cf. *The Middle East*, July 1984, pp. 28–9; Asad's address, Damascus Radio, 12 March 1985; *Al-Thawra* (Syria), 17 May 1985.

21 Even according to Asad himself; see his speech, Damascus Radio, 27 February 1986.

22 *Financial Times* (London), 2 June 1980; *MEED*, 26 April 1986, p. 57; Agence France Presse, Joyce Starr in *International Herald Tribune*, 27 August 1984.

23 *New York Times*, 18 May and 3 December 1986; *Financial Times* (London), 2 June 1986; *Al-Dustur* (London), 31 March 1986; *Al-Watan Al-Arabi* (Lebanon), 10 May 1985.

24 See chapter 7, and *Observer* (London), 4 May 1982; *Al-Dustur* (London), 4 March 1985, 19 May 1986; *Al-Talia Al-Arabiyya* (Paris), 16 December 1985.

25 See chapter 12, and cf. *Al-Watan Al-Arabi* (Lebanon), 10 May 1985.

26 See chapter 6.

27 See chapter 8, and cf. R. A. Hinnebusch, 'Syria', pp. 193ff.

28 See for example Asad's address to the Syrian students' union, Damascus Radio, 4 May 1985; see also *Al-Ba'th* (Syria), 18 May 1984, 27 November 1980.

Index